The Play of Fictions

MICHIGAN MONOGRAPHS IN CLASSICAL ANTIQUITY

The Play of Fictions: Studies in Ovid's Metamorphoses *Book 2*
  A. M. Keith

The Play of Fictions

Studies in Ovid's *Metamorphoses* Book 2

A. M. Keith

Ann Arbor
THE UNIVERSITY OF MICHIGAN PRESS

Copyright © by the University of Michigan 1992
All rights reserved
Published in the United States of America by
The University of Michigan Press
Manufactured in the United States of America

1995 1994 1993 1992   4 3 2 1

Library of Congress Cataloging-in-Publication Data

Keith, A. M., 1962–
   The play of fictions : studies in Ovid's Metamorphoses Book 2 / A.M. Keith
      p.   cm. — (Michigan monographs in classical antiquity)
   Revision of the author's doctoral dissertation (University of Michigan).
   Includes bibliographical references (p.   ) and index.
   ISBN 0-472-10274-5 (alk.)
   1. Ovid, 43 B.C.-17 or 18 A.D. Metamorphoses. Liber 2.
2. Mythology, Classical, in literature. 3. Metamorphosis in literature. 4. Narration (Rhetoric). 5. Rhetoric, Ancient.
   I. Ovid, 43 B.C.-17 or 18 A.D. Metamorphoses. Liber 2. II. Title.
III. Series.
PA6519.M9K4   1992
873'.01—dc20   91-42073
                                                                         CIP

OPTIMIS PARENTIBUS

Acknowledgments

This study is a revised version of my University of Michigan doctoral dissertation, and I am grateful to the members of my committee, Professors D.O. Ross, A. Clej, S.E. Hinds, and C. Witke for their encouragement and advice. It is my pleasure to acknowledge the generous financial support of the Social Sciences and Humanities Research Council of Canada and the Horace H. Rackham School of Graduate Studies, which funded the original project.

Cathy Connors, Alex Kurke, and Liz Warman have helped me to rethink the nature of this study and contributed several acute observations. Stephen Hinds generously read through the complete manuscript, correcting a number of significant errors and suggesting many substantive improvements. I have also benefited substantially from the remarks of the two anonymous readers for the University of Michigan Press. My friend and editor, Ellen Bauerle, has been extremely helpful in the final stages of preparing the manuscript for publication. Finally, I would like to express my heartfelt gratitude to my parents, the dedicatees of this work, for their loving support through the years.

Contents

Abbreviations	xi
Introduction	1
Chapter	
1. The Crow's Tale: *Met.* 2.549–95	9
2. The Metamorphosis of the Raven: *Met.* 2.531–632	39
3. Chiron's Daughter and the Art of Prophecy: *Met.* 2.633–79	63
4. Battus and the Rewards for Telling Tales: *Met.* 2.676–707	95
5. The Petrifaction of Aglauros: *Met.* 2.708–835	117
Epilogue	135
Appendices	
1. Swans in *Metamorphoses* 2	137
2. The Cercopes	147
3. Text of Callimachus' *Hecale* (Hollis frr. 70–74)	151
Bibliography	153
Index	163

Abbreviations

Abbreviations of the names of classical authors and works follow or are more explicit than Liddell-Scott-Jones, *A Greek-English Lexicon,* and Glare, *Oxford Latin Dictionary.* Titles of periodicals are abbreviated according to the system of *L'Année philologique.* Works of modern scholarship are cited by the author's name and date of publication, as they are listed in the bibliography. Except where noted, I quote from W.S. Anderson's *Ovidius, Metamorphoses* (Leipzig, 1977). Unless otherwise indicated, translations are my own. The following abbreviations may be noted:

Atti	*Atti del Convegno Internazionale Ovidiano,* vols. I and II. 1959.
Chantraine	P. Chantraine. *Dictionnaire etymologique de la langue grecque, histoire des mots.* Paris, 1968–1980.
Ernout-Meillet	A. Ernout and A. Meillet. *Dictionnaire etymologique de la langue latine, histoire des mots.* 4th ed. Paris, 1959.
FGrH	F. Jacoby, ed. *Die Fragmente der griechischen Historiker.* 15 vols. Berlin, then Leiden, 1923–1969.
Frisk	*Griechisches Etymologisches Worterbuch.* 2 vols. Heidelberg, 1960.
GRF	G. Funaioli, ed. *Grammaticae Romanae Fragmenta.* Leipzig, 1907.
Lewis and Short	C.T. Lewis and C. Short, *A Latin Dictionary.* Oxford, 1879.
LSJ	H.G. Liddell and R. Scott, revised by H. Stuart Jones, *A Greek-English Lexicon.* 9th ed. Oxford, 1940.

M-W	R. Merkelbach and M.L. West, eds. *Fragmenta Hesiodea*. Oxford, 1967.
OCD	N.G.L. Hammond and H.H. Scullard, eds. *Oxford Classical Dictionary.* 2d ed. Oxford, 1970.
OLD	P.G.W. Glare, ed. *Oxford Latin Dictionary.* Oxford, 1968–82.
PMG	D. Page, ed. *Poetae Melici Graecae.* Oxford, 1962.
RE	*Paulys Real-Encyclopädie der classischen Altertumswissenschaft.* Stuttgart, 1894– .
SH	H. Lloyd-Jones, and P. Parsons, eds. *Supplementum Hellenisticum.* Berlin, 1983.
TLL	*Thesaurus Linguae Latinae.* Leipzig, 1900– .

Introduction

Ovid's *Metamorphoses,* his only extant venture into hexameter epic, has enjoyed the admiration of readers since its "publication" in A.D. 8, but the poet's interpreters have had difficulty in accounting for the popularity of a work that has been called "the most difficult major poem that the Graeco-Roman world has bequeathed to us."[1] In spite of this assessment, the *Metamorphoses* has not received a great deal of detailed critical attention. Broad overviews of the Ovidian corpus tend not to offer close and detailed readings of short passages in the *Metamorphoses,* while book-length studies of the *Metamorphoses* have been concerned less with the organization of narrowly defined passages than with overarching literary interpretation of the poem as a whole.[2] The scope of this study, by contrast, is purposefully narrow, in that it offers the first literary interpretation of the sequence of dense and sophisticated narratives at

---

1. Anderson 1968, 93. Ovid tells us that the *Metamorphoses* was nearly complete upon his relegation to Tomis (*Tr.* 1.1.117, 3.14.[15]19), and he confidently predicts the success of the poem at its conclusion (*Met.* 15.871–79; cf. *Tr.* 1.7). There are several references to the poem in the literature of the first century A.D., which offer incontrovertible evidence that the poem was being read: see, e.g., Seneca the Elder, *Contr.* 2.2.8, Seneca the Younger, *Apocolocyntosis* 9, and Quintilian, *Inst. Or.,* 4.1.77. Cf. also G. Williams (1978, chap. 5 *passim*), mentioning widespread allusion to Ovid's *Metamorphoses* in poetry of the first century A.D. On the circumstances of literary publication at Rome, see Kenney 1982b, 10–27.

2. For broad overviews of the corpus, see Fränkel 1945, Wilkinson 1955, Herescu 1958, and *Atti* 1959. Book-length studies of the *Metamorphoses* include those of Ludwig 1964, Otis 1970, Little 1972, Due 1974, Galinsky 1975, Knox 1986, and Solodow 1988. Within the last ten years two book-length studies have appeared that offer more closely focused analyses of narrowly defined passages of the poem: Davis 1983 offers an interpretation of *Met.* 7.661–862; Hinds 1987 examines *Met.* 5.250–678 (and its relationship to *Fasti* 4.393–620). See also now W.C. McCarty n.d., a discussion of the Cadmus cycle (*Met.* 3.1–4.603) with particular attention to the Narcissus episode.

2 / *The Play of Fictions*

Met. 2.531–835: the transformation of the raven from white to black (*Met.* 2.531–632); the embedded narrative of the crow in which she recounts, among other tales, her metamorphosis from the royal daughter of Coroneus into a bird (*Met.* 2.549–95); the transformation of Chiron's daughter Ocyroe into a mare (*Met.* 2.633–79); the petrifaction of Battus (*Met.* 2.680–707); and the petrifaction of Aglauros in an episode with a lengthy excursus on the personified figure of *Invidia* (*Met.* 2.708–835).

This passage has been neglected by most of Ovid's interpreters, perhaps because of its context in the *Metamorphoses,* for the sequence follows the Callisto episode, which reprises the divine amours of the first book of the poem (Daphne, Io, Syrinx, and Phaethon's mother, Clymene), and precedes the much-admired Theban cycle of *Met.* 3.1 through *Met.* 4.603. H. Fränkel suggested that the theme of indiscretion linked the episodes at *Met.* 2.531–835, while N.G.G. Davis has identified the theme of tale-telling, *indicium,* as the focus of this passage.[3] Other critics, however, have been less willing to discover thematic connections linking the episodes of the crow, the raven, Ocyroe, Battus, and Aglauros, and have therefore been tempted to condemn the sequence.[4] One critic even suggests that the episodes narrated at *Met.* 2.401–875 can be interpreted as Ovid's self-referential reflection on the potential monotony of his poetic aims in the *Metamorphoses,* and he implies that this passage must ultimately be considered a failure:

> In fact, Ovid may well have intended the [stories at *Met.* 2.401–875] to serve as an object lesson of what happens when metamorphosis is emphasized at the expense of other constituent parts of a myth. The stories of Battus, Herse, and Europa break off with the metamorphosis although, especially in *Herse,* a great many details are given that are irrelevant to the metamorphosis and make the reader expect the completion of the story. These stories, however, are left incomplete because of the abandonment of themes that are equally as or more integral to the stories than is the metamorphosis theme, and the result is unsatisfactory.[5]

Even Fränkel may imply a similar judgment of this section of the poem

---

3. See Fränkel 1945, 221 n. 7, and Davis 1969, 18–39.
4. For unflattering assessments of this passage, see Wilkinson 1955, 235; Otis 1970, 379; Little 1972, 98; and Galinsky 1975, 93–96.
5. Galinsky 1975, 95.

in his discussion of the *Metamorphoses,* for he opens the chapter with a loose paraphrase of the *Metamorphoses,* beginning with the first lines of the poem and running thence, uninterrupted, up to the conclusion of the Callisto episode (*Met.* 2.530), but then turns abruptly to Book 9.[6] This study argues on the contrary that Ovid's control of, and commitment to, his material did not fail at this point in the poem.

Among scholarly discussions of the *Metamorphoses* there has been one point alone "on which the interpreters seem to be unanimous, and that is the dominant importance of narrative in the *Metamorphoses.*"[7] Ovid repeatedly draws attention to his own act of story-telling in a poem in which story-telling is such a prominent feature. The poem opens in the narrative voice of the poet (*Met.* 1.1–4), identified throughout this study as "first-layer narrative," but as early as *Met.* 1.209 the first internal narrator, Jupiter, begins to tell a story; and indeed elsewhere in the poem it is possible to find up to three layers of narrative embedded one within another.[8] Scholarship investigating the characteristics of a distinctly Ovidian narrative aesthetic has shown a tendency to focus on paired embedded narratives and their relationship to one another, reducing the complexity of Ovidian narrative discourse to a neat schema: in the different pairs of embedded narratives, scholars have seen paradigms of the "bad" poem and the "good" poem, according to their theories of Ovidian poetics.[9] After detailed analysis of the paired embedded narratives, such studies generally conclude with the suggestion that the "good" embedded poem provides a model for Ovid's "good" poem, the *Metamorphoses* as a whole.[10]

---

6. Fränkel 1945, 75–81.

7. Kenney 1973, 117; cf. Solodow 1988, 34–36.

8. At *Met.* 5.300–678, for example, an unnamed Muse recounts to Athena a song delivered by Calliope in a contest with the Pierids (*Met.* 5.341–661), which contains a first-person narrative of Arethusa's transformation into a spring reported by Arethusa to Ceres (*Met.* 5.577–641), a character in Calliope's narrative. Five books later Calliope's son Orpheus delivers a song, taking as his subjects the illicit passions of women and mortal youths beloved by gods (*Met.* 10.148–739). Orpheus' narrative includes Venus' recital to Adonis of the transformations of Atalanta and Hippomenes into lions (*Met.* 10.560–707). On *Met.* 5.250–678, see Hinds 1987; on *Met.* 10.148–739, see Knox 1986, 48–64, and Barchiesi 1989, 64–73.

9. See especially Anderson 1968, 93–104 (cf. Galinsky 1975, 82–83), and Hofmann 1985, 223–41. Nagle 1985, 28 discusses Calliope's song at *Met.* 5.341–661 by itself as a paradigm of Ovid's narrative aesthetic in the *Metamorphoses.*

10. For a less schematic interpretation of paired embedded narratives, see now Hinds 1987, 126–33 and 166–67 n. 40, who shows that both the Pierid's song (reported by an unnamed Muse to Athena at *Met.* 5.318–31) and Calliope's song (*Met.* 5.341–661) share

Critics have only very recently begun to explore the relationship between embedded narrative and first-layer narrative in the *Metamorphoses,* even though the poem invites critical analysis not only of the stories told by internal narrators, but also of the ways in which the poet/narrator interacts with the embedded tales and reflects upon them.[11] In addressing the question of the relationship between embedding and embedded narrative, scholars have focused on identifying the voice of the internal narrator. Two opposing positions have been adopted: some scholars suggest that there is no essential distinction between internal narrators and the poet/narrator, while others argue, to the contrary, that there are significant distinctions to be made between the two. J.B. Solodow, the foremost proponent of the former view, takes the position that "there is basically a single narrator throughout, who is Ovid himself. The introduction of other speakers is more formal than consequential; the words are heard as those of the poet."[12] Short of an exhaustive examination of every embedded narrative and all of the first-layer narrative of the poet, however, there seems no way either to support or to challenge this view, and Solodow himself discusses in detail only the song of Orpheus at *Met.* 10.148-739.[13] F. Ahl and B.R. Nagle argue, on the other hand, that we must be careful to distinguish the internal narrators from the poet/narrator, and their analyses of individual embedded narratives in the *Metamorphoses* have contributed much to our understanding of an Ovidian narrative aesthetic. Ahl suggests that "in contemplating any tale told in the *Metamorphoses* by a character within the work, we must consider not only what Ovid may wish to suggest to *us* but what the secondary narrator seeks to suggest to his audience... [for] it is often important to our understanding of why the Ovidian version of a myth differs from common versions found elsewhere."[14] In accordance with this premise, Ahl investigates in detail the embedded narrative of Cephalus (*Met.* 7.675-862) and demonstrates that "Ovid's

---

features that are characteristic of the finely crafted Alexandrian poetry it is presumably Ovid's desire to produce.

11. For discussion of some of the embedded narratives in the *Metamorphoses* see, in addition to the material cited in notes 8-10 above, Leach 1974, Due 1974, 123-33, Lateiner 1984, and Knox 1986, 48-64.

12. Solodow 1988, 38. In practice this assumption dominates critical discussion of the *Metamorphoses,* for scholars often fail to distinguish the poet/narrator from internal narrators in analyses of individual passages.

13. Solodow 1988, 39-41.

14. Ahl 1985, 202-3.

story of Cephalus... is shaped by its narrator to the needs of his particular situation."[15] Nagle's studies of thematically related embedded narratives and first-layer narrative in the poem have confirmed the utility of distinguishing between poet/narrator and internal narrator.[16]

The sequence of episodes at *Met.* 2.531–835, which includes the themes of indiscreet loquacity and an interest in story-telling as well as two embedded but unpaired narratives (*Met.* 2.549–95 and 642–64), provides an ideal testing ground for an analysis of the formal characteristics of Ovidian narrative. The present study offers a detailed discussion of *Met.* 2.531–835 in order to elucidate the narrative structures that organize this sequence of episodes. The following issues, in particular, inform my discussion of the sequence of episodes at *Met.* 2.531–835. I am concerned to identify the narrating voice of each episode, whether that of the poet/narrator in first-layer narrative or of distinctive internal narrators in "embedded" or "inset" or "second-layer" narratives, and to examine the circumstances (Genette's "narrating instance") in which an embedded narrative is recounted to an internal narratee.[17] In addition to such problems of narrative point of view that are well known to narratologists, this study investigates the structures that organize the narrative of each brief episode in the sequence. Opening and closing narrative structures are of particular interest to the student of an Ovidian narrative aesthetic, for Ovid accomplishes the continuous narrative of the *Metamorphoses* (*perpetuum... carmen, Met.* 1.4) not by recounting one tale but by effecting transitions from tale to tale. Is it nonetheless possible to identify the beginning and end of an Ovidian episode?[18] Other questions posed in this study will seem more familiar to students of ancient literature, in their attention to recurrent formal and thematic structures that organ-

---

15. Ahl 1985, 211.
16. Nagle 1983, 301–15; 1985, 28; 1988a, 76–77; and 1988b.
17. De Jong (1987, xiv) defines the "recipient of the narration by the narrator" as the "narratee." The phrase *instance narrative,* "narrating instance," is first used by Genette (1972, 227), who explains:

> Une situation narrative, comme toute autre, est un ensemble complexe dans lequel l'analyse, ou simplement la description, ne peut *distinguer* qu'en déchirant un tissu de relations étroites entre l'acte narratif, ses protagonistes, ses déterminations spatio-temporelles, son rapport aux autres situations narratives impliquées dans le même récit, etc.

18. On beginnings see E. Said, *Beginnings: Intention and Method* (New York, 1975); on closure see Kermode 1966, Smith 1968, and Fowler 1989.

ize the progression of Ovidian narrative. Thematic structures will emerge from consideration of the plot, while etymological wordplay and literary allusion constitute two common formal structures employed as organizational features of the narrative. Throughout, this study takes account of critical developments in narratology, a field of study that undertakes "the systematic investigation of different codes and contexts of narrative."[19]

Chapter 1 explores in detail the embedded narrative of the crow at *Met.* 2.549-95. Taking as a starting point the principal modelling text for the crow's speech, Callimachus' *Hecale* (Hollis frr. 70-74; = fr. 260 Pf.; = *SH* 288), the chapter traces the recurrent thematic and formal structures that organize this embedded narrative. The crow's garrulity is the point of departure for every ancient description of the bird, and while the Ovidian crow's narrative develops in accordance with this characterization there are several features of the narrative that may be expected to show points of contact with the organization of the poet/narrator's first-layer narrative. Chapter 2 explores the relationship between the first-layer account of the raven's metamorphosis (*Met.* 2.531-632) and the crow's narrative and suggests that Ovid's treatment of the raven's metamorphosis (as a punishment for tale-bearing) functions as a sophisticated reinterpretation of the crow's story. Chapter 3 examines the narrative role of prophecy in the tale of Chiron's daughter Ocyroe (*Met.* 2.633-79), with particular attention to the function of etymological wordplay in narrative. Chiron's daughter is the first mortal prophet we meet in the *Metamorphoses* and she offers a melancholy paradigm for the place of the *vates* (both prophet and poet) in the world, for Ocyroe's metamorphosis and loss of the faculty of speech are inflicted upon her as a punishment for uttering prophecies. Chapter 4 examines the poet's treatment of language and story-telling in the episode of Battus (*Met.* 2.680-707), a character whose avarice prompts his foray into tale-bearing. Chapter 5 investigates the structure of Ovid's account of the fate of the daughters of Cecrops, and particularly that of Aglauros, the wicked sister (*Met.* 2.708-835). This episode concludes the thematically

---

19. Steiner 1988, 95. The modern study of narratology begins with Auerbach 1946. Other works that have proved useful for this study include Kermode 1966, Barthes 1970 and 1977, Todorov 1971, Genette 1972, Hollander 1981, Prince 1982, Kermode 1983, and Bal 1985. Classical scholarship has not been slow to employ the new theoretical models: see Nagle 1983, 1985, 1988a, and 1988b; Winkler 1986; de Jong 1987; Barchiesi 1989; and R. Hexter, "What Was the Trojan Horse Made of? Interpreting Vergil's *Aeneid*," *Yale Journal of Criticism* 3.2 (1990): 109-31.

related sequence by returning to characters first introduced in the embedded narrative of the crow and by reversing the thematic structure that organizes the rest of the sequence. A brief epilogue considers some of the broader implications of Ovid's interest in language and narrative, and suggests that this interest in the "appropriate" use of speech may reflect—and reflect upon—political developments under the institution of the principate, *viz.*, the imperial controls encroaching upon all modes of discourse.

Chapter 1

The Crow's Tale: *Met.* 2.549-95

> tum cornix plena pluviam vocat improba voce
> et sola in sicca secum spatiatur harena.
> —Virgil, *Geo.* 1.388-89

A convenient point of departure in considering the speech of Ovid's *cornix* is its principal model, the speech of the Callimachean κορώνη in the *Hecale*. Let us begin our discussion by reexamining the text of the Callimachean passage in order to determine as closely as possible its context, for an accurate assessment of that context is the key to understanding Ovid's *imitatio*. It will be salutary at the outset to argue directly from the *Hecale* and independently of the Ovidian narrative to which scholars reconstructing the Callimachean version have usually had recourse.[1] We will then ensure that the long-standing agreement regarding Ovid's debt to Callimachus has not been based on circular argument. The newly detailed demonstration of Ovid's dependence on Callimachus that follows will be on the firmest possible ground.[2]

The longest of our fragments of the *Hecale* (Hollis frr. 69-74; = frr. 260, 261, 346, 351, and 374 Pf.; *SH* 288 and 289) can be reconstructed from four papyri, although there are significant problems with the restoration of the text.[3] We are missing approximately twenty-two lines

---

1. See Haupt, Ehwald, and Albrecht 1966, 120-25; Cola 1937, 43; Pfeiffer 1949, 249, *ad* 27ff.; Barigazzi 1954, 319; Lloyd-Jones and Rea 1968, 140; Bömer 1969, 371; Otis 1970, 119, 381, and 388-89; Boillat 1976, 124-25; Moore-Blunt 1977, 115; Hill 1985, 207; Bulloch 1985, 563, with H. Lloyd-Jones' review of P.E. Easterling and B.M.W. Knox, eds., *The Cambridge History of Classical Literature 1* (Cambridge, 1985), *CP* 82 (1987): 264; and the cautious remarks of Hollis 1990, 33.

2. The following discussion is greatly indebted to Pfeiffer 1949, 247-53; Lloyd-Jones and Rea 1968, 133-45; and Hollis 1990, 217-62. Wherever they depend on *Met.* 2.535-95 for the reconstruction of the Callimachean fragment, however, I have attempted to argue the point from the remains of the *Hecale* alone.

3. 1) *Tabula Vindobonensis,* first published by T. Gomperz, *MPER* VI (1897) 1 (=

10 / *The Play of Fictions*

between the first and second columns of the *Tabula Vindobonensis* (our most important witness); twenty-two lines again between the second and third columns; and approximately eleven lines between the third and fourth columns. Moreover, the reconstruction of the second and third columns, the most important for our study, is the least secure. It is nonetheless possible to establish several elements of the narrating situation from the narrative itself: we can identify first who is speaking; second, what the subject of the narrative is; and third, to whom the narrative is addressed.[4]

> until the time when to the daughters of Cecrops... secret, not to be spoken, and whence his lineage I neither knew nor learned... [but a story reached the][5] birds, that Gaia bore him to Hephaistos. Then she [i.e., Athena], in order to set up a bulwark for her land which she had recently acquired by vote of Zeus and the twelve other immortals and by witness of the snake, came to Achaian Pellene. But during that time the girls, his guardians, planned to accomplish a wicked deed, to release [the bonds of] the chest...
>
> (Hollis fr. 70.5-14)

[approximately 22 verses missing][6]

> [Athena], bearing aloft a great chunk of Hypsizorus, was going up to the city, when I met her at the beautiful, ever-gleaming, gymnasium of Lycean Apollo.... But she, turning livid and with her eyes looking grimly askance....
>
> (Hollis frr. 71-72)

> ...crows... for I once... your anger, mistress... many things of ill-

---

P.Rainer VI, 1-18), is the main witness. It is supplemented by 2) *P.Oxy.* 2217, first published by E. Lobel in *P.Oxy.* vol. 19 (1948, 44ff.); 3) *P.Oxy.* 2398, published by E. Lobel in *P.Oxy.* vol. 24 (1957, 97ff.); and 4) *P.Oxy.* 2437, published by E. Lobel in *P.Oxy.* vol. 25 (1959, 123ff.). H. Lloyd-Jones has twice published a text of this passage: first with J. Rea (1968), and more recently still with P. Parsons (1983, 130-34). The most recent edition of the *Hecale* is that of Hollis 1990, whose frr. 69-74 (pp. 95-100) correspond to Pfeiffer 1949, frr. 260, 261, 346, 351, and 374, and to Lloyd-Jones and Parsons 1983, frr. 288 and 289: all quotations of the *Hecale* are from Hollis 1990 unless otherwise noted.

4. For the full text of this section of the *Hecale,* see Appendix 3.

5. Hollis 1990, 235.

6. Hollis 1990, 96-97 locates frr. 71 and 72 in this passage: see pp. 237-40 of his commentary.

omen the nimble birds never..., and at that time they ought to have... [your]... on the one hand... [but] our... she laid low... nor ever from her spirit; for Athena's anger is always grievous. But I was present as a little child; for already is come my eighth[7] generation....

(Hollis fr. 73.6-14)

[approximately 11 verses missing]

May I only have remedies against wretched hunger for my belly... but Hecale... and of a posset which dripped coarse barley meal to the ground... ah, you will get no thanks for your audacity[8]... messenger of bad news. For would that you were... living still throughout that time, that... thus the Thriae inspire the old crow. Yes, by—for not yet have all the days [elapsed]—by my shrivelled hide, by this tree, dry though it is—not all suns have yet shattered their pole and axle, and set their feet in the west, but there will come an evening or night, midday or dawn when the raven, who now at least could rival swans and milk in complexion, and the foam on the crest of the wave, will have on him a thick plumage as dark as pitch, the reward for tale-bearing which Phoebus will grant him at the time when he learns the abominable deed of Koronis, the daughter of Phlegyas, who followed horse-driving Ischys." So saying, sleep came over her and her listening companion.

(Hollis fr. 74.1-21)

The first person verbs ἔγνων and ἐδάην (Hollis fr. 70.6-7)[9], the first person pronouns ἐγώ, ἔγωγε, and μοι (Hollis frr. 70.4, 71.2, 73.7, 13, 14), and the first person pronominal adjectives ἡμετερ[..] and ἐμόν (frr. 73.11, 74.11), combine to show that the narrative voice of the passage is the first singular. We can also conclude, again from the evidence of the fragment itself, that the speaker is not the poet of the *Hecale* as a whole but an internal narrator, for the resumptive φαμένην at Hollis fr. 74.21, an epic convention, shows that the preceding passage is reported in direct discourse: τὴν μὲν ἄρ' ὣς φαμένην ὕπνος λάβε, τὴν δ'

---
7. On the reading [ὀ]γδ[ο]άτ[η] at Hollis fr. 73.13, see Appendix 3.
8. Hollis 1990, 245, quoting Lloyd-Jones.
9. The readings of both verbs are secure. Cf. also ἔ]χοιμι at Hollis 1990, 98, fr. 74.1, where the first singular personal ending of the verb is also secure.

ἀΐουσαν, "so saying, sleep came over her and her listening companion."[10] The passage itself also provides evidence to suggest that the speaker is a crow. It is the old crow, γρῆῦν . . . κορώνην (Hollis fr. 74.9), whom the Thriae inspire and it must therefore be the crow (despite the third person reference at Hollis fr. 74.9) who swears the oath immediately following (Hollis fr. 74.10–11),[11] and who then goes on to prophesy that the raven will lose Apollo's favor by informing him of Coronis' infidelity (Hollis fr. 74.14–20). The ancients commonly attributed the gift of prophecy to the crow.[12] Moreover, the crow was commonly characterized as garrulous in antiquity, and such a characterization is particularly appropriate to the speaker in the *Hecale,* who continues at considerable length (Hollis frr. 70–74.20).[13] Since we are missing numerous lines at the start of our text and the narrative is already in progress when the text resumes in column ii (Hollis fr. 70), we cannot know when the internal narrator began speaking. Nevertheless, we can calculate that the narrative must be at least seventy-nine lines long, for the total must include the thirty-four lines missing between the second and third, and the third and fourth columns of the *Tabula Vindobonensis,* as well as the number of lines we actually have.[14] At an early point in our passage, the speaker seems to have referred to begging (Hollis fr. 74.1), and both greed and begging feature prominently in ancient descriptions of the crow.[15] Finally, we

---

10. Cf. Homer *Il.* 5.290, 835, *Od.* 10.446, etc. I. de Jong 1987, 197 discusses the speech formulae that open and close direct discourse in the *Iliad* and concludes that the "capping" formula (i.e., the closural formula) "normally contains: an anaphoric (demonstrative) pronoun [and a] verb of speaking." See further de Jong 1987, 200–3.

11. Cf. Lloyd-Jones and Rea 1968, 143. Note also the first singular personal pronominal adjective ἐμόν (Hollis fr. 74.11).

12. See Ap. Rhod. 3.927–39; Aes. *Fab.* 202; Nonnus, *Dionys.* 3.97–98; Plaut. *Asin.* 260; Virg. *Ecl.* 9.15; Prop. 4.1.105; Prud. *Apoth.* 298; Isid. *Or.* 12.7.44. Cf. also Ernout-Meillet 143, s.v. *cornix,* and 145, s.v. *corvus;* Thompson 1936, 171–72 s.v. ΚΟΡΩΝΗ; and *R-E* 11.1564, s.v. *Krähe.* I would like to thank Professor T.D. Barnes for drawing to my attention Appian fr. 19, a passage that presupposes knowledge of the crow's well-known role as a prophet.

13. For the proverbial garrulity of the crow in antiquity, see Hesiod fr. 304 M-W (= fr. 171 [Rz]); Ap. Rhod. 3.929; [Ovid] *Amores* 3.5.21–22; Ovid, *Fasti* 2.89; Plin. *N.H.* 10.30; Macrobius, *Sat.* 2.4.29–30; cf. Varro, *L.L.* 6.56 with Kent 1938, vol. 1, *ad loc.* See further Thompson 1936, 168–72, s.v. ΚΟΡΩΝΗ; and cf. Lloyd-Jones and Rea 1968, 142.

14. Cf. Hollis 1990, 224–25, who calculates the crow's speech to be at least eighty-two lines in length.

15. Cf. Arist. *H.A.* 9.593b 14; Archil. 44, *ap.* Athen. 594 (= M. West, *Iambi et Elegi Graeci* 1 [Oxford 1971] fr. 331, p. 108). See further Thompson 1936, 169 and 172, s.v. ΚΟΡΩΝΗ; and Lloyd-Jones and Rea 1968, 141. Hollis 1990, 258 suggests that his fr. 75, γίνεό μοι τέκταινα βίου δαμάτειρά τε λιμοῦ, "be my provider of livelihood and subduer of hunger" (= fr. 267 Pf.), refers to the crow's voracious appetite and may have been

know that the ancients believed the crow to be very long-lived, and the narrator in our passage seems to refer to her great age at several points in the narrative: ὀ]γδ[ο]άτ[η] γὰρ / ἤδη μοι γενεὴ (Hollis fr. 73.13-14, with Gomperz' supplement); ζώουσα κατὰ χρόνον (Hollis fr. 74.8);[16] ναὶ [μ]ὰ τὸ ῥικνὸν / σῦφαρ ἐμόν (Hollis fr. 74.10-11).[17] The most likely candidate for the speaker in this passage, therefore, is a crow.

The first subject of the inset narrative of the crow in the *Hecale* seems to be an aetiological explanation of Athena's hatred for the race of crows (Hollis frr. 70-73). Antigonus Carystius reports an explanation for this feeling of Athena, which supplements our understanding of the Callimachean narrative.

> Amelesagoras the Athenian, who wrote the *Atthis,* says that the crow does not fly up to the acropolis, nor could he say that he had seen one there; and he gives the reason in a story. For he says that Athena was given in marriage to Hephaestus, but when she had lain with him she disappeared and Hephaestus, falling to the ground, ejaculated his seed. Later the earth gave birth at that place to Erichthonius, whom Athena took into her keeping; she shut him into a chest, entrusted it to the daughters of Cecrops—Agraulos, Pandrosos, and Herse— and instructed them not to open the chest until she returned. And upon reaching Pellene, Athena carried off a mountain in order to set up a bulwark for the acropolis; but two of the daughters of Cecrops, Agraulos and Pandrosos, unfastened the chest and saw two serpents around Erichthonius. He says that a crow met Athena carrying the mountain which is now called Lykabettos, and told her that Erichthonius had been revealed. Upon hearing this Athena threw down the mountain where it now stands and for reporting bad news she told the crow that it would no longer be lawful for her to approach the acropolis. (Antigonus Carystius, *Hist. mirab.* 12)[18]

---

part of her speech in the "lacuna between frs. 73 and 74 (less probably in the lacuna between frs. 69 and 70)."

16. Trypanis (1958, 195) supposes this to refer to Hecale's age, in a wish that she had lived even longer. The present fragmentary state of the text makes certainty unattainable.

17. Cf. Lloyd-Jones and Rea 1968, 143-44. Hesiod fr. 304 M-W attests to both long life and garrulity as characteristics of the crow: ἐννέα τοι ζώει γενεὰς λακέρυζα κορώνη / ἀνδρῶν ἡβώντων, "the chattering crow lives through nine generations of full-grown men." Cf. Aratus, *Phaenomena* 1022, ἐννεάγηρα κορώνη, "the crow, nine times [as] old [as a man]," which is modeled on the Hesiodic tag (as also Ap. Rhod. 3.927, cited above, nn. 12 and 13). Cf. Ar. *Av.* 967; *Greek Anthol.* 2.193; Lucr. 5.1083; Hor. *C.* 3.17.13, *C.* 4.13.25; Martial 10.67. See further Thompson 1936, 169 and 172, s.v. ΚΟΡΩΝΗ.

18. Ἀμελησαγόρας δὲ ὁ Ἀθηναῖος, ὁ τὴν Ἀτθίδα συγγεγραφώς, οὔ φησι κορώνην

It is clear that, although fragmentary, the embedded narrative in the *Hecale* and the account of Antigonus Carystius concern the same story. In Callimachus' account, Aglauros, Pandrosos, and Herse are introduced as Cecrops' daughters, Κεκροπίδ[η]σιν (Hollis fr. 70.5).[19] Cecrops himself is also apparently alluded to, in his role as the judge who casts the deciding vote in the contest between Athena and Poseidon for possession of Athens (Hollis fr. 70.10–11). We meet the infant Erichthonius immediately following the daughters of Cecrops (Hollis fr. 70.6–8), and although Erichthonius' name does not occur in our remains of the *Hecale,* we can be sure that these lines refer to him, for Nonnus uses λάθριον of Erechtheus (= Erichthonius) at *Dionys.* 27.115, in the same metrical *sedes,* at the beginning of the hexameter.[20] Moreover, we learn elsewhere that Erichthonius was the offspring born to Hephaestus from Earth.[21] The narrator in our passage of the *Hecale* then returns to the

---

προσίπτασθαι πρὸς τὴν ἀκρόπολιν, οὐδ' ἔχοι ἂν εἰπεῖν ἑορακὼς οὐδείς. Ἀποδίδωσιν δὲ τὴν αἰτίαν μυθικῶς. φησὶν γὰρ Ἡφαίστῳ δοθείσης τῆς Ἀθηνᾶς, συγκατακλιθεῖσαν αὐτῷ ἀφανισθῆναι. τὸν δὲ Ἥφαιστον, εἰς γῆν πεσόντα, προίεσθαι τὸ σπέρμα. τὴν δὲ γῆν ὕστερον αὐτῷ ἀναδοῦναι Ἐριχθόνιον, ὃν τρέφειν τὴν Ἀθηνᾶν, καὶ εἰς κίστην καθεῖρξαι, καὶ παραθέσθαι ταῖς Κέκροπος παισίν, Ἀγραύλῳ καὶ Πανδρόσῳ καὶ Ἔρσῃ, καὶ ἐπιτάξαι μὴ ἀνοίγειν τὴν κίστην, ἕως ἂν αὐτὴ ἔλθῃ. ἀφικομένην δὲ εἰς Πελλήνην, φέρειν ὄρος, ἵνα ἔρυμα πρὸ τῆς ἀκροπόλεως ποιήσῃ· τὰς δὲ Κέκροπος θυγατέρας τὰς δύο, Ἄγραυλον καὶ Πάνδροσον, τὴν κίστην ἀνοῖξαι, καὶ ἰδεῖν δράκοντας δύο περὶ τὸν Ἐριχθόνιον. τῇ δὲ Ἀθηνᾷ, φερούσῃ τὸ ὄρος, ὃ νῦν καλεῖται Λυκαβηττός, κορώνην φησὶν ἀπαντῆσαι, καὶ εἰπεῖν, ὅτι Ἐριχθόνιος ἐν φανερῷ· τὴν δὲ ἀκούσασαν, ῥῖψαι τὸ ὄρος ὅπου νῦν ἐστι. τῇ δὲ κορώνῃ, διὰ τὴν κακαγγελίαν, εἰπεῖν ὡς εἰς ἀκρόπολιν οὐ θέμις αὐτῇ ἔσται ἀφικέσθαι. (*Hist. mirab.* 12 = *FGrH* 330 1)

Jacoby demonstrated that it was very likely that the account of Amelesagoras (mentioned by Antigonus Carystius) was Callimachus' source for this passage in the *Hecale*. See *FGrH* IIIb, vol. 1, 602–3 (with vol. 2, 490–92) for a full exposition of the argument. We can reconstruct the course of the Callimachean narrative relatively securely using this evidence (and cf. Apollodorus 3.14.6). For hostility between Athena and the crow, cf. Paus. 10.15.5, Plutarch, *De pyth. orac.* 8, Lucr. 6.751-55, and Ovid, *Amores* 2.6.35: see Thompson 1936, 170, s.v. ΚΟΡΩΝΗ. κακαγγελία is a distinctive characteristic of the crow: see Labate 1986, 141–43.

19. Pfeiffer 1949, 248; Lloyd-Jones and Rea 1968, 126 and 131; Lloyd-Jones and Parsons 1983, 131; and Hollis 1990, 96 all restore some form of the patronymic. Pfeiffer assumes them to be the daughters of the first Athenian king Cecrops in his note *ad loc.*

20. According to Harpocration s.v. Αὐτόχθονες, Pindar was the first to distinguish between Erichtheus and Erichthonius (*Pyth.* 7.10, fr. 253). The *Et. Mag.* too shows that Erechtheus was also called Erichthonius (s.v. Ερεχθεύς): see Burkert 1983, 156, and cf. Lloyd-Jones and Rea 1968, 136.

21. Cf. the discussion in Pfeiffer 1949, who quotes Schol. AD to Homer, *Il.* 2.547: "Erichthonius... was born of Hephaestus. For this god was in amorous pursuit of Athene... and he ejaculated on the goddess' thigh. Disgusted, she wiped it off with wool

daughters of Cecrops, calling them guardians (presumably of Erichthonius) and telling the story of the crime they planned (Hollis fr. 70.12-14). Later in the passage we find Athena very angry: βαρὺς χόλος αἰὲν Ἀθήνης "Athena's anger is always grievous" (Hollis fr. 73.12). Lloyd-Jones suggests that the immediately preceding lines be restored to read something like οὕτως ὑμε]τέρην μὲν... ἀλλὰ γενέθλην / ἡμετέρ[ην] ἔκλεινε, with the sense "Your race she [i.e., Athena] exalted, mine she depressed."[22] Such a reconstruction of the text would make the crow the object of Athena's anger, through what must certainly be the first person pronominal adjective, ἡμετέρην (Hollis fr. 73.11).

Thus far we have established that an internal narrator, whom we have identified as a crow, explains her loss of Athena's favor at the outset of her narrative (Hollis frr. 70-73). The badly preserved central section of the narrative (Hollis fr. 74.1-5 and presumably some of the eleven missing lines) seems to take up a different subject, and it has been suggested that the crow here reviews the close relationship that subsequently developed between herself and Hecale.[23] The crow's narrative then closed with a prophecy of the downfall of the raven as a consequence of reporting bad news to Apollo (Hollis fr. 74.10-20). It is clear from this summary of the narrative progression of the passage that the Callimachean κορώνη told her interlocutor more than one tale, although the lacunose central section makes it impossible for us to be sure whether she told two distinct stories (an explanation for Athena's hatred of the race of crows and the prophecy of the raven's metamorphosis) or three (an account of the crow's relationship with Hecale in addition to the aetion of Athena's hatred for crows and the prophecy of the raven's metamorphosis).

The identity of the crow's interlocutor in the *Hecale* remains a vexed problem, but some facts can be established nevertheless. First, we may note that the narrative itself can be best understood if the crow's audience is another bird,[24] who is sitting in the tree mentioned in the crow's oath

---

and hurled the seed onto the ground. Whence was born the child Erichthonius, given back from the ground, and he was named for the wool [*erios*] and the ground [*chthon*]. Callimachus tells this story in the *Hecale*." The tale is also recounted at Apollodorus, 3.14.6; Eur. fr. 925 N² *ap.* [Eratosth.] *Cataster.* 13; Nonnus, *Dionys.* 13.177ff.; Amelesagoras, *FGrH* 330 F 1 (= Antigonus Carystius, *Hist. mirab.* 12); and Hyg. *Astr.* II 13. B. Powell (1906) collects (pp. 56-64) and discusses (pp. 1-7) all the relevant material.

22. Lloyd-Jones and Rea 1968, 140.
23. Lloyd-Jones and Rea 1968, 141.
24. Cf. Pfeiffer 1949, 248. For another pair of chattering birds (one of which is a crow)

(Hollis fr. 74.11). It has been suggested that the other bird is an owl, and this is an attractive proposal for a number of reasons.[25] Other fragments of, or at least attributable to, the *Hecale* suggest that the owl appeared in it.[26] In our passage, the crow apparently warns her interlocutor against bringing bad news (κακάγγελον, Hollis fr. 74.7; cf. κακαγγελίαν, Antig. Caryst., *Hist. mirab.* 12), first by describing her own experience with Athena's wrath and then by foretelling the raven's metamorphosis because of Apollo's wrath. The bird to whom the crow is talking seems to be one who enjoys Athena's favor, as the reconstruction of Lloyd-Jones quoted earlier would suggest. If this reconstruction could be shown to be correct, the owl would be a most appropriate audience for the crow's narrative, since the owl is the bird most commonly associated with Athena in antiquity.[27] It would be particularly suitable for the former favorite of Athena to use her experience to warn her new favorite.[28] Nor need we suppose that the two are not on speaking terms.[29] I conclude with Wilamowitz and Lloyd-Jones, therefore, that the owl is the most attractive candidate for the identity of the bird to whom the crow's narrative is addressed.

Reexamination of the narrating instance of this fragment of Callimachus' *Hecale,* without recourse to the Ovidian evidence, has confirmed

---

conversing in a tree, cf. Call. *Iamb.* 4.61ff.: on the relationship between the talking birds of *Iamb.* 4.61ff., and those of the *Hecale,* see Clayman 1980 and Hollis 1990, 26–27. Garrulous crows speaking from trees also appear at Ap. Rhod. 3.929–37, in a passage with a number of Callimachean resonances: see Hunter 1989, 200–201 *ad loc.* and Hollis 1990, 26–27. The theory that Hecale is the crow's interlocutor has been decisively refuted by Lloyd-Jones and Rea 1968, 142–44.

25. First suggested by U. von Wilamowitz-Moellendorff, "Über die *Hekale* des Kallimachos," *Kleine Schriften* (Berlin and Amsterdam 1935–72), 2:30–47 (first published 1893). Lloyd-Jones and Rea (1968, 142–43) support this suggestion.

26. Hollis frr. 77 (= fr. 326 Pf.), 167 (= fr. 519 Pf.), and 168 (= fr. 608 Pf.); cf. perhaps fr. 803 (Pf.).

27. The fragmentary state of the *Hecale* precludes certainty; cf. Lloyd-Jones and Rea 1968, 140–41 and Hollis 1990, 225–26. For the owl as the bird of Athena, cf. Ar. *Av.* 516 and *Eq.* 1092; see further Thompson 1936, 80, s.v. ΓΛΑΥΞ. For the owl on the reverse of Athenian coins bearing the head of Athena, see B.V. Head, *Historia Numorum* (Oxford 1911): 368–76; cf. Ar. *Av.* 1106 and Schol. *ad* Ar. *Eq.* 1091.

28. For the crow as the bird of Athena see Nonnus, *Dionys.* 3.122; Paus. 4.34.6, where Pausanias reports that in Corone ("Crow-town") in Messenia, a bronze statue of Athena holding a crow in her hand could be found; and Paus. 2.11.7, with Frazer 1898, *ad loc.*

29. Cf. the discussion in Lloyd-Jones and Rea 1968, 142. For enmity between crow and owl, however, see Thompson 1936, 169–70, s.v. ΚΟΡΩΝΗ; cf. Aelian, *Nat. Anim.* 3.9, 5.48; Antigonus Carystius, *Hist. mirab.* 57 (62); Arist. *H.A.* 9.609 a 8; Plut. *Mor.* 537 C; Ovid, *Fasti* 2.89.

that the speaker is an internal narrator who can be securely identified as a crow. We can conclude, moreover, that the crow delivered a narrative at least seventy-nine lines in length, which comprised two or three sections: her narrative opened with the story of how Athena came to hate the race of crows (Hollis frr. 70-73); she may then have reviewed her close relationship with Hecale herself or continued to describe the disastrous results of her tale-bearing (Hollis fr. 74.1-5);[30] and she concluded with a prophecy of the raven's fall from grace and subsequent punishment by Apollo (Hollis fr. 74.6-20). Lastly, the crow's audience is another bird, possibly the owl (Hollis fr. 74.11, 21).

We are now in a position to investigate the nature of the relationship between the narratives of the Callimachean κορώνη (Hollis frr. 70-74) and the Ovidian *cornix* (*Met.* 2.549-95). Foremost among the similarities between the passages are the circumstances in which the embedded narratives are situated in their respective texts. Ovid's *cornix*, following the example of the Callimachean κορώνη in the *Hecale,* delivers a first-person narrative about herself to another bird, in this case the raven. The organization of the Ovidian narrative also parallels, in abbreviated form, that of our passage in the *Hecale*. In the first story that Ovid's *cornix* tells, we find the daughters of Cecrops in charge of a chest containing Erichthonius (*Met.* 2.552-61), just as we saw them in the crow's narrative in the *Hecale* (Hollis frr. 70-73). The Cecropids have received instructions concerning this chest from Pallas Athena (*Met.* 2.552-56; cf. Hollis fr. 70.5-6), but in the *Metamorphoses,* as in the *Hecale,* the sisters disobey the goddess' explicit injunction not to unfasten the chest and look into it (*Met.* 2.558-61; cf. Hollis fr. 70.12-14). The crow, who has witnessed the crime of Cecrops' daughters, reports it to the goddess (*Met.* 2.557-62; cf. Hollis frr. 71 and 74.7). Minerva then conceives anger against the crow herself and remains hostile (*Met.* 2.562-68; cf. Hollis frr. 72-73). The structure of the first part of the Ovidian crow's narrative is, insofar as we can compare the two versions, essentially the same as the first part of the Callimachean crow's narrative, and lexical points of contact between the two versions have often been noted.[31] Ovid uses the same word to designate the chest in which Erichthonius lies as that which Callimachus seems to have used in the *Hecale*

---

30. Lloyd-Jones and Rea 1968, 141 suggest that the crow's narrative may at some point have touched on the subject of Hecale herself; cf. Hutchinson 1988, 60 and Hollis 1990, 243.

31. See Pfeiffer 1949, 248-50; Lloyd-Jones and Rea 1968, 133-45; and Hollis 1990,

(*cista, Met.* 2.554; cf. κ.ίστη, Hollis fr. 70.14).³² The crime the daughters of Cecrops commit is lexically equivalent in both versions (δεσμά τ' ἀνεῖσαι, Gomperz' supplement, Hollis fr. 70.14; *nodos . . . manu diducit,* "one unbound the fastenings with her hand" *Met.* 2.560).³³ The daughters of Cecrops are introduced in both passages by the name of their father (Κεκροπίδῃσιν, Hollis fr. 70.5; *virginibus tribus gemino de Cecrope natis,* "the three maidens, daughters of biform Cecrops," *Met.* 2.555).³⁴ Moreover, the contents of the *cista* / κίστη are characterized in both versions as secret and concealed (*secreta, Met.* 2.556; λάθριον ἄρρητον, Hollis fr. 70.6). Ovid even specifies the Attic setting of the tale with the pointed phrase *Actaeo . . . de vimine,* "from Athenian osier" (*Met.* 2.554), recalling the opening of Callimachus' *Hecale* that explicitly sets the scene in Attica: Ἀκταίη τις ἔναιεν Ἐρεχθέος ἔν ποτε γουνῷ, "A woman of Attica once dwelt in the hill country of Erechtheus" (Hollis fr. 1; = fr. 230 Pf.).³⁵

The relationship of the remaining two-thirds of the crow's narrative in the *Metamorphoses* to the narrative of the κορώνη in the *Hecale* is less clear, however, since the Ovidian *cornix* neither mentions Hecale nor prophesies the raven's metamorphosis. Nonetheless, it is likely that the structure of the Ovidian crow's narrative alludes to the κορώνη's narrative in the *Hecale* as its model in two ways. First, we may note that after recounting the misdeeds of the Cecropids and the disastrous results of her report, the *cornix* embarks on a review of her personal history (*Met.* 2.569-88), which may be analogous to the central section of the Callimachean κορώνη's narrative (Hollis fr. 74.1-5), if at that point the κορώνη did indeed reminisce about her past relationship with Hecale. Second, by having the *cornix* conclude her narrative with complaints

---

226-52. Cf. also Haupt, Ehwald, and Albrecht 1966, 120-25; Bömer 1969, 374-79; and Moore-Blunt 1977, 115-16.

32. Lloyd-Jones and Rea (1968, 129) doubt Gomperz' reading κείστης for reasons of paleography, although the sense of the passage certainly seems to require the reading. Hollis (1990, 237) notes that κᾳιστης is possible and remarks that it is the appropriate word. Indeed, κίστη is the technical term for the basket in which the sacred objects are carried in ritual, and it frequently appears in accounts of the myth of Erichthonius: see the sources collected by Powell 1906, 56-64, and the discussions of Burkert 1983, 150-52 and 1985, 229, with notes, 439. So also Robertson 1983, 248 n. 23: "The literary sources for the fostering of Erichthonius . . . mostly say κίστη, *cista, cistula.*"

33. The reading accepted by Pfeiffer 1949, 249. Lloyd-Jones and Rea (1968, 129) report "δέσματ'" unconfirmed"; cf. Lloyd-Jones and Parsons 1983, 133. Hollis (1990, 96) notes of Gomperz' supplement, *"non excluditur"*: see further his discussion *ad loc.,* 1990, 237.

34. Cf. Pfeiffer 1949, 248; Lloyd-Jones and Rea 1968, 128; and Hollis 1990, 233.

35. Cf. Bömer 1969, 376; Moore-Blunt 1977, 119; and Hollis 1990, 137.

about the owl, the bird which has supplanted her in Minerva's favor (*Met.* 2.589-95), Ovid transforms the owl from the probable interlocutor of Callimachus' κορώνη in the *Hecale* into a subject of his crow's narrative, and in turn the raven, a subject of the narrative in the *Hecale*, is recast as the crow's interlocutor.[36] Ovid would thus retain the three birds Callimachus had used in the *Hecale* (the crow, the owl, and the raven), redeploying them in his own narrative in such a way as to point the *doctus lector* back to the modelling passage. This analysis accounts for the single discrepancy between the narrating instances of the two passages, the different interlocutors.

Perhaps a final point of contact between the two passages is to be found in their respective versions of Coronis' infidelity to Apollo and the raven's role in carrying this information to Apollo. Callimachus' crow delivers a prophecy concerning the raven's fall from grace and subsequent color change (Hollis fr. 74.15-20), probably in order to deter the owl from reporting bad news. In Ovid's version the crow tells the story of her own fall from grace in order to deter the raven from making this very journey to Apollo.

> ... quem garrula motis
> consequitur pennis, scitetur ut omnia, cornix
> auditaque viae causa 'non utile carpis'
> inquit 'iter: ne sperne meae praesagia linguae.'
>
> (*Met.* 2.547-50)

[... whom (i.e., Phoebus' bird, the raven) the chattering crow followed on her flapping wings in order to learn all his gossip, but when she heard the reason for his trip she said, "You undertake a useless journey: dɔ not disdain my tongue's prophetic warnings."]

Her story is explicitly a warning to the raven rather than a prophecy: ... *mea poena volucres / admonuisse potest, ne voce pericula quaerant* (*Met.* 2.564-65), "my punishment can warn birds not to court danger with their talk."[37] The crow merely warns the raven that Apollo will not be pleased and adduces her own story in order to deter the raven from reporting Coronis' infidelity, foregoing the prediction of the raven's

---

36. Cf. Lloyd-Jones and Rea 1968, 142.

37. Avery 1937, 37 characterizes the speech at *Met.* 2.549-95 as an "argument against some line of conduct." Cf. Boillat 1976, 125; and Nagle 1988b, 43.

metamorphosis that her counterpart in the *Hecale* gives. But the first words of the *cornix* seem to allude to the Callimachean crow's prophecy: *ne sperne meae praesagia linguae* (*Met.* 2.550), "do not disdain my tongue's presentiments." Ovid has chosen the crow's diction here very carefully, for *praesagium* is a "forewarning," "presage," or "portent," and thus carries with it a connotation of prophecy.[38] In the first words of the *cornix* narrative, then, Ovid alludes to the prophetic narrative that closes the longer speech of the Callimachean κορώνη.[39]

It seems certain, therefore, that the long-standing agreement that the literary impulse behind Ovid's narrative at *Met.* 2.549-95 was offered by Callimachus' *Hecale* need not be challenged. Such a source is likely on *a priori* grounds also, inasmuch as the *Hecale* and the *Aetia* were Callimachus' most famous works in antiquity,[40] and we know that Ovid used the *Hecale* as a source for other stories in the *Metamorphoses* (e.g., the story of Baucis and Philemon, narrated at *Met.* 8.620-724).[41] Ovid's adaptation of this passage gestures deftly towards the *Hecale* as its model, not only in embedding the crow's narrative, but also in the organization of that embedded narrative. Ovid retains the interlocutors and subjects of the Callimachean narrative, rearranging them to suit the purposes of his own narrative.

At this point we are ready to consider more closely the Ovidian narrative itself, as distinct from its Callimachean model. We may begin by noting that the crow's speech to the raven at *Met.* 2.549-95 comprises three discrete tales: she opens with an explanation of Minerva's hatred for the crow (*Met.* 2.549-68); she then reviews her lineage and metamorphosis (*Met.* 2.569-88); and she concludes with complaints that the owl, who has displaced her from Athena's favor, is unworthy of that honor (*Met.* 2.589-95).[42] The crow begins her speech with a reference to the raven's journey, making her narrative immediately relevant to the raven by saying *non utile carpis . . . iter: ne sperne meae praesagia lin-*

---

38. *OLD* s.v. *praesagium* 2.

39. Zetzel (1983, 261) notes that "it seems to be a convention of Alexandrian and neoteric poetry to reverse beginnings and ends." Thus Catullus, for example, alludes to the end of Apollonius' *Argonautika* (4. 1773-75) at the opening of poem 64 (22-25). Zetzel (1983, 261 n. 28) offers further examples.

40. Crinagoras *Anth. Pal.* 9.545. See Hollis 1990, 26-40 on the influence and survival of the *Hecale*.

41. See the discussion of Bömer 1977, 190-96, *ad loc.*; cf. also Wilkinson 1955, 154 and 187; Bulloch 1985, 563; Hutchinson 1988, 346-48; and Hollis 1990, 33-34.

42. Boillat (1976, 117) analyzes the inset narrative of the crow with precisely the same divisions between tales.

guae, "You undertake a useless journey: do not disdain my tongue's prophetic warnings" (*Met.* 2.549-50). She then explains her warning, anticipating the moral of her story before beginning the narrative proper: *quid fuerim quid simque, vide meritumque require: / invenies nocuisse fidem...* (*Met.* 2.551-52), "look at what I was and what I am, and then ask what I deserved: you will find that loyalty was my undoing." With this introduction, the *cornix* supplies the raven with the specific conclusion to be drawn from her tale, namely, *invenies nocuisse fidem* (*Met.* 2.552).

The narrative proper opens with the tale of the transgression of the Cecropids, the daughters of Cecrops, who disobey Pallas Athena's instructions by opening the chest containing Erichthonius and looking in upon the infant.

>...nam tempore quodam
Pallas Erichthonium, prolem sine matre creatam,
clauserat Actaeo texta de vimine cista
virginibusque tribus gemino de Cecrope natis
et legem dederat, sua ne secreta viderent.
 ...commissa duae sine fraude tuentur
Pandrosos atque Herse; timidas vocat una sorores
Aglauros nodosque manu diducit, et intus
infantemque vident adporrectumque draconem.
(*Met.* 2.552-56, 558-61)

[... for once upon a time Pallas enclosed Erichthonius, child born without a mother, within a chest woven from Athenian osier, and gave to the three maiden daughters of biform Cecrops the injunction that they not look upon her secrets... Two of the girls, Pandrosos and Herse, guarded their commission without deceit; one, Aglauros, called her sisters timid, unbound the fastenings with her hand, and within they saw the child and a serpent stretched out at his side.]

The Cecropids' actions do not go unobserved, however, for it transpires that the crow has been watching from a nearby elm tree: *abdita fronde levi densa speculabar ab ulmo, / quid facerent...*, "hidden in the thick foliage I watched what they did from a slender elm" (*Met.* 2.557-58). The crow then flies off to inform the goddess of the Cecropids' transgression of her instructions.

acta deae refero; pro quo mihi gratia talis
redditur, ut dicar tutela pulsa Minervae
et ponar post noctis avem....

(*Met.* 2.562-64)

[I reported their deeds to the goddess; for which my reward is such that I am reported to be banished from Minerva's favor and am esteemed after the owl, the bird of night....]

Oddly enough, it is the crow whom Athena punishes. In most of the other extant versions of the story the focus is on the punishment of the daughters of Cecrops, and it is commonly reported that the Cecropids went mad and leaped from the Acropolis to their deaths.[43] The crow herself, however, leaves untold the fate of the Cecropids, concentrating instead upon her own punishment: *mea poena volucres / admonuisse potest, ne voce pericula quaerant,* "my punishment can warn birds not to court danger with their talk" (*Met.* 2.564-65). Thus the crow brings her Cecropid narrative to a close with a statement that recapitulates her opening warning to the raven.[44]

We might expect the crow to bring her recital to an end after she has drawn the moral of her story in accordance with that announced at the outset.[45] Instead of falling silent, however, the garrulous crow moves immediately into a second story, provoked by a suspicion that the raven may not believe her:

at, puto, non ultro nec quicquam tale rogantem
me petiit!—ipsa licet hoc a Pallade quaeras:
quamvis irata est, non hoc irata negabit.

(*Met.* 2.566-68)

[But, I suppose, she did not seek me of her own accord, when I asked no such thing! You can ask Pallas herself about this: though she was angered, she will not deny it out of anger.]

---

43. See the material collected in Powell 1906, 7. It is typical of the *doctus poeta,* of course, to choose the most obscure variant of a story for his learned poetry; the significant point here, however, is that the most obscure account of this story also helps the crow to establish the veracity of her moral, *invenies nocuisse fidem* (*Met.* 2.552).

44. Cf. Boillat 1976, 125.

45. Cf. Boillat 1976, 125.

The subsequent tale, an account of her own earlier history, is organized in a fashion similar to her first. As with her first tale, the crow offers the moral of her story at the outset: *forma mihi nocuit,* "my beauty was my undoing" (*Met.* 2.572).[46]

> nam me Phocaica clarus tellure Coroneus
> (nota loquor) genuit fueramque ego regia virgo
> divitibusque procis (ne me contemne) petebar;
> forma mihi nocuit. nam cum per litora lentis
> passibus, ut soleo, summa spatiarer harena,
> vidit et incaluit pelagi deus, utque precando
> tempora cum blandis absumpsit inania verbis
> vim parat et sequitur; fugio densumque relinquo
> litus et in molli nequiquam lassor harena.
>
> (*Met.* 2.569–77)

[For famous Coroneus bore me in the land of Phocis (I tell a well-known tale); I was a royal maiden and I was sought (do not scorn me) by wealthy princes. My beauty was my undoing. For when I went walking along the shore with slow steps over the top of the sand, as was my wont, the god of the sea saw me and blazed with passion; but when he had wasted time in vain in entreaty and flattering words he readied force and gave pursuit. I fled and left the hard-packed shore, and grew tired on the soft sand, but to no avail.]

She characterizes herself as a royal maiden, *regia virgo,* in order to underscore the propriety of her attendance upon the maiden goddess Pallas Athena:

> inde deos hominesque voco, nec contigit ullum
> vox mea mortalem: mota est pro virgine virgo
> auxiliumque tulit...
> . . . .
> ...mox acta per auras

---

46. Her story is typical of many in the *Metamorphoses,* in which a *virgo* is no sooner seen by a god (here Neptune, *pelagi deus, Met.* 2.574) than desired; see Anderson 1971, 686. Like many other such victims (although unlike Callisto, the nearest preceding *virgo* in *Metamorphoses* 2) the *cornix* escapes her would-be ravisher and receives timely help from the maiden goddess, Minerva.

evehor et data sum comes inculpata Minervae.

(*Met.* 2.578-80, 587-88)

[Then I cried out to gods and men, nor did my cry reach any mortal. Moved by a maiden the maiden goddess brought aid ... soon, borne through the breezes I was carried aloft, and became the blameless companion of Minerva.]

Coroneus' daughter resembles the Cecropids who are also royal maidens (*virgines, Met.* 2.555) and attend upon the goddess Minerva.[47]

The crow's reminiscences include a lengthy description of her metamorphosis into a bird, and, as the only metamorphosis in the crow's narrative, the passage is easily explicable in terms of the intentions of the poet regarding the structure of the *Metamorphoses* as a whole.[48]

... tendebam bracchia caelo:
bracchia coeperunt levibus nigrescere pennis;
reicere ex umeris vestem molibar: at illa
pluma erat inque cutem radices egerat imas;
plangere nuda meis conabar pectora palmis,
sed neque iam palmas nec pectora nuda gerebam;
currebam, nec ut ante pedes retinebat harena,
sed summa tollebar humo; mox acta per auras
evehor et data sum comes inculpata Minervae.

(*Met.* 2.580-88)

[... I tried to stretch out my arms to the sky: my arms began to grow dark with slender feathers. I was trying to cast my clothing from my shoulders: but it was plumage and had driven roots deep into my skin. I strove to beat bared breasts with my palms but neither did I have palms nor bared breasts. I tried to run, nor did the sand restrain my feet as before, but I skimmed over the top of the ground; soon I was carried aloft, borne through the breezes, and became the blameless companion of Minerva.]

---

47. Boillat (1976, 125-26) notes the crow's insistence on her elevated social status before her transformation but does not connect this to the Cecropids or Nyctimene.

48. For "*Metamorphoses*" as the title of the poem, see Seneca the Younger, *Apocolocyntosis* 9, and Quint. *Inst. Or.* 4.1.77.

In addition to the poet's need for a metamorphosis in this embedded narrative, however, the crow's characteristic loquacity motivates a lengthy account of her metamorphosis. Nor does the crow conclude her speech with this description of her own transformation. Rather, she continues to chatter jealously on the subject of her rival Nyctimene's elevation to Athena's favor (*Met.* 2.589-95).

After the focus of the crow's previous stories, we might expect to find in the tale of Nyctimene a royal maiden who once again enjoys Minerva's favor. A fuller account of the version alluded to in the crow's narrative is preserved by Hyginus and it does indeed fulfill our expectations, for Nyctimene's story corresponds in broad outline to the crow's own history.[49]

> Nyctimene is said to have been the daughter of Epopeus, king of the Lesbians, and a very beautiful maiden. Her father Epopeus, inflamed with lust, raped her: her virtue sullied, she hid in the woods. Minerva took pity on her and changed her into a night-owl, a bird which does not go out into the daylight because of her shame, but is subject to the night. (Hyginus, *fab.* 204)

Both royal maidens, the daughters of Coroneus and Epopeus, are rescued from sexual aggression by timely metamorphosis into birds at the instigation of Pallas Athena, and both thereupon become attendants of the maiden goddess.

The crow herself, however, rejects any attempt to liken Nyctimene's circumstances to her own, insisting that the two are entirely different.

> quid tamen hoc prodest, si diro facta volucris
> crimine Nyctimene nostro successit honori?
> an, quae per totam res est notissima Lesbon,
> non audita tibi est, patrium temerasse cubile
> Nyctimenen? avis illa quidem, sed conscia culpae
> conspectum lucemque fugit tenebrisque pudorem

---

49. *Nyctimene Epopei regis Lesbiorum filia virgo formosissima dicitur fuisse. hanc Epopeus pater amore incensus compressit: quae pudore tacta silvis occultabatur. quam Minerva miserata in noctuam transformavit, quae pudoris causa in lucem non prodit sed noctu paret* (*fab.* 204). Cf. Hyginus, *fab.* 253: [*Quae*] *contra fas concubuerunt: Nyctimene cum Epopeo patre rege Lesbiorum,* "[Women who] engaged in sexual intercourse against divine law: Nyctimene, with her father Epopeus, king of the Lesbians."

celat et a cunctis expellitur aethere toto.

(*Met.* 2.589-95)

[Nonetheless what good is this if Nyctimene, who became a bird because of a dreadful crime, accedes to our position of honor? Or have you not heard—a tale very well-known through all of Lesbos—how Nyctimene violated her father's bed? Yes she is a bird, but well-aware of her crime she flees being seen in the light of day, conceals her disgrace in the shadows, and is outcast by all from the whole of the sky.]

The thematic elements that linked the *virgines* of the crow's two earlier stories seem conspicuously absent from the crow's final story. She avoids acknowledging, in this section of her narrative, that it was Minerva who took pity on Nyctimene and turned her into a bird, as we saw her do in the crow's own case. Minerva's favor is only briefly mentioned (*Nyctimene nostro successit honori, Met.* 2.590),[50] and the goddess herself is not even mentioned by name in this section of the narrative at all. Indeed, the crow seems to do her jealous best to separate physically the names of Minerva and Nyctimene in her narrative and this contributes to the poet's characterization of the *cornix* as officious, jealous, and loquacious. The crow effectively ignores Nyctimene's metamorphosis, saying only *diro facta volucris / crimine* (*Met.* 2.589-90), because she has already given an exhaustive description of her own transformation. Thus the crow emphasizes her own importance at the expense of the owl's, denying to her rival an extensive description of her metamorphosis, and dissociating Nyctimene from Minerva.

Examination of the structural progression of the *cornix*' narrative reveals striking similarities from tale to tale. We have seen that the crow opens each story with the moral to be drawn from it: *invenies nocuisse fidem* (*Met.* 2.552); *forma mihi nocuit* (*Met.* 2.572); *quid tamen hoc prodest, si diro facta volucris / crimine Nyctimene nostro successit honori?* (*Met.* 2.589-90). Moreover, the plots of the crow's three stories share other features. Her protagonists are all royal *virgines,* favorites of the maiden goddess Pallas Athena. In two of the three stories the maidens commit some kind of crime for which they go unpunished in the crow's

---

50. Although her favor has already been mentioned earlier by the crow: *dicar tutela pulsa Minervae / et ponar post noctis avem,* "I am reported to be banished from Minerva's favor and am esteemed after the owl, the bird of night" (*Met.* 2.563-64).

narrative. In the first story, the crow's silence implies that the Cecropids go unpunished.[51] In Nyctimene's case, the crow states explicitly not only that she was not punished for her crime, but that she was even rewarded: *diro facta volucris / crimine Nyctimene nostro successit honori.* In the center of the crow's narrative, her own history, the crow explains her metamorphosis as a favor, but her audience already knows that when she tried to do her patroness a favor she lost not only Minerva's goodwill, but even Minerva's patronage (*Met.* 2.562-64). The patterns that emerge from this analysis of the individual stories of the crow's narrative can be seen to support the moral with which she opened her speech, *invenies nocuisse fidem* (*Met.* 2.552). Her stories suggest, on the one hand, that Nyctimene and the daughters of Cecrops, who are all guilty of *crimina* according to the crow's narrative, have flourished. The only "guiltless" character in the crow's narrative is the crow herself. On the other hand, the crow's urge to report everything to the goddess, a quality that she calls *fides* but that is, perhaps, more accurately characterized by Antigonus Carystius as κακαγγελία, has resulted in the withdrawal of Minerva's favor.[52]

This analysis of the narrative organization of the crow's three stories does not reveal a simple chronological structure, although it is possible to situate most of the events of the crow's narrative in a strictly linear order. First, the crow is saved by metamorphosis from rape and becomes the favorite of Athena (*Met.* 2.569-88); second, she reports the transgression of the Cecropids to Minerva and thereby loses her privileged status (*Met.* 2.552-64); and third, Nyctimene accedes to that status (*Met.* 2.564, 589-90).[53] The crow herself, however, seems indifferent to the temporal sequentiality of the events of her narrative, preferring to relate her three stories thematically.[54] In each story she explores the relationship between Minerva and her attendants: within each discrete story we find the crow reexamining the same relationship (divine patronage) between the same characters (royal *virgines* in the service of Pallas Athena) in the same plot (attaining and retaining the goddess' favor). Such narrative

---

51. It is only much later, and in the surrounding first-layer narrative, that we learn more of the Cecropids: see Chap. 5.

52. Boillat (1976, 125-26) analyzes the three tales with particular attention to the cumulative contribution each individual tale makes to the crow's warning.

53. It does not seem possible to set Nyctimene's metamorphosis into our chronology, unless her metamorphosis and her accession to favored status are envisaged as contemporaneous (as in Hyginus, *fab.* 204, quoted above n. 49).

54. Cf. Boillat 1976, 117.

organization, wherein each episode in a series of tales shares recurrent plot features and thereby offers a commentary on its companions, has been called "collocative."[55]

Another consistent feature of the crow's narrative is her remarkable emphasis on the activity of story-telling itself.[56] The crow's first words to the raven point the way: *non utile carpis . . . iter: ne sperne meae praesagia linguae,* "You undertake a useless journey: do not disdain my tongue's prophetic warnings" (*Met.* 2.549-50). The crow here seems to raise fundamental questions about speech and story-telling, and she returns to the subject repeatedly. Her account of the Cecropids' transgression suggests that the misdeeds of the daughters of Cecrops begin with Aglauros' use of her *vox: timidas vocat una sorores / Aglauros* (*Met.* 2.559-60). The *cornix* herself then compounds the crime of the Cecropids by reporting their transgression to Minerva: *acta deae refero* (*Met.* 2.562). The crow concludes her first story by posing the question of the proper use of the *vox: mea poena volucres / admonuisse potest, ne voce pericula quaerant* (*Met.* 2.564-65). Antigonus Carystius explicitly ascribes Minerva's hatred of the crow to the crow's reporting of bad news to her: τῇ δὲ κορώνῃ διὰ τὴν κακαγγελίαν εἰπεῖν ὡς εἰς ἀκρόπολιν οὐ θέμις αὐτῇ ἔσται ἀφικέσθαι, "She told the crow that, for reporting bad news, it would no longer be lawful for her to come to the acropolis" (*Hist. mirab.* 12; = *FGrH* F 330 1). It is as a result of κακαγγελία, for telling tales, that the crow is punished.[57] It is therefore all the more fitting that the crow's punishment for telling Athena of the Cecropids' transgression is for this very story to be told and retold:

acta deae refero; pro quo mihi gratia talis
redditur, ut dicar tutela pulsa Minervae

(*Met.* 2.562-63)

[I reported their deeds to the goddess; for which my reward is such that I am reported to be banished from Minerva's favor.]

In the crow's phraseology, the result of her *fides* to Minerva is the report of her rejection. Indeed, the crow seems to envisage her punishment as

---

55. McCarty n.d.
56. Cf. Bernbeck 1967, 54-55.
57. Cf. Lloyd-Jones and Rea 1968, 141-42 and Zetzel 1987, 356.

the general circulation of this very tale. Her punishment for telling Minerva about the Cecropids' transgression is to be talked about herself.

In recounting her own personal history too, the crow emphasizes that her tale is well-known, *nota loquor* (*Met.* 2.570). This seems a rather extraordinary claim, however, since her story appears nowhere else in the extant literature of antiquity.[58] In what sense can the crow's story be said to be well-known? Ovid has his *cornix* explain that she was accustomed to walk along the shore before she was transformed into a bird: *nam cum per litora lentis / passibus, ut soleo, summa spatiarer harena,* "for when I went walking along the shore with slow steps over the top of the sand, as was my wont..." (*Met.* 2.572-73). The poet here has recourse to a Latin model that supplies much of the diction for his crow's tale, the Virgilian characterization of the *cornix* at *Geo.* 1.388-89: *tum cornix plena pluviam vocat improba voce / et sola in sicca secum spatiatur harena,* "then the shameless crow calls for rain in her full voice and alone on the dry sand takes her walk."[59] Ovid redeploys almost every word of this short passage in the story that his *cornix* calls her own, with the words *ut soleo* functioning as the learned poet's "footnote" to his literary source.[60] The Virgilian passage is evoked in several ways. A specific verbal reminiscence is contained in the words *spatiarer harena* (Ovid, *Met.* 2.573, and cf. Virg. *Geo.* 1.389), and this verbal allusion is further reinforced by Ovid's alliteration on "s" (*... ut soleo, summa spatiarer...*, *Met.* 2.573), recalling Virgil's heavily alliterative line (*... sola in sicca secum spatiatur...*, *Geo.* 1.389).[61] In the *Georgica*, Virgil emphasizes the *cornix'* *vox* with another alliterative collocation, the *figura etymologica, vocat... voce.* This is echoed by the Ovidian *cornix* in her explanation of her attempts to elude the advances of the god Neptune: *inde deos hominesque voco, nec contigit ullum / vox mea*

---

58. The commentators remark that Coroneus, the crow's father, is otherwise unknown: see Bömer 1969, 379; Moore-Blunt 1977, 121-22; and Hill 1985, 207. Haupt, Ehwald, and Albrecht (1966, 123) observe: "Die Quelle für diese wohl erst von Ovid eingelegte Met. ist unbekannt. 569 bis 588 ist wohl nach Einleitung und Schluß Zusatz Ovids."

59. On the borrowing see Haupt, Ehwald, and Albrecht 1966, 123; Bömer 1969, 380; and Moore-Blunt 1977, 122; on Ovid's linguistic debt to Virgil, see Bömer 1968; and in general on Ovid's debt to Virgil, see Lamachia 1960 and Döpp 1968.

60. On the "Alexandrian footnote" see Ross 1975, 78, following Norden 1957, 123-24; cf. Cairns 1979a, 132; Conte 1986, 57-60; and Hinds 1987, 40. In his useful discussion of literary *imitatio*, Russell 1979, 12 notes that "the borrowing had to be acknowledged."

61. Ovid's *soleo* perhaps assists this verbal reminiscence by recalling the sound of the Virgilian *sola*. Difference in vowel quantity is unimportant in ancient etymological discussion: see Chap. 3 n. 2.

mortalem, "Then I cried out to gods and men, nor did my cry reach any mortal" (*Met.* 2.578-79). The extensive use to which the Ovidian *cornix* puts the Virgilian material does indeed, therefore, support her claim that she is narrating an already well-known tale. But the structure of the Ovidian narrative owes nothing to Virgil's *Georgica,* and it can in no way be described as a simple reworking of the Virgilian material.

G.B. Conte has suggested, in discussing an allusion to Ennius' *Annales* at *Met.* 14.812-16, that one of the features of an Ovidian reference to an earlier text is "the 'authentication' of a new text by an authoritative old one."[62] In our passage (*Met.* 2.569-88), however, it is also true that while Virgil's description of the crow in the *Georgica* "authenticates" Ovid's text, the later poet "authenticates" the earlier description of the crow fully as much, since the Ovidian daughter of Coroneus walks on the beach while still a maiden, and thus before she is metamorphosed into the Virgilian crow who frequents the same shore. In this way Ovid inserts himself seamlessly into the literary tradition in which he writes, becoming, in fact, indispensable to that tradition.[63] Such an adaptation of a literary model is a technique typical of the *doctus poeta,* and Ovid's control of this material confirms both his knowledge of the literary tradition and his claim to inclusion within it. In this connection it is worth noting that the words that assert the crow's narrative authority, *nota loquor,* recall a famous fragment of Callimachus, ἀμάρτυρον οὐδὲν ἀείδω (fr. 612 Pf.), "I sing nothing unattested."[64] The Ovidian crow knows whereof she speaks because she "remembers" walking on the beach in Virgil's *Georgica.*[65] Ovid may imply, through his adherence to this tenet of Callimachean poetics, that only tales drawn from the literary tradition, like the one the crow has

---

62. Conte 1986, 57-60. In his subsequent discussion of Ovid's treatment of Ariadne in *Fasti* 3 and her relation to Catullus' Ariadne of poem 64, Conte (1986, 61), observes that Ariadne "has 'lived' her experience as a poetic self, in Catullus' poem, and she remembers the tears she wept there." This observation also offers a useful insight into the Ovidian crow's reworking of Virgilian material at *Met.* 2.573: the crow "remembers" walking on the beach in the *Georgica.*

63. Cf. Conte 1986, 42-43: "The classical poet . . . respects the tradition that confers respect on him and through which he can claim, 'I *too* am a poet!' He learns by reference to a tradition that also prompts him to experiment; he examines worthy examples and reuses them."

64. Cf. *nota cano* at *Ars* 1.297 with Hollis 1977, 93-94 *ad loc.*

65. Cf. the insightful discussion of Labate (1986, 141 n. 20) on the temporal relationship between the Callimachean crow's prophecy and the Ovidian crow's reminiscences: ". . . la cornacchia, che nell' *Ecale* profetizzava, nelle *Metamorfosi* ricorda: sicché, nel completo rovesciamento, viene però rispettata la 'cronologia relativa' stabilita da Callimaco."

just told the raven about the Cecropids (since it has been told elsewhere—by the crow herself in Callimachus' *Hecale*) and her own (since it appears in the *Georgica,* however briefly), should be retold.[66]

At the conclusion of her narrative, the crow does not so much tell the story of Nyctimene as assume that it has been told and retold a number of times.

> an, quae per totam res est notissima[67] Lesbon,
> non audita tibi est, patrium temerasse cubile
> Nyctimenen?
>
> (*Met.* 2.591-93)

[Or have you not heard—a tale that is very well-known through all of Lesbos—how Nyctimene violated her father's bed?]

This claim is remarkably similar to the terms in which she set out her own story, *nota loquor,* and in one sense it is true enough, for the owl's metamorphosis was a well-known fable in antiquity even if the story to which the crow here alludes was not the best known version of the tale.[68] The literary obscurity of this particular version of the owl's metamorphosis, however, allows the crow to underscore the secretive natural habits of the owl. Moreover, the crow's fascination with the process of storytelling gives the poet ample opportunity to document the accuracy of his characterization of the chattering crow, whose loquacity he emphasizes at the beginning of the episode: *garrula motis / consequitur pennis, scitetur ut omnia, cornix* (*Met.* 2.547-48).[69]

A final important technique that characterizes the organization of the crow's narrative remains to be considered. The Ovidian *cornix* reveals a

---

66. We may compare the concerns of the Minyades in *Met.* 4, who are not interested in telling tales that are already too well-known, as they explain before embarking on a story (*Met.* 4.36-54 and 276-84). Note the adjective *utile* used of story-telling (*Met.* 4.39); and the rejection of the well-known story, in favor of the little-known story, *hoc placet; haec quoniam vulgaris fabula non est...,* "the final suggestion pleases her, since this story is not commonly known" (*Met.* 4.53). On this motif see Bernbeck 1967, 54-55.

67. Cf. *fabula notissima,* of the tale of Mars and Venus caught by Vulcan, at *Ars* 2.561.

68. The owl's metamorphosis was the subject of a number of different tales in antiquity: see Thompson 1936, 79, s.v. ΓΛΑΥΞ. We know of literary treatments of the owl's metamorphosis by Nicander (*apud* Ant. Lib. 10; for this story cf. Ovid, *Met.* 4.1-415); Corinna (fr. 12, *PMG* 338); and Boio(s), in an *Ornithogonia* (*apud* Ant. Lib. 15.4).

69. Further aspects of the poet's characterization of the crow are discussed in Chap. 2.

consistent interest in etymological exploration of the names of her characters, in order to emphasize recurrent features of plot configuration in her narrative.[70] We shall see in the following chapters that the crow's interest in *lusus etymologici* reflects an Ovidian interest in etymological play not merely for the display of erudition, but also as a means of organizing the narrative framework of an extended passage in the *Metamorphoses*. The crow makes narrative capital through etymological play most obviously with the name of her rival for Minerva's favor, Nyctimene. Nyctimene is not named in the narrative until five lines from its end (*crimine Nyctimene nostro successit honori, Met.* 2.590), but the crow alludes to the owl at the conclusion of her first story when she tells the raven how Minerva punished her by elevating the owl to first place in her favor, *et ponar post noctis avem* (*Met.* 2.564). The *noctis avis* is the owl, and although there are several species of owl (e.g., *bubo, strix, scopes*) the crow here points specifically to the night owl, *noctua*.[71] Varro had already suggested that the night owl, *noctua,* derived its name from night, *nox: Sunt quae aliis de causis appellatae, ut noctua, quod noctu canit et vigilat,* "There are some [birds] which are named for other reasons, such as the *noctua,* 'night owl,' because it sings and stays awake by night" (*L.L.* 5.76).[72] Ovid's crow draws out the meaning of the Greek name Nyctimene with the Latin translation of the Greek word νύξ, the first element in that name, in an etymology that works across the two

---

70. Ancient interest in the meanings of names can be seen already in the Homeric poems and archaic Greek literature: see, e.g., Homer, *Od.* 5.339-40 with Pucci 1987, 183 n. 6; *Od.* 19.407-9 with Pucci 1987, 65; Hesiod *Theog.* 77-79 with the discussion of West 1966, 180-81 *ad loc.;* Aes. *Ag.* 686-90; Eur. *Phoinissae* 499-502; etc. Snyder (1980, 62) draws attention to the fact that "the only rhetorical use for any kind of word-play which [Aristotle] especially recommends is the argument which can be drawn from an etymological analysis of a proper name (*Rh.* 1400b 16-25)." Etymological interest in names is also a fundamental feature of the literature of Rome, enjoying particularly high standing amongst the Augustan Latin poets. Roman etymological interests are best exemplified by M. Terentius Varro's important *De lingua latina*. On Varro's place in the ancient scholarly tradition, see *R-E* Suppl. 6.1172ff., and cf. also Collart 1978, 3-21, 135-92, and 293-336. On the influence of Varro's etymological investigations on Augustan poetry, see Cairns 1979b, 90-97, and Ahl 1985, 35-40. In general, on etymological play in Ovid see Ahl 1985.

71. The commentators recognize the reference to the owl's nocturnal habits: see Haupt, Ehwald, and Albrecht 1966, 123; Bömer 1969, 378-79; and Moore-Blunt 1977, 120-21.

72. All quotations from Varro's *De lingua latina* are from the Loeb edition of R.G. Kent (1938), unless otherwise specified. With the etymology offered by Varro here, we may compare the implicit etymology in Hyginus' account of the same story (*fab.* 204), quoted above n. 49.

languages.⁷³ She pursues the implications of this etymology later in her narrative too, when she describes Nyctimene as shunning the light.

> ... avis illa quidem, sed conscia culpae
> conspectum lucemque fugit tenebrisque pudorem
> celat et a cunctis expellitur aethere toto.
>
> (*Met.* 2.593-95)
>
> [... Yes she is a bird, but well-aware of her crime she flees being seen in the light of day, conceals her disgrace in the shadows, and is outcast by all from the whole of the sky.]

Here the etymology of the owl's name underscores the crow's complaints about her rival's character flaws, and indeed the etymology itself seems to prompt the direction the crow's narrative takes at its conclusion.⁷⁴

A second example of such word-play can be found in an implied etymology for Minerva's Greek epithet, Pallas. We have seen that the crow's stories center around royal *virgines* in attendance upon the maiden goddess Athena, and the Ovidian crow underlines this narrative pattern by directing attention to Pallas' maidenly status with an emphatic use of polyptoton: *mota est pro virgine virgo / auxiliumque tulit,* "Moved by a maid the maiden goddess brought aid" (*Met.* 2.579-80). With this juxtaposition Ovid exploits one of the ancient etymological interpretations of Athena's epithet Pallas, giving it the meaning "Maiden." Thus Strabo, for example, explains,

> and to Zeus, whom they honor in particular, they dedicate a maiden [παρθένος] of very great beauty and the best family; such maidens [ἅς] the Greeks call "Pallas-es" [παλλάδας]. (Strabo 17.816)⁷⁵

---

73. That Ovid is both interested in, and capable of, punning across the two languages is clear from the employment of Greek proper names with their Greek inflections throughout the crow's narrative (e.g., *Nyctimenen* = Νυκτιμένην, *Met.* 2.593; *Lesbon* = Λέσβον, *Met.* 2.591; cf. also *Coronida* = Κορωνίδα, *Met.* 2.599; etc.). On Ovid's predilection for Greek proper names throughout the *Metamorphoses,* see Kenney 1973, 126-27.

74. So also André 1975, 193, who proposes an etymology of νύξ + μένω for Nyctimene.

75. τῶι δὲ Διί, ὃν μάλιστα τιμῶσιν, εὐειδεστάτη καὶ γένους λαμπροτάτου παρθένος ἱερᾶται, ἃς καλοῦσιν οἱ Ἕλληνες παλλάδας· (Strabo, 17.816). Cf. Eur. *Tro.* 971, παρθένον τε Παλλάδα, where παρθένος, "maiden," supplies an etymological gloss on the meaning of the goddess' epithet Pallas; and Nonnus, *Dionys.* 27.114. Burkert (1985, 139) reports that the etymology of "Pallas remains obscure; it was interpreted sometimes as Maiden, and sometimes as the weapon-brandishing, but it might equally have had a non-Greek origin." "Pallas" occurs at *Met.* 2.553 and 567; "Minerva" at *Met.* 2.563 and 588.

The crow implies this etymology of Pallas through her association of the goddess with *virgines* and her explicit reference to the goddess as *virgo*. Pallas, of course, alternates regularly with the Roman name Minerva throughout the *Metamorphoses,* but the etymology seems attractive here for two reasons. First, the goddess is never referred to as *virgo* in earlier Latin literature without an adjective that describes one of her functions in myth.[76] More importantly, at one point in his exile poetry Ovid explicitly calls Pallas *virgo* in another reference to the story of Erichthonius, with a collocation that gestures towards this very etymology.

> Pallade conspecta, natum de crimine virgo
> sustulerit quare, quaeret, Erichthonium.
>
> (*Tr.* 2. 293–94)

[When Pallas is considered, one wonders how she, a modest maid, came to take charge of Erichthonius, a child of sin.]

---

76. The Roman poets reserve the use of *virgo* without an adjective (though often in combination with *dea*) for the goddess Diana: see Lewis and Short s.v. *virgo* IA and B. Ovid himself calls Minerva *virgo* only twice elsewhere in the *Metamorphoses.* In the first instance, he adds an adjective, *bellica,* which immediately identifies this *virgo* as Minerva, and then he names her in the following line:

Dis tribus ille focos totidem de caespite ponit,
laevum Mercurio, dextrum tibi, bellica virgo,
ara Iovis media est: mactatur vacca Minervae,
alipedi vitulus, taurus tibi, summe deorum.

(*Met.* 4.753–56)

[To the three gods he builds the same number of hearths of sod; the left for Mercury, the right for you, warrior maiden, the middle altar Jove's; to Minerva a cow is sacrificed, a calf to the wing-footed god, and a bull to you, greatest of the gods.]

Cf. Silius 7.459–60: *iam bellica virgo / aegide deposita,* "now the warrior maiden, her aegis laid aside...". The second instance in the *Metamorphoses* may recall the passage in *Met.* 2 under discussion: *Naryciusque heros a Virgine virgine rapta / quam meruit poenam solus, digessit in omnes,* "and the Narycian hero, Ajax, brought down upon us all the punishment that he alone had earned from the Maiden for ravishing a maid" (*Met.* 14.468–69).

For other references to Minerva's status as virginal maiden, in none of which the word *virgo* appears, cf. Hor. *C.* 1.7.5, *intactae Palladis,* and Prop. 3.20.7, *castae Palladis.* It seems possible that the adjectives used in the examples from Horace and Propertius, both of which denote virginity and modify Minerva's name Pallas, were chosen for their etymological significance.

Etymological sophistication may also explain Ovid's singular choice of Aglauros as the sole Cecropid responsible for disregarding Athena's instructions. Other accounts of the Cecropids' transgression differ from this passage in the *Metamorphoses* by identifying 1) all three sisters as equally culpable; 2) Aglauros and Herse as guilty, with Pandrosos alone innocent; 3) Aglauros and Pandrosos as culpable, with Herse, presumably, innocent; or 4) either Herse or Pandrosos as blameworthy, while the other two are, presumably, innocent.[77] Ovid's version, however, identifies Pandrosos and Herse as equally innocent. This variation in the tradition may be etymologically motivated, for the names of both Pandrosos and Herse mean "dew": Pandrosos can be explained as the combination of πᾶν, "all," and δρόσος, "dew," with the meaning "all-bedewed," while Herse too, according to Hesychius, is a Greek word meaning "dew."[78] By contrast, Aglauros' name is an adjective related both morphologically and semantically to the adjective ἀγλαός, which means "splendid," "shining," or "bright."[79] The Ovidian crow's narrative may isolate Aglauros on the level of plot, therefore, because her name has no intrinsic etymological link to those of her sisters, whose names both mean "dew."

The crow's most important etymological commentary, however, is offered when she calls herself the daughter of the Phocian king Coroneus.

nam me Phocaica clarus tellure Coroneus
(nota loquor) genuit fueramque ego regia virgo....

(*Met.* 2.569-70)

---

77. All three sisters are guilty in Euripides, *Ion* 273-74, and probably also in Callimachus' *Hecale* (Hollis fr. 70.12-13); Pandrosos is singled out as innocent by Pausanias (1.18.2; 1.27.3; cf. Apollodorus 3.14.6); Amelesagoras identifies Agraulos and Pandrosos as culpable (according to Antigonus Carystius, *Hist. mirab.* 12); Euphorion (fr. 9 Powell = 11 van Groningen) isolates Herse as the guilty sister while a fragment of Philodemus' *De pietate* (*PHerc.* 243 II.1-6) seems to imply that Callimachus singles out Pandrosos alone for blame on another score (for not giving up her sister Herse to Hermes). On *PHerc.* 243 II.1-6 and its relationship to the *Hecale*, see my Chap. 5 n. 14; on the relationship between *PHerc.* 243 II.1-6 and the sequence of episodes at *Met.* 2.531-835, see Chap. 5. On the Cecropids' transgression, see further the discussions of Powell 1906, 7-8 and 38; Simon 1983, 45-46 and Plate 12. 2; and Hollis 1990, 229-31.

78. Hesychius s.v. ἔρση reports, ἔρση· δρόσος (C 598). Cf. Powell 1906, 39 and 49, of Herse, "She is but the double of Pandrosos..."; and so also Simon 1983, 45-46.

79. LSJ s.v. ἄγλαυρος, -ον. The Hellenistic poet Nicander, whose four-book Ἑτεροιούμενα (*Transformations*) was an important literary model for Ovid's *Metamorphoses*, uses the adjective in the sense of "brilliant, radiant, gleaming" at *Ther.* 62 and 441.

[For famous Coroneus bore me in the land of Phocis (I tell a well-known tale); I was a royal maiden....]

She explicitly asserts that her father is the Phocian (and therefore, Greek) king Coroneus (= Κορωνεύς), and in this way Ovid alludes to the Greek word for crow, κορώνη, and the Callimachean model of the narrative.[80] We shall see in Chapter 2 that the reference to the crow's father has a further importance in that it provides the reader with an opportunity to formulate a patronymic for the crow, Coronis (= Κορωνίς).[81] The narrative complexities that result when a crow, *cornix,* named Coronis tells her own story to a raven, *corvus,* who intends to tell another Coronis' story to Apollo, will be explored in the next chapter.

The crow's narrative implicitly suggests that the meaning of a name can be established through etymological play, and that the meaning thus established reveals some innate quality of the name's bearer that contributes to our understanding of their character. Nyctimene, the crow complains, shuns the light because she is ashamed of her criminal past (*Met.* 2.593-95): the crow implies that her very name may also help to explain this characteristic. The crow's thematic concern with *virgines* is reinforced by an implicit etymology of Pallas meaning "Maiden." And the "dew-sisters," Pandrosos and Herse, are distinguished from the guilty Aglauros through the similarity in meaning of their names and through their initial obedience to Athena's instructions.[82] Thus the crow's playful etymological exploration of the meanings of her characters' names underscores the thematic associations that link her stories.

This chapter has been concerned with identifying recurrent organizational features of the embedded narrative of the crow. The crow herself justifies Ovid's characterization of her as *garrula* (*Met.* 2.547) by speaking

---

80. Cf. Hill 1985, 209. Κορώνη is, of course, the word employed by Callimachus in the *Hecale* (Hollis frr. 73.6 and 74.9).

81. *Pace* Hill 1985, 209, who writes *ad Met.* 2.569, "Her name is certainly not 'Coronis', as in the plot summaries of some mediaeval manuscripts and renaissance editions, for that would produce intolerable confusion." That the audience is supposed to formulate the crow's own name from these hints seems assured from the crow's insistence on naming everyone who appears in her narrative. Cf. Ahl 1985, 198: "As the *CORvus* flies off to tell the god of his mistress' indiscretion, he is intercepted by the talkative *female* crow, *CORnix*. She explains that she was once human before being punished for telling tales: the daughter of *CORoneus* of Phocis (2.542-52). So her name would also have been *CORonis.*"

82. For the application to Pandrosos and Herse of the term "dew-sisters," see Simon 1983, 45.

at such length to the raven and by her fascination with story-telling. While the crow presents each tale she tells as already well-known, the poet playfully alludes to the literary model that lies behind her tales. The crow also takes an interest in the meanings of her characters' names in order to underline certain patterns in the plots of her stories. These devices of plot construction are characteristic of the chattering crow. In the next chapter we shall investigate the ways in which the crow's techniques of narrative construction reflect, and reflect upon, a peculiarly Ovidian narrative aesthetic.

Chapter 2

The Metamorphosis of the Raven: *Met.* 2.531–632

The embedded narrative of the crow (*Met.* 2.549–95) interrupts the poet's account of the metamorphosis of the raven from a white bird to a black bird, promised at *Met.* 2.540–41, before it is fully started. Having traced the thematic and formal structures that organize the crow's narrative in the previous chapter, it will now be feasible to consider the organizational structures of the embedding narrative (the first-layer account of the raven's metamorphosis, *Met.* 2.533–632), as well as the complex nature of the relationship between the embedding narrative and the embedded narrative (the crow's stories, *Met.* 2.549–95). Although the thematic coherence of the embedding and embedded narratives at *Met.* 2.533–632 has not been doubted, the intricacies of the structure have gone unappreciated.[1] We may begin by exploring the details of Ovid's transition into the story of the raven's metamorphosis (*Met.* 2.531–40).

Ovid moves away from the extended narratives of Phaethon and Callisto into a smaller series of short episodic tales that conclude the second book, and the transition from the Callisto episode into the tale of the raven's metamorphosis foreshadows the new direction that the subsequent stories will take. The poet moves swiftly from the catasterism of Callisto and her son Arcas (*Met.* 2.505–7) through Juno's angry visit to the deities of the ocean (*Met.* 2.508–30) and her subsequent return to the aether in the chariot drawn by her bird, the peacock (*Met.* 2.531–32). The peacock's tail then becomes the immediate pretext for the transition

---

1. There are sensitive discussions of the relationship between the embedded narrative of the crow and the first-layer narrative of the raven's metamorphosis in Haupt, Ehwald, and Albrecht 1966; Bömer 1969, 370–90; Galinsky 1975, 94; Hill 1985, 206–7; and Kenney 1986, 387–88.

from Callisto's story to that of the raven, a transition generally considered unsuccessful, although typical of Ovidian ingenuity.[2] Careful consideration of the details of the connection, however, shows how skillfully Ovid has organized the transition in order to impart narrative continuity and coherence to the *Metamorphoses* as a whole, as well as to introduce the themes that will assume importance not only in the course of the crow's narrative, but also in the following sequence of stories.

When he gives prominence to the peacock's tail (*Met.* 2.532-33) the poet alludes to Argus, whose death he narrates in the first book of the *Metamorphoses* in the course of the story of Io (*Met.* 1.568-746). Ovid concludes his account of Argus' death with the translation of Argus' eyes to the tail of Juno's bird, the peacock.

> Arge, iaces, quodque in tot lumina lumen[3] habebas,
> exstinctum est, centumque oculos nox occupat una.
> excipit hos volucrisque suae Saturnia pennis
> conlocat et gemmis caudam stellantibus inplet.
>
> (*Met.* 1.720-23)

[Argus, you lay prostrate, the light that you had in so many eyes was

---

2. Quintilian's judgment of Ovid's transitions is the earliest and most famous:

illa vero frigida et puerilis est in scholis adfectatio, ut ipse transitus efficiat aliquam utique sententiam et huius velut praestigiae plausum petat, ut Ovidius lascivire in Metamorphosesin solet; quem tamen excusare necessitas potest, res diversissimas in speciem unius corporis colligentem. (*Inst. Or.* 4.1.77)

[That is indeed a flat and childish conceit in the schools, for the transition itself to effect some epigram and demand applause for this trick, as Ovid is accustomed to indulge this affectation in his *Metamorphoses*. Nonetheless, he can be pardoned because of the necessity to combine tales on the most diverse subjects into the semblance of a unified whole.]

Modern assessments of Ovid's transitions generally conform: see Miller 1921, 464-76; de Saint Denis 1940, 1; Steiner 1958, 218-36; Frécaut 1968, 255; Kenney 1973, 117; Galinsky 1975, 42 and 79-109; and Kenney 1986, xxi. For assessments of the transition at *Met.* 2.531-35, see Wilkinson 1958, 235; Frécaut 1968, 249; Otis 1970, 379; Little 1972, 98; Galinsky 1975, 93-96; and Solodow 1988, 42-43.

3. The polyptoton *lumina lumen* deftly dramatizes the action in these lines. The semantic tension between the contrasting senses of *lumen* is emphasized by their close collocation: for *lumen* of "life" see *TLL* 7.2.1812.66ff., and cf. *OLD* s.v. *lumen* 3; for *lumina* of "eyes" see *TLL* 7.2.1812.54ff., and cf. *OLD* s.v. *lumen* 9. But the collocation also playfully underlines the meaning of the prepositional phrase in which the first *lumen* occurs (*in tot lumina*), for Ovid has reproduced materially on the *pagina* the very plurality of *lumina* that his narrative has ascribed to Argus.

extinguished, and a single night seized your hundred eyes. Saturnian Juno took these eyes and placed them on the feathers of her bird, the peacock, filling its tail with starry jewels.]

The poet reprises this earlier passage at *Met.* 2.531-41 in order to effect the transition from the story of Callisto, a second *paelex*[4] of Jove hated by Juno, to the metamorphosis of another bird, in this case the raven.[5]

> ... habili Saturnia curru
> ingreditur liquidum pavonibus aethera pictis,
> tam nuper pictis caeso pavonibus Argo
> quam tu nuper eras, cum candidus ante fuisses,
> corve loquax, subito nigrantes versus in alas.
>
> (*Met.* 2.531-35)

[... Saturnian Juno entered the clear air in her swift chariot drawn by colorful peacocks, peacocks bedecked so recently, upon the death of Argus; as recently indeed as you, chattering raven, though earlier you had been white, were transformed suddenly into black wings.]

Juno's name Saturnia (*Met.* 1.722; 2.531) as well as the references to Argus (*Met.* 1.720; 2.533) and to the peacock (*Met.* 1.722; 2.532-33) combine to signal an allusion to the earlier passage. Ovid exploits his reader's memory of the peacock's recent transformation, which is the first bird metamorphosis of the poem, in order to introduce another tale that concludes with the metamorphosis of a bird. The poet's reference to a story told earlier in the poem perhaps also serves to suggest that

---

4. The diction is exactly parallel. Io is identified as *paelex* by the poet/narrator, at a point where Juno's perspective colors the narrative, towards the conclusion of the story of Io (*Met.* 1.724-27); Juno herself calls Callisto *paelex* at the end of her speech to the divinities of the sea at *Met.* 2.527-30. Otis (1970, 379-89) also interprets the Callisto and Io tales as complementary. In the appendix "On the Sources Used by Ovid," Otis groups together the stories of Daphne-Apollo, Io (*Met.* 1.452-746), Callisto (*Met.* 2.401-530), and Coronis (*Met.* 2.531-632), and notes their structural relations: "The important point about these stories is that they are *arranged* in symmetrical sequence around the *Phaethon*.... The two amours of Apollo and two amours of Jupiter correspond in chiastic order. Ovid clearly arranged the liaison as well as the counterpoint of motifs...."

5. The many different types of metamorphosis (catasterism, petrifaction, bird metamorphoses, etc.) found in the poem are conveniently collected and classified by Lafaye 1904, 245-49.

the world of the *Metamorphoses* generates its own framework for the coherence of the poem as a whole.[6] In this way the *Metamorphoses* itself seems to ensure its own narrative continuity.

The subject of the new tale, the raven's transformation from a white bird into a black bird, is dwelt upon in a brief catalog of birds whom the raven once rivalled in whiteness.

> nam fuit haec quondam niveis argentea pennis
> ales, ut aequaret totas sine labe columbas
> nec servaturis vigili Capitolia voce
> cederet anseribus nec amanti flumina cygno.
>
> (*Met.* 2.536–39)

[For at one time this bird was silver-hued with white feathers, so that it could equal doves entirely without stain nor would it yield to geese, birds who would prove saviors of the Capitoline with their watchful cry, nor to the river-loving swan.]

The foremost reason for this particular selection of dove, goose, and swan is, of course, the whiteness of their feathers. But in addition the swan, the final bird of the comparison, is the second metamorphosis of a bird narrated thus far in the *Metamorphoses* (2.367–80). With his choice of the swan at the close of this transition, as with that of the peacock's tail at the start, Ovid is careful to recall his own earlier passage. The three-word phrase describing the swan at *Met.* 2.539 is reminiscent of the conclusion of Cygnus' metamorphosis as it was narrated earlier in the book. The words *amanti flumina cygno* (*Met.* 2.539) pointedly refer the reader to the closing lines of the metamorphosis of Cygnus.

> stagna petit patulosque lacus ignemque perosus,

---

6. It is, I suspect, Ovid's facility with syntactical connection that is condemned by the poet's critics. Even so sensitive a reader of Ovid as L.P. Wilkinson could see little purpose behind the forced ingenuity he perceived in this transition; of it Wilkinson (1958, 235) remarked that "only very occasionally is [a transition] so flimsy as to be ineffectual, as when we are told (2, 533–4) that as lately as the peacock's tail had been decked with Argus' eyes, the raven's plumage had been turned from white to black." Otis, too (1970, 379), is unimpressed by the "curious introduction of Coronis by means of a comparison between the crow and the peacock (Argus' eyes)." For other similarly unflattering assessments of this passage see, in addition to the references collected in n. 2 above, my Introduction n. 4.

quae colat, elegit contraria flumina flammis.

(*Met.* 2.379-80)

[He seeks pools and open lakes, and hating fire he chose rivers, the opposite of flames, in which to make his home.]

They recall as well the first reference to "swans" in the poem (*flumineae volucres, Met.* 2.253).[7] The significance of Ovid's choice of the birds that frame the transition from the story of Callisto to the story of the raven's metamorphosis lies precisely in the fact of their existence in the physical world of the *Metamorphoses*.

The implications of the swan's presence in this transition are worth pursuing somewhat further. The Callimachean κορώνη too, in the prophecy of the raven's metamorphosis with which she concludes her narrative (Hollis fr. 74.12-20), had emphasized the raven's originally white plumage by means of a comparison.[8] In the *Hecale*, the κορώνη had compared the raven's plumage to three things: the white plumage of the swan, the color of milk, and the color of the crest of a wave.

εὖτε κόραξ, ὅς νῦν γε καὶ ἂν κύκνοισιν ἐρίζοι
καὶ γάλακι χροιὴν καὶ κύματος ἄκρωι ἀώτωι,
κυάνεον φὴ πίσσαν ἐπὶ πτερὸν οὐλοὸν ἕξει

(Hollis fr. 74.15-17)

[when the raven, who now at least could rival swans and milk in complexion, and the foam on the crest of the wave, will have on him a thick plumage as dark as pitch]

Ovid reproduces the three-point comparison he found in the embedded narrative of the *Hecale*'s κορώνη, but of the three Callimachean com-

---

7. Appendix 1 contains a full discussion of the swans of *Metamorphoses* 2 and includes detailed comments on the swanlike river birds of *Met.* 2.253.

8. For an extensive discussion of Ovid's reworking of the Callimachean material in the speech of the crow, see Chap. 1. The observation of Zetzel (1983, 261) that it is a convention of Alexandrian and neoteric poetry to allude to a literary model by reversing beginnings and endings also seems relevant to this discussion, since Ovid's comparison of the raven's white feathers to those of the swan, at the opening of his account of the raven's metamorphosis, adapts a comparison placed at the end of Callimachus' account in the *Hecale*. On Ovid's reminiscences of Callimachus' *Hecale* in the first-layer narrative surrounding the inset narrative of the crow, see also Labate 1986, 140-42.

paranda our poet has retained only the swan (κύκνοισιν, Hollis fr. 74.15; *cygno, Met.* 2.539).

> ales, ut aequaret totas sine labe columbas
> nec servaturis vigili Capitolia voce
> cederet anseribus nec amanti flumina cygno.
>
> (*Met.* 2.537-39)

[a bird, that could equal doves entirely without stain, nor would it yield to geese, birds who would prove saviors of the Capitoline with their watchful cry, nor to the river-loving swan.]

In the *Metamorphoses*, Ovid represents the concept of competition in Callimachus' ἐρίζοι with the verbs *aequaret* (*Met.* 2.537) and *cederet... nec* (*Met.* 2.539), by which he compares the raven to the dove and the goose, as well as to the swan.[9] In this way, then, the swan offers our *doctus poeta* at the outset of the new tale an opportunity to acknowledge, with considerable economy, Callimachus' *Hecale* as his literary model. Moreover, Ovid's revision of the Callimachean comparison results in a more tightly focused comparison. In confining himself to a list of three birds, Ovid emphasizes the raven's former whiteness by comparing the *corvus* directly to comparanda of essentially the same type (i.e., *aves*).

Even the Ovidian description of the raven's discovery of Coronis' infidelity echoes the words of Callimachus' κορώνη. The Callimachean crow prophesies the raven's color change upon learning of Coronis' relations with Ischys.

> ἀγγελίης ἐπίχειρα τά οἵ ποτε Φοῖβος ὀπάσσει
> ὁππότε κεν Φλεγύαο Κορωνίδος ἀμφὶ θυγατρός
> Ἴσχυϊ πληξίππῳ σπομένης μιαρόν τι πύθηται.
>
> (Hollis fr. 74.18-20)

[the reward for tale-bearing that Phoebus will grant him at the time when he learns the abominable deed of Coronis, the daughter of Phlegyas, who followed horse-driving Ischys]

In Ovid's account, the raven's perception of the crime is an important element of the narrative.

---

9. On the lexical correspondences between the two passages, see Haupt, Ehwald, and Albrecht 1966, 121; Bömer 1969, 372; Moore-Blunt 1977, 116; and Hollis 1990, 250.

>   ... sed ales
> sensit adulterium Phoebeius, utque latentem
> detegeret culpam, non exorabilis index,
> ad dominum tendebat iter. . . .
>
> (*Met.* 2.544–47)

[. . . but Phoebus' bird discovered her adultery, and upon detecting the hidden crime, he set off to find his master, an unyielding informer. . . .]

Thus, *sensit adulterium* reproduces the sense of Callimachus' μιαρόν τι πύθηται. Ovid's debt to Callimachus' poem is apparently satisfied with the fulfillment of the prophecy of the κορώνη, which is accomplished by the actual metamorphosis of the raven that closes the narrative.[10]

> sperantemque sibi non falsae praemia linguae
> inter aves albas vetuit consistere corvum.
>
> (*Met.* 2.631–32)

[Phoebus Apollo forbade the raven, who was expecting a reward for his accurate tale, to stand in the ranks of the white birds.]

The goose is apparently included in the Ovidian comparison because of the whiteness of its feathers, and not because of the well-known legend that the Capitoline geese saved Rome by the noise they made when the Gauls attacked, presumably because that event will occur far in the future of the world of the *Metamorphoses,* as Ovid hints with the coy use of the future participle (*servaturis . . . anseribus, Met.* 2.538–39).[11] Although

---

10. Cf. Labate 1986, 140–42.

11. This is one of the poet's devices for reminding the audience of the grand chronological design that unifies the epic, as he promises in the proem of the work:

>   . . . di, coeptis (nam vos mutastis et illa)
> adspirate meis primaque ab origine mundi
> ad mea perpetuum deducite tempora carmen.
>
> (*Met.* 1.2–4)

[Gods, inspire my undertakings (for you have transformed even these), and spin a fine thread of song without a break from the world's first origin all the way down to my own times.]

46 / *The Play of Fictions*

the white color of the goose is well-attested in antiquity, the inclusion of the goose also allows the poet to develop a further contrast between the raven and the goose.[12]

> corve loquax, subito nigrantes versus in alas.
> nam fuit haec quondam niveis argentea pennis
> ales, ut aequaret totas sine labe columbas
> nec servaturis vigili Capitolia voce
> cederet anseribus nec amanti flumina cygno.
> lingua fuit damno: lingua faciente loquaci,
> qui color albus erat, nunc est contrarius albo.
>
> (*Met.* 2.535–41)

[Chattering raven, you were transformed suddenly into black wings: for at one time this bird was silver-hued with white feathers, so that it could equal doves entirely without stain nor would it yield to geese, birds who would prove saviors of the Capitoline with their watchful cry, nor to the river-loving swan. His tongue was his downfall: his chattering tongue made the raven, whose hue had been white, now the opposite of white.]

The phrase *vigili . . . voce,* situated between two occurrences of the adjective *loquax* applied to the raven, explicitly contrasts the goose's appropriate use of his *vox* with the raven's inappropriate use of his *lingua*.[13]

Allusions to the future are found most numerously in the early books of the poem, for obvious reasons, and examples of the technique in Books 1 and 2 include: *nondum laurus erat,* "the laurel-tree was not yet in existence" (*Met.* 1.450), which functions as the transition into the tale of Apollo and Daphne; *nondum Oeagrius,* "not yet Oeagrian" (*Met.* 2.219) of Mt. Haemus, to which *Met.* 10.76–77 responds; and Jupiter's choice of devastation by flood at *Met.* 1.254–58, foreshadowing the devastation by fire that Phaethon will wreak at *Met.* 2.200–78. The technique is clearly related to that of redeploying characters from stories already narrated in the course of the poem. On Ovid's extensive use of the future participle in the *Metamorphoses,* see Solodow 1988, 61–63. On Ovid's debt to Callimachus and other Hellenistic poets in marking the relative chronology of mythical times, see Labate 1986; and Hollis 1990, 235–36. On the reading *illa* at *Met.* 1.2, see Kenney 1976.

12. On the whiteness of the goose cf. Lucretius, *D.R.N.* 4.683, *Romulidarum arcis servator candidus anser,* "the white goose, savior of the Romans' citadel," and see further Bömer 1969, 372, *ad Met.* 2.539. Moore-Blunt (1977, 115) and Hill (1985, 204) suggest, in my view rightly, that Ovid owes the adjective *argentea* by which he characterizes the raven to the Virgilian description of the savior of the Capitol as *argenteus anser* (*Aen.* 8.655).

13. The story of the Capitoline geese saving the Capitol is narrated at length by Livy,

The raven's overly zealous use of his tongue, after all, will be the cause of his metamorphosis.[14]

This analysis of the organization of the transition into the tale of the raven, Apollo, and Coronis has shown it to be both playfully original and extremely efficient. Ovid redeploys the two birds whose metamorphoses he has already narrated, and which therefore exist independently within the world of the poem. Outside the world of the *Metamorphoses*, but in the literary tradition within which that poem stands, the poet has deftly reworked the Callimachean comparison of the raven's former whiteness to, among other things, the swan, thus enabling him to acknowledge his immediate literary model. Finally, the inclusion of the goose in the Ovidian comparison presages the cause of the raven's metamorphosis. By characterizing the goose as *vigili . . . voce* in contrast to the raven, the poet fleetingly raises the subject of an appropriate use of the *vox*, an issue which emerges as significant in the course of the crow's narrative.[15] Moreover, the suggestion that the use of the voice will assume thematic importance in this episode, implicit in the transition, is activated in the subsequent narrative when the poet explicitly offers the moral of the story at the outset.

> lingua fuit damno: lingua faciente loquaci
> qui color albus erat, nunc est contrarius albo.
>
> (*Met.* 2.540-41)

---

who attributes the safety of the city to the noise made by the geese:

> Quae res saluti fuit; namque clangore eorum alarumque crepitu excitus M. Manlius qui triennio ante consul fuerat, vir bello egregius, armis arreptis simul ad arma ceteros ciens vadit et dum ceteri trepidant, Gallum qui iam in summo constiterat umbone ictum deturbat. (Livy 5.47.4)

> [This was the thing that saved Rome: for the geese, with their shrieking and the rustling of their wings, awakened Marcus Manlius, who had been consul three years before and was distinguished in battle; he snatched up his weapons at once and, calling the rest of his companions to arms, he strode past his bewildered comrades and with a blow of his shield dislodged a Gaul who had already reached the summit.]

Cf. also the references to the story at Lucretius, *D.R.N.* 4.683, Cic. *Pro Sex. Roscio* 56, Prop. 3.3.12, and Virg. *Aen.* 8.655.

14. For the ancient tradition of the raven's garrulity, see Hesiod fr. 60, Ael. 2.51, Porph. *De abst.* 3.4, and Plin. 10. (43) 60; cf. Labate 1986, 141. For other ancient traditions concerning the raven see Thompson 1936, 159–64, s.v. ΚΟΡΑΞ.

15. On the crow's interest in story-telling, see Chap. 1. Cf. Altieri 1973, 35, who draws attention to the raven's misuse of language.

[His tongue was his downfall: his chattering tongue made the raven, whose hue had been white, now the opposite of white.]

Ovid pointedly centers our attention, at the opening of this new episode, upon the element that brings about the raven's metamorphosis, his *lingua*. This is echoed in the crow's opening words to the raven, when she calls into question the efficacy of the raven's plan to tell Apollo of Coronis' infidelity (*Met.* 2.549–50). The anaphora *lingua...lingua* (*Met.* 2.540) in the introduction to the raven's story focuses our attention upon language and utterance, and thereby invites our investigation of the ways in which the language of the text meditates upon the efficacy of storytelling in the course of a "narrative about narratives."[16]

The raven is characterized from the outset as a garrulous bird, *corve loquax* (*Met.* 2.535; cf. 540), and the emphasis on the loquacity of the raven is complemented by the introduction of the crow in identical terms: *quem garrula motis / consequitur pennis, scitetur ut omnia, cornix*, "the chattering crow followed the raven on her flapping wings, in order to hear all the gossip" (*Met.* 2.547–48). Ovid's chiastic arrangement of the birds and their epithets is calculated to emphasize their garrulity, for the *garrula cornix* corresponds neatly to the *corve loquax*. That the poet considered indiscreet loquacity to be the salient characteristic of both birds and, indeed, the primary theme of this narrative is also suggested by some evidence from his contemporaneous compendium of Roman myth and legend, the *Fasti*.[17] In the entry under the third day of the month of February, Ovid offers an aetiology for the constellation of the

---

16. Winkler (1986, p. x of the Preface), in a discussion concerning Apuleius' *Metamorphoses*.

17. The relative chronology of the individual works of Ovid's oeuvre is a notorious problem: see the discussions of Cameron 1968, 320–33; Syme 1978, chap. 1; Barsby 1978, 4–5; and Kenney 1982a, 421. Ovid's poetry from Tomis testifies to the existence of two poems in progress at the time of his relegation: see *Tr.* 1.7.13–14, and *Tr.* 2.549–56, and on the reliability of the poet's statements here, see Hinds 1987, 137 n. 23. It is generally assumed that the *Fasti* and the *Metamorphoses* are contemporaneous compositions, products of the years A.D. 1 to 8: for this view see Heinze 1919, 1 [= 1960, 308]; Wilkinson 1955, 241; Otis 1970, 21–22; Frécaut 1972, 271; Wormell 1979; and Kenney OCD^2, 764. Fränkel believed that the bulk of the *Fasti* as we have it (the first six books) was composed in A.D. 7 and 8, on the assumption that the parallels between subject matter in the last books of the *Metamorphoses* and in the *Fasti* are exactly contemporaneous: see Fränkel 1945, 143, and 238 nn. 2–4. Fränkel does not discuss the rather more famous cases involving the duplicated subject matter of Callisto (*Met.* 2.401–530 and *Fasti* 2.153–92) and the Rape

Dolphin (*Fasti* 2.79–118), and his narrative centers around the poetic powers of the singer Arion.[18]

> quod mare non novit, quae nescit Ariona tellus?
>   carmine currentes ille tenebat aquas.
> saepe sequens agnam lupus est a voce retentus,
>   saepe avidum fugiens restitit agna lupum;
> saepe canes leporesque umbra iacuere sub una,
>   et stetit in saxo proxima cerva leae,
> et sine lite loquax cum Palladis alite cornix[19]
>   sedit, et accipitri iuncta columba fuit.
>
> (*Fasti* 2.83–90)

[What sea does not know Arion, what land? He could hold back the running waters with his song. Often the wolf chasing the lamb was held fast by his voice and often the lamb fleeing the greedy wolf halted in her tracks; often hounds and hares lay in a single patch of shade, the deer on a rock stood next to the lion, the chattering crow sat without quarrel beside the bird of Pallas, and the dove was next to the hawk.]

One of the adynata offered in this passage is the cessation of hostilities between the chattering crow and Athena's bird, the owl.[20] The poet

---

of Proserpina (*Met.* 5.346–571 and *Fasti* 4.417–618). Bömer (1957, 15) suspends judgment on the question. Syme (1978, 21–36) argues that the period of the composition of the *Fasti* should be confined to the years A.D. 1–4. Recently Lefèvre (1976) and Fantham (1983, 210–16, and 1985, 243–81) have reexamined the case for extensive reworking of the *Fasti* by the poet in exile at Tomis. Hinds (1987, 154 n. 11), while pointing out that the details are ultimately unrecoverable, concedes in the end "the simultaneity of the *Metamorphoses* and the *Fasti* as a whole"; cf. also Hinds 1987, 10–11 and 42–44. Only within the last decade have scholars begun to investigate the potential literary implications of the contemporaneous composition of the two poems: see Hinds 1982, Hinds 1987 *passim,* and Newlands 1991.

18. On Arion, see Herodotus, *Hist.* 1.23–24.

19. The line is full of characteristically Ovidian sound- and wordplay. The caesura after *loquax* and line end after *cornix* throw both words into prominence and emphasize the crow's loquacity. The similarity of the sound patterns of the immediately preceding word in each case underscores this internal "rhyme," with *alite* (though different in quantity) echoing the sound of *lite*. The poet may even fleetingly suggest that *sine lite* is equivalent to *alite,* with a bilingual pun in reference to the Greek alpha-privative.

20. For the popular tradition of their mutual hostility, see the references collected in Chap. 1 n. 29.

underscores the crow's garrulity with the adjective *loquax* (*Fasti* 2.89-90). This adjective may constitute, in the *Fasti,* a cross-reference to the interrelated stories of the raven and the crow that the poet tells together in the *Metamorphoses* (Book 2), by conflating the *corve loquax* (*Met.* 2.535) and the *garrula cornix* (*Met.* 2.547-48) into the *loquax cornix.*[21] Ovid's emphasis on the garrulity of both the crow and the raven is clearly the basis of his characterization in the corresponding passage of the *Metamorphoses.*[22] This is no chance characterization, for neither *loquax* nor *garrula* occurs frequently in the *Metamorphoses* or the *Fasti.*[23] Moreover, the crow herself complains about the owl in her speech to the raven in this very section of the *Metamorphoses* (2.589-95). Indeed, the crow of the *Fasti* shares with her counterpart in the *Metamorphoses* not only garrulity, but also a hostile relationship to the owl, Athena's favorite.[24]

A second passage in Book 2 of the *Fasti* offers further oblique comment on the episode at *Met.* 2.531-632. *Fasti* 2.243-66 offers an account of Apollo's punishment of the raven that is rather different from that of *Metamorphoses* Book 2, and concludes with the raven's catasterism instead of a color transformation. In the *Fasti,* the raven is ordered by Apollo to fetch water in a bowl for sacrifice (*Fasti* 2.249-50). However,

---

21. But cf. Frazer 1929, 2.305 *ad Fasti* 2.89, who remarks:

The epithet 'chattering' which the poet here applies to the crow seems to allude to a story told about the raven. It is said that when Coronis, a damsel beloved by Apollo, proved false to her divine lover, tidings of her infidelity were officiously carried by the raven to Apollo, who in his anger turned the bird jet black, whereas up to that time the plumage of the raven had been as white as driven snow. Ovid has himself told the story of the raven's unseasonable loquacity and called the bird a chatterer.

On the verbal parallels between the raven episode in the *Fasti* and that in the *Metamorphoses,* see Bömer 1958, 88; and Moore-Blunt 1977, 115, *ad Met.* 2.535, and 118, *ad Met.* 2.547.

22. Cf. Fränkel 1945, 221 n. 7; Altieri 1973, 35; and Fredericks 1977, 244.

23. The adjective *garrulus* occurs twice elsewhere in the *Metamorphoses*. Echo is characterized as *garrula* at *Met.* 3.360, and the *perdix* is so qualified at *Met.* 8.237 (where there is, however, a textual problem). The adjective occurs once only in the *Fasti,* of a burbling brook (*Fasti* 2.316). The noun *garrulitas,* formed from the adjective, occurs once in Ovid's oeuvre, of the Pierids, the rivals of the Muses (*Met.* 5.678). The adjective *loquax* occurs only once elsewhere in the two poems, at *Met.* 9.137. In three of these five occurrences, the words appear in tales in which the poet explores the nature of story-telling (*Met.* 3.360; 5.678; 9.137). For the comparative rarity of *garrulitas,* see *TLL* 6.2.1697.21-75; of *garrulus,* see *TLL* 6.2.1698.5-1699.39; and of *loquax,* see *TLL* 7.2.1653.55-1655.67 s.v. *loquax;* and cf. *OLD* s.v. *loquax.*

24. Hollis (1990, 225) suggests that *Fasti* 2.89-90 may "distantly reflect the situation" of Callimachus' *Hecale,* frr. 70-74.

he delays discharging this task by gorging himself on figs, and then he returns not with the water but with a snake (*Fasti* 2.251-58), justifying the delay to Apollo by fabricating the story that the snake prevented him from getting the water.

> iamque satur nigris longum rapit unguibus hydrum,
>   ad dominumque redit, fictaque verba refert:
> 'hic mihi causa morae, vivarum obsessor aquarum:
>   hic tenuit fontes officiumque meum.'
>
> (*Fasti* 2.257-60)

[And now, sated, he snatched up a long water snake in his black talons, and returning to his master, brought back a false tale: "This snake was the cause of my delay, blockading the pure waters: this held the spring and held up my task."]

Phoebus Apollo then punishes the bird for both his guilt and his mendacity (*addis . . . culpae mendacia,* "you compound your guilt with lies," *Fasti* 2.261), banishing him from icy cold fountains (*Fasti* 2.264). The account concludes with the catasterism of the Raven, the Snake, and the Bowl (*Fasti* 2.265-66). It has been suggested that Ovid's conflicting tales of the raven in the *Fasti* and the *Metamorphoses,* both in the second books of their respective poems, challenge one another in an extended cross-reference between the two poems.[25] Indeed, the two accounts are broadly parallel, for in both poems the raven, as the bird of Apollo (*ales / . . . Phoebeius, Met.* 2.544-45; *mea avis,* spoken by Apollo, *Fasti* 2.249) performs a service for his divine patron. In the *Fasti,* the bird does not perform his appointed task and lies to Apollo to justify his negligence (*fictaque verba refert, Fasti* 2.258); in the *Metamorphoses,* on the other hand, the bird officiously tells Apollo of Coronis' faithlessness (*Met.* 2.598-99). In both versions it is the raven's tale-telling that prompts Apollo to punish his bird, and in both poems the raven's punishment is accomplished by a metamorphosis. There is, however, an intriguing difference in the progress of the narrative in the different versions, for that of the *Fasti* focuses closely on the raven while that of the *Metamorphoses* is first interrupted by the inset narrative of the crow and,

---

25. Newlands 1991, 252-54.

even when resumed, centers upon Apollo's reaction to the raven's talebearing rather than on the raven's account of Coronis' infidelity.

Let us return to the point in the *Metamorphoses* when the inset narrative of the crow gives way to the first-layer narrative of the raven's transformation from white to black. Ovid underscores the crow's garrulity by suggesting that the raven cuts her off in mid-narrative in order to be off on his errand to Apollo.

> Talia dicenti 'tibi' ait 'revocamina' corvus
> 'sint precor ista malo: nos vanum spernimus omen.'
> nec coeptum dimittit iter dominoque iacentem
> cum iuvene Haemonio vidisse Coronida narrat.
>
> (*Met.* 2.596–99)

[As she was speaking, the raven said, "May your ominous reminiscences, summons to return, bode you ill: we disdain your empty prophecy." Nor did he put off the journey he had undertaken; he told his master that he had seen Coronis abed with a Thessalian youth.]

The continuous aspect of the present participle *dicenti* evocatively dramatizes the crow's relentless chattering, but the raven has had enough and contemptuously rejects her warnings as *revocamina* (*Met.* 2.596). The word *revocamen* is an Ovidian coinage, and it has the sense of "a summons to return."[26] In the context, however, of the crow's obsession with language and story-telling, revealed in the course of her narrative, it seems not only possible but also desirable to recover from the raven's use of the word further nuances along the lines of "retelling," and even "recalling" (hence my translation, "reminiscences"). Such a meaning is the more compelling since the verb *revoco,* from which the noun *revocamen* is derived, is itself used in the works of Cicero to signify "encore" (literally "re-cite"), specifically of literary texts.[27] Indeed *revocamen* may here perform the function of another "footnote" to the Callimachean

---

26. See Linse 1891, 32; Bömer 1969, 383–84; Kenney 1973, 126–27 and 148 n. 80; and Moore-Blunt 1977, 125. The word occurs only twice elsewhere in extant Latin literature, at Ovid, *Her.* 13.135 and *Fasti* 1.561. On the meaning, see *OLD* s.v. *revocamen*.

27. Of considerable interest is *Tusc.* 4.29.63: *cum Orestem fabulam doceret Euripides, primos tris versus revocasse dicitur Socrates,* "when Euripides produced his tragedy 'Orestes,' Socrates is said to have called for an encore of the first three verses." See *OLD* s.v. *revoco* 2b; cf. also *OLD* s.v. *revocatio*.

modelling passage.²⁸ Moreover the raven's response to the crow offers further echoes of this Callimachean context. Both *precor* and *omen* recall the undertones of augury in the crow's use of *praesagia* at the beginning of her speech (*Met.* 2.550), in an allusion to her Callimachean counterpart's actual prophecy in the *Hecale* (Hollis fr. 74.10-20). The connotation of augury is also implicit in *revocamen*,²⁹ and of course the fulfillment of the prophecy of the Callimachean κορώνη will actually occur at the conclusion of this episode as the poet narrates the metamorphosis of the raven and thus "authenticates" the prophecy of Callimachus' κορώνη.

Once the raven has informed Apollo of Coronis' infidelity, the first-layer narrative again defers an account of the raven's fate (just as it was earlier interrupted by the inset narrative of the crow), and our attention is directed to Apollo's reaction to his bird's report.

> laurea delapsa est audito crimine amantis,³⁰
> et pariter vultusque deo plectrumque colorque
> excidit, utque animus tumida fervebat ab ira,
> arma adsueta capit flexumque a cornibus arcum

---

28. For the term see Chap. 1 n. 60; for another example of Ovid's use of this technique see Chap. 1. The use of *revocamen* at *Fasti* 1.561, in an account of Hercules' dealings with Cacus (*Fasti* 1.543-86), illuminates our passage further. The density of allusions to Ovid's predecessors in the literary tradition suggests that *revocamen* also functions in the *Fasti* passage as a "footnote" acknowledging his literary debts. Ovid gestures to the versions of both Virgil and Propertius: compare *Fasti* 1.560 and *Aen.* 8.215-18; *Fasti* 1.551-58 and *Aen.* 8.193-98; *Fasti* 1.543 and Prop. 4.9.2; *Fasti* 1.550 and Prop. 4.9.12 (and cf. also Livy 1.7.5). On *Fasti* 1.543-86 and its literary models, see Bömer 1958, 61-65.

29. Thus Paley (1881, 39, *ad Fasti* 1.561) notes: "'*accipio revocamen*,' like the Greek δέχομαι τὸν οἰωνὸν, said when anyone acts on a hint dropped or an expression used which can be interpreted as an omen." Ovid's third (though chronologically first?) use of the noun implicitly activates this meaning:

> Sed quid ago? revoco? revocaminis omen abesto,
> blandaque compositas aura secundet aquas!
>
> (*Her.* 13.135-36)

[But what am I doing? Recalling you? Be the omen of recall far from me, and may a gentle breeze favor travel over the peaceful waters!]

See further Palmer's note *ad loc.* (1898, 408), and cf. Virg., *Aen.* 6.128. Note also Ovid's play on the derivation of noun from verb in *revoco? revocaminis...* (*Her.* 13.135).

30. I follow Kenney (1973, 125 and 149 n. 75) in preferring the manuscript reading of *amantis* to Heinsius' emendation *amanti*, which Anderson (1977) accepts, and also in interpreting *amantis* as a reference to Coronis rather than to Apollo.

54 / *The Play of Fictions*

> tendit et illa suo totiens cum pectore iuncta
> indevitato traiecit pectora telo.
>
> <div align="right">(<i>Met.</i> 2.600-5)</div>

[When the god had heard the charge of her infidelity, the laurel wreath fell from his head; his face fell, his complexion paled, and his quill slipped from his hands; as his heart blazed with tumultuous anger he snatched up his customary weapons, strung the curving bow from the horns, and pierced her breast, so often joined to his own, with an unerring shaft.]

There is considerable humor in the syllepsis of *Met.* 2.601, and the figure mimics the speed of Apollo's actions in the narrative.[31] The inevitable finality of Coronis' death is movingly evoked by the heavily spondaic *indevitato,* which concludes the account of the god's first reactions to the raven's news. The dying woman has time for only the briefest response: '*potui poenas tibi, Phoebe, dedisse, / sed peperisse prius. duo nunc moriemur in una,*' "I could have paid the penalty you impose, Apollo, but after giving birth. Now two of us shall die in one" (*Met.* 2.608-9). With another syllepsis, *et pariter vitam cum sanguine fudit,* "and she lost her life as the blood gushed forth" (*Met.* 2.610), the poet picks up the pace and turns his attention to Apollo's more thoughtful reaction upon his rash killing of mother and child (*Met.* 2.612-30). As befits second thoughts, the narrative is more expansive in delineating Apollo's grief at his haste, and Ovid emphasizes Apollo's parental concerns (*Met.* 2.621-30) at the expense of his amatory woes (*Met.* 2.617-19).

The episode concludes with the brief statement of the raven's metamorphosis that we have expected since the opening lines of the tale (*Met.* 2.533-41) promised an account of this very metamorphosis as a punishment for the raven's excessive loquacity.

> sperantemque sibi non falsae praemia linguae
> inter aves albas vetuit consistere corvum.
>
> <div align="right">(<i>Met.</i> 2.631-32)</div>

[And the raven, who was expecting a reward for his accurate tale,[32] was forbidden to stand in the ranks of the white birds.]

---

31. On Ovid's predilection for syllepsis, see Kenney 1973, 149 n. 76.
32. The raven of the *Metamorphoses* seems to expect a reward for his accurate report

The actual accomplishment of this metamorphosis, therefore, is an effective signal of the episode's conclusion, and indeed the account of the raven's transformation is strongly marked off from what precedes and follows. The first words of the episode shift the narrative abruptly away from Callisto, while the conclusion of the episode is emphatically marked by ring composition (*Met.* 2.631-32 reprising *Met.* 2.540-41). By contrast, we saw in our discussion of the inset narrative of the *cornix* that the crow was more interested in continuing to tell stories than in bringing her warning to a speedy close. The crow's narrative is not irrelevant to this discussion, however, for the sound pattern of the moral that Ovid states at the end of the embedding narrative, *praemia linguae* (*Met.* 2.631), recalls that of the warnings offered by the *cornix* to the raven at the outset of her embedded narrative, *praesagia linguae* (*Met.* 2.550). The result is that the conclusion of the first-layer narrative of the raven's metamorphosis also effectively closes the embedded narrative.

As this discussion of the closural effects of the epigrammatic conclusion to the episode suggests, there are several points of contact between the embedding and embedded narratives in our passage. The several thematic similarities that we have already observed may now be summarized. The raven and crow, prophets and story-tellers in the literature of antiquity, are characterized by Ovid as chattering (*Met.* 2.535, 540, 547-48) tattle-tales (*Met.* 2.546, 562).[33] The Latin words for crow and raven, *cornix* and *corvus* respectively, are etymologically related and easily confused.[34] Both birds tell stories about women who share with the birds the syllable c-r in their names—the Cecropids, the daughter of Coroneus (whose name would presumably be either Corone or Coronis), and Coronis of Larissa—and indeed, the poet seems to have delighted in including in this passage as many stories as possible with figures whose names participate in this syllabic configuration.[35] Moreover, the stories that Ovid's crow tells the raven, in a lengthy meditation on her relationship to her own divine patron Athena, are intended to document the inefficacy of the raven's journey, which was undertaken in order to tell a story to his divine patron Apollo. The crow's narrative

---

of Coronis' infidelity, because he was punished by Apollo for telling a lying tale at *Fasti* 2.261-62.

33. For ancient testimony of the raven's skill in augury, see Ael. 1.48, Aes. *Fab.* 212, Plin. 10 (12), 15, Cic. *De divin.* 1.39.85, Plaut. *Aulul.* 4.3.1, *Asin.* 2.1.12, Hor. *C.* 3.17, etc. See also Thompson 1936, 162-63, s.v. ΚΟΡΑΞ.

34. See Ernout-Meillet 143 s.v. *cornix,* and Ernout-Meillet 145 s.v. *corvus.*

35. Cf. Ahl 1985, 198.

consists of three tales, all of which are concerned with exploring the relationship between Athena and her attendants. In plot, therefore, the crow's stories complement the first-layer narrative of the raven, since the raven tells his patron Apollo of a third party's transgression, just as the crow reported the transgression of the Cecropids to her patron. The two tales thus form a "Chinese box" pattern of nested narratives.[36]

In addition to the manifold thematic connections already considered, we may note that both the crow and the raven are originally motivated to officious tale-bearing out of greed. The raven's metamorphosis comes as an unexpected "reward" for his tale-bearing, *non falsae praemia linguae* (*Met.* 2.631), and we may recall that the crow had also posed the question of just "recompense" for fidelity to her divine patron Athena.

> acta deae refero; pro quo mihi gratia[37] talis
> redditur, ut dicar tutela pulsa Minervae
> et ponar post noctis avem...
> quid tamen hoc prodest, si diro facta volucris
> crimine Nyctimene nostro successit honori?
>
> (*Met.* 2.562–64, 589–90)

[I reported their actions to the goddess; for which my reward is such that I am expelled from Minerva's protection and I am replaced by the night bird.... Nonetheless what good is this, if Nyctimene, who became a bird because of a dreadful crime, accedes to our position of honor?]

At the outset of the embedded narrative too, the crow directs the raven's attention to the question of the worth of his narrative (*Met.* 2.547–50), for with her opening words she queries the "utility" of the raven's purpose in reporting Coronis' infidelity to Apollo. The crow is well-placed to discuss the practical utility of story-telling with the raven, for this is not the first time, after all, that she has told her story. We know from the beginning of her tale that the crow has already related the Cecropids' transgression to Pallas Athena (*Met.* 2.562). From the outcome, the crow has learned that her narrative was not "worth" the punishment she

---

36. Kenney 1986, xxvii and 387–88.
37. On the financial connotations of *gratia*, see *TLL* 6.1.2228.26ff., and cf. *OLD* s.v. *gratia* 4.

earned, as she explains to the raven: *mea poena volucres / admonuisse potest, ne voce pericula quaerant* (*Met.* 2.564-65). The crow brings this knowledge to her encounter with the raven, so that the motivation of the second narrating instance can no longer be characterized as financial or economic. It is clear, however, that the crow recognizes the implicitly economic motivation of the raven in the structure of her response: her first story lays out the risks of telling stories for a price.[38]

Thus far, we have been concerned with elucidating the parallels between the characters of the *corvus* and the *cornix,* but at this point it is worth considering the points of contact between the crow's stories and the story of Coronis that the raven tells Apollo. In Chapter 1, we saw that the *cornix'* narrative was organized by recurrent themes and structures that combine to characterize the tales' actors as royal maidens, attendants of Minerva. In the course of her narrative she suggests that they are all guilty of some sort of crime against Minerva for which it is implied that they all, with the significant exception of the crow herself, go unpunished. Does the crow, in thus setting into motion this pattern linking her characters, inadvertently suggest to the raven that she herself bears a certain similarity to Coronis, the cause of the raven's expedition to Apollo?

The poet's description of Coronis is brief and typical of many of the introductions of women in the early books of the poem.[39]

Pulchrior in tota quam Larissaea Coronis
non fuit Haemonia: placuit tibi, Delphice, certe

(*Met.* 2.542-43)

[There was no woman in the whole of Thessaly more beautiful than Coronis of Larissa: certainly, she pleased you, god of Delphi.]

Coronis' beauty is underscored in order to emphasize Apollo's amatory interest in her, and the crow's own story begins similarly, with the claim that she was beautiful and much sought after.

---

38. See further my discussion in Chap. 4, pp. 101-3, of the recurrent theme of an economic motivation for narrative throughout the sequence of episodes at *Met.* 2.531-835.

39. Cf. the poet's address to Daphne (*Met.* 1.488-89), Jupiter's remarks to the comely Io (*Met.* 1.589-90), and the introductions of Callisto (*Met.* 2.409-16) and Herse (*Met.* 2.722-26). In the first two books of the *Metamorphoses* alone, we meet Daphne, Io, Syrinx, Callisto, and Europa, all of whom suffer a fate similar to that of Coroneus' daughter: see Otis 1970, 379-89 and Anderson 1971, 686.

> ...fueramque ego regia virgo
> divitibusque procis (ne me contemne) petebar;
> forma mihi nocuit. nam cum per litora lentis
> passibus, ut soleo, summa spatiarer harena,
> vidit et incaluit pelagi deus, utque precando
> tempora cum blandis absumpsit inania verbis,
> vim parat et sequitur....
>
> (*Met.* 2.570-76)

[I was a royal maiden and I was sought (do not scorn me) by wealthy princes. My beauty was my undoing. For when I went walking along the shore with slow steps over the top of the sand, as was my wont, the god of the sea saw me and blazed with passion; but when he had wasted time in vain in entreaty and flattering words he readied force and gave pursuit....]

Both maidens are described as beautiful (*pulchrior... Coronis, Met.* 2.542; *forma, Met.* 2.572), and receive advances from a god (*placuit tibi, Delphice, Met.* 2.543; *vidit et incaluit pelagi deus, Met.* 2.574). These similarities in themselves are, of course, hardly unusual in the world of the *Metamorphoses,* but a more significant parallel between the two maidens is the similarity of their names. In telling her own history, the *cornix* included the name of her father Coroneus, who is otherwise unknown to the tradition.[40] D.E. Hill alone suggests that the name Coroneus is relevant to our interpretation of the passage, remarking that "the name was presumably chosen to encourage the reader to supply for the name of the crow herself the Greek word for that bird, 'Corone'."[41]

---

40. See Bömer 1969, 379 *ad loc.*; Moore-Blunt 1977, 121; and Hill 1985, 209. Haupt, Ehwald, and Albrecht (1966, 123) imply the same in their note *ad loc.*, quoted in Chap. 1 n. 58.

41. Hill 1985, 209, noting further that "the stories of Coronis, Corone, the Owl and Athene were...connected long before Ovid..."; cf. Frazer 1898, 3.72-73. Gildersleeve (1885, 272) in his note on the adjective Λακέρειαν *ad* Pindar, *Pyth.* 3.34, suggests that the connection had been made as early as Pindar: "Van Herwerden has called attention to the resemblance between Koronis of Lakereia and Hesiod's λακέρυζα κορώνη (*Erga* 745)." Young, too (1968, 38 n. 2), apparently assumes the connection between the raven's story and the crow's story to have been current in Pindar's time. Hollis (1990, 252) observes that Callimachus "makes nothing special of the fact that the κορώνη prophesies about Κορωνίς" and therefore suggests that Ovid "may be indulging in free invention when he makes his crow the transformed daughter of Coroneus."

The large number of Greek proper nouns in this passage, and their appearance in Greek forms of the oblique cases, suggests that an evocation of the feminine form of the Greek patronymic, Coronis, is also potentially appropriate to this context. Moreover, the occurrence of Coronis' name before the crow's narrative (*Larissaea Coronis, Met.* 2.542) and its recurrence in an oblique case at the resumption of the first-layer narrative after the crow's speech (*cum iuvene Haemonio vidisse Coronida narrat, Met.* 2.599) may also help the *doctus lector* toward the formulation of the patronymic Coronis.[42] It has been argued that such an ambiguity would "produce intolerable confusion," but it is clear that the story of the crow is meant to complement that of the raven in a variety of ways and we are likely on firm ground when we find yet another aspect of the crow's story that illuminates the raven's.[43] Moreover, the story of Coroneus' daughter, the *cornix* herself, receives the longest treatment of any subject in her narrative (*Met.* 2.569–88), and its relevance to the context can surely be allowed to go beyond the poet's need for a metamorphosis. Once we recognize that the poet has set into motion a pattern that suggests an affinity between the *cornix* and Coronis, as well as that between the *cornix* and the *corvus,* we can see another reason for the *corvus'* disdainful dismissal of the *cornix'* warning. When the *cornix* consistently returns in her narrative to a plot pattern in which maidens go unpunished for crimes they have committed against their divine patron, when she identifies herself among them, and when she implicitly identifies herself with the criminal of the raven's story, the

---

42. The intellectual climate at Rome at the time when Ovid was writing was thoroughly Hellenized, and had been at least since Catullus' day: see Wiseman 1979, 154–66, and E. Rawson, *Intellectual Life in the Late Roman Republic* (London 1985).

43. I quote Hill 1985, 209. Cf. the similar remarks of Young (1968, 38 n. 2) about Pindar's Third Pythian Ode: "Mere mention of the raven might have produced some confusion due to the similarity of κορώνη ('crow') to Κορωνίς." Conte (1986, 194), however, points out that poetry works "by surrounding the individual word with connotations that are dense with implicit significance," rather than by careful statements of linear logic. In this respect, therefore, poetry differs significantly from modern conceptions of philosophy, history, and logic; cf. the cautionary discussion of Ross 1987, 8–9, concerning the poetry of Virgil. For a valuable discussion of the fluidity of ancient (as opposed to modern) conceptions of philosophy, history, etc., see Wiseman 1979 *passim.*

The technique of an inset narrative illuminating an epic narrative is common in Hellenistic and Roman poetry. See further Crump 1931, 23–24; Gutzwiller 1981; Hinds 1987, 92, and 158 n. 47; and Hutchinson 1988, 57–61 on the relationship between the Callimachean crow's account of her life-history in the *Hecale* and the life-history of Hecale herself as it emerges in the poem.

60 / *The Play of Fictions*

corvus can easily refuse to see the parallels between himself and his interlocutor, the *cornix*.⁴⁴

In exploring the complexities of the relationship between the account of the raven's metamorphosis and the embedded narrative of the crow we have seen that they complement each other in several ways (thematically, syllabically, in plot configuration, recurrent character types, etc.). Are there then no significant differences from a narratological perspective between the embedded and embedding narratives? On the contrary, it seems possible to make (at least) four important distinctions, and we are now in a position to consider the divergences between the narrative aesthetic of the crow and the poet. Ovid's organization of the introduction to the story of the raven's metamorphosis differs significantly from the crow's brief introduction to her own set of stories, in that the poet tells us not only the moral of the story that he will tell, but also the outcome of this story, *viz.*, that the raven will be transformed from a white bird into a black bird, *qui color albus erat, nunc est contrarius albo* (*Met.* 2.541). We may even interpret this remark about the fate of the raven

---

44. Name "doublets" are not unusual in the *Metamorphoses*. For example, from *Met.* 5.300 to *Met.* 6.2 an unnamed Muse tells Athena of a contest in which she and her sisters, called *Mnemonides (Met.* 5.268, 280) and *Aonides* (*Met.* 6.2; only Uranie, *Met.* 5.260, and Calliope, *Met.* 5.339 are mentioned by name), took part against the daughters of the Greek king Pieros: *Pieros has genuit Pellaeis dives in arvis*, "wealthy Pieros sired these girls in Pellan lands" (*Met.* 5.302). The daughters of Pieros could presumably be identified by the patronymic "Pierides," yet in the ancient literary tradition the Pierides are the Muses, so called because of their associations with Pieria in southwest Macedon: see Hes. *Sc.* 206; Pind. *Ol.* 10(11).96 and *Pyth.* 1.14; Virg., *Ecl.* 3.85, 6.13, 8.63, 9.33, and 10.72; Prop. 2.10.12; Hor. *C.* 4.3.18 and *C.* 4.8.20. Ovid himself elsewhere calls the Muses *Pierides:* cf. *Am.* 1.1.16; *Ars* 3.548; *Fasti* 2.269, 4.222, 5.109, 6.798-99; *Tr.* 3.2.3, 7.4, 4.1.28, 9.16, 5.1.34, 3.10, and 7.32; *ex Pont.* 2.5.63, 4.2.45, 8.70, and 16.42. On the name "doublet" in *Met.* 5, see Hinds 1987, 166-67 n. 40.

Ovid deploys several similar names in closely related episodes of the fourth book of the *Metamorphoses*. Early on we find the Minyad Leuconoe (*Met.* 4.168) telling the story of Leucothoe (*Met.* 4.196), while later Ino's name is changed to Leucothoe (*Met.* 4.541-42). Another of the stories in *Metamorphoses* 4 is told by the Minyad Alcithoe (*Met.* 4.274), whose name also seems confusingly close to Leucothoe and Leuconoe. Antoninus Liberalis' prose account of the Minyades' transformation identifies the sisters by the names Leucippe, Arsippe, and Alcathoe (Ant. Lib., *Met.* 10.1), and the discrepancy between the names there preserved and those used by Ovid in *Met.* 4 (Leuconoe and Alcithoe are named while the third Minyad goes unnamed) suggests that Ovid may have manipulated the names in this sequence of episodes in order to achieve closer homonymy.

Finally, in a rather different use of "doublets," Ovid narrates in the course of the poem three swan metamorphoses (*Met.* 2.367-80, 7.371-81 and 12.71-167), two Alcyone metamorphoses (*Met.* 7.400-1 and 11.410-750), two Scylla metamorphoses (*Met.* 8.17-151 and 13.730-14.74), two accounts of Atalanta (*Met.* 8.317-444 and 10.560-707), and the tales of two different men both named Iphis (*Met.* 9.666-797 and 14.698-771).

as an assurance that there will indeed be a metamorphosis at the end of this story, in a promise that the *cornix,* as an internal narrator, does not have to offer either to her (internal) interlocutor or to the audience of the first-layer narrative. Secondly, the first-layer narrative of the raven's metamorphosis, although interrupted and foreshadowed by the embedded narrative of the crow, follows the logic of temporal sequentiality, while no such claim can be made for the embedded narrative.[45] A concern with temporal sequentiality is a striking feature of the whole of the *Metamorphoses,* and it accords with the final clause of the proem to the work wherein the poet undertakes to "spin a fine thread of continuous song from the original creation of the world down to [his own] day" (*primaque ab origine mundi / ad mea perpetuum deducite tempora carmen, Met.* 1.3–4). Thirdly, we have seen that the crow does not bother to close one story before she hurries on to the next, and in this respect too the embedded narrative is very different from the first-layer narrative, with its clearly marked opening (*quam tu nuper... subito nigrantes versus in alas, Met.* 2.534–35) and epigrammatic conclusion (*Met.* 2.631–32). Finally, there is every reason to suppose that the crow's narrative is organized as it is in order to underscore the poet's initial characterization of the speaking crow as a loquacious chatterer (*Met.* 2.547). The personality of the poet/narrator of the *Metamorphoses* as a whole, however, remains considerably more elusive.[46]

---

45. For the confusion of temporal sequence in the crow's narrative, see Chap. 1.
46. On the personality of the poet/narrator of the *Metamorphoses*, see Galinsky 1975, 99, and Solodow 1988, 37–73.

Chapter 3

Chiron's Daughter and the Art of Prophecy: *Met.* 2.633-79

A striking feature that emerged from our analysis of the transition from the Callisto episode into that of the raven and crow (*Met.* 2.531-41) was the poet's reuse of characters whose metamorphoses had been narrated earlier in the *Metamorphoses*, the translation of Argus' eyes onto the peacock's tail and Cygnus' transformation into a swan. In effecting the transition into the Ocyroe episode from that of the raven, Ovid once again redeploys characters from an earlier episode, in this case the immediately preceding episode. Before the raven's metamorphosis Coronis tells Apollo of their unborn child (*Met.* 2.609), and this child, along with his guardian Chiron, is the focus of the transition from the tale of the raven's metamorphosis into the Ocyroe episode.

> non tulit in cineres labi sua Phoebus eosdem
> semina, sed natum flammis uteroque parentis
> eripuit geminique tulit Chironis in antrum,
> sperantemque sibi non falsae praemia linguae
> inter aves albas vetuit consistere corvum.
>   Semifer interea divinae stirpis alumno
> laetus erat mixtoque oneri gaudebat honore.
> ecce venit rutilis umeros protecta capillis
> filia Centauri....
>
>   (*Met.* 2.628-36)

[Phoebus did not suffer his own seed to perish in the same ashes but tore his son from his mother's womb out of the flames, and carried him to the cave of biform Chiron; and the raven, who was expecting a reward for his accurate tale, was forbidden to stand in the ranks of the white birds. Meanwhile Chiron, half-beast, rejoiced in the care of a divine child and was gladdened by the prospect of honor along with the task. Look the Centaur's daughter comes, her glowing red hair covering her shoulders. . . .]

The temporal adverb *interea* (*Met.* 2.633), besides functioning as a chronological signpost within the framework of the poem's continuous narrative (*perpetuum carmen, Met.* 1.4), effectively signals a new direction for the narrative. In this connection we may recall that the transition into the account of the raven's metamorphosis was also accomplished with a strongly marked temporal referent.

tam nuper pictis caeso pavonibus Argo,
quam tu nuper eras, cum candidus ante fuisses,
corve loquax, subito nigrantes versus in alas.

(*Met.* 2.533-35)

[As recently as the peacock was bedecked upon the death of Argus (with his hundred eyes), so recently were you, chattering raven—though you had previously been white—suddenly transformed into black wings.]

Recurrent structures of plot configuration also link the tales of the raven and Ocyroe. In the conclusion to the account of the raven's metamorphosis, Apollo's parental interests figured more prominently than his amatory interest in Coronis, while in the subsequent tale Chiron's daughter Ocyroe is quickly introduced (*Met.* 2.635-38), and both the children, Aesculapius and Ocyroe, are the focus of the new episode. Moreover, the emphasis in the tale of the raven's metamorphosis upon Apollo's inability to heal Coronis' wounds, despite his prowess in the medical arts (*Met.* 2.617-19), is complemented in the next episode by Ocyroe's prophecy of Aesculapius' healing powers (*Met.* 2.642-46).

Further etymological play with the names of characters around the syllabic nexus c-r, which we identified as an important principle of narrative organization in the preceding episode, occurs at the outset of Ovid's account of Ocyroe's transformation, thereby strengthening the narrative links between the two episodes. Chiron's name itself, along with that of his wife Chariclo, may facilitate the transition from the metamorphoses of the raven (*corvus*) and the crow (*cornix*) into the tale of the centaur's daughter, introduced without delay by the Greek name Ὠκυρόη, Ocyroe.¹ The difference in the quantities of the vowels, and even in the vowels themselves, is of little importance in ancient etymologizing, as many Varronian instances suggest.² Ovid draws etymological attention to the name of the centaur's daughter, as the commentators remark, by glossing it with a Latin translation, *rapidum flumen*, "swift river."

> ecce venit rutilis umeros protecta capillis
> filia Centauri, quam quondam nympha Chariclo
> fluminis in rapidi ripis enixa vocavit
> Ocyroen....
>
> (*Met.* 2.635-38)

[Look the Centaur's daughter comes, her glowing red hair covering her shoulders, a girl whom once the nymph Chariclo bore on the banks of a swift river and called Ocyroe, "Swift River." ...]

It is a typical feature of Alexandrian etymologizing to emphasize such a gloss by introducing in close conjunction a verb or noun of naming, and the prominent placement of *vocavit* (*Met.* 2.637) underscores Ovid's

---

1. On the importance of the syllable as the fundamental basis for ancient etymological discussion, see Quint. *Inst. Or.* 1.1.26, 1.1.30, 1.1.37, 9.4.84-93, and 12.10.32-33. For modern discussion see D.L. Blank, *Ancient Philosophy and Grammar,* American Classical Studies 10 (Chico, CA, 1982), 6-10, and Ahl 1985, 35-40.

2. For example, Varro offers an etymology for Venus' name in which not only the quantities of the vowels differ, but also the vowels themselves: *Venus... quae ab hoc etiam dicitur nuncupata, quod sine vi femina virgo non esse desinat,* "Venus, who is said to get her name from this, the fact that a woman does not cease to be a virgin without violence." The passage is cited by Augustine, *De civ. dei* 6.9, and quoted by Ahl 1985, 39. Cf. Varro *L.L.* 5.61-62:

> ...et horum vinctionis vis Venus. Hinc comicus: Huic victrix Venus, videsne haec? Non quod vincere velit Venus, sed vincire.
>
> [... the force of the binding of these is Venus. Hence the comic poet says, "Venus is victorious over this man, do you see it?" not because Venus wishes to conquer [*vincere*] but to bind [*vincire*].]

See also Snyder 1980, 106; Ahl 1985, 35-40; and Ross 1987, 43.

etymological play here.³ The emphasis on Ocyroe's name and the Latin gloss that precedes it at the opening of the episode is paralleled at its conclusion, where Ovid makes oblique allusion to the more common Greek names for Chiron's daughter, Hippe ("Ιππη, "Mare") or Melanippe (Μελανίππη, "Black Mare"):⁴ *in equam cognataque corpora vertor... nomen quoque monstra dedere,* "I am turned into a mare, a kindred form, ... the wonderful transformation even supplied her with a name" (*Met.* 2.663, 675).⁵ The usual name of Chiron's daughter is hinted at rather than stated, not only because it is better known, but also because the translation of the name Ocyroe at the outset of this episode has already given the *doctus lector* a model for forming a Greek name from a gloss.⁶ More significantly still, the obscure name Ocyroe contributes to the effectiveness of the transition by its verbal similarity (-cyro-) to the syllabic nexus c-r, for neither Hippe nor Melanippe bears any resemblance to the names of the characters in the preceding episode, the daughters of Cecrops, the raven (*corvus*), the crow (*cornix,* Greek κορώνη), the Phocian king Coroneus, and the Thessalian princess Coronis. The *lusus etymologici* that cluster around the names of Chiron's daughter draw attention to the poet's choice of the obscure name Ocyroe over the more common Hippe or Melanippe, and thereby effect the narrative progression of our passage from the account of the raven's metamorphosis into that of Ocyroe's transformation through the syllabic association.

Even Ocyroe's prophetic prowess may be related to the proverbial

---

3. O'Hara (1986, 15-16 and n. 21) collects a number of examples of explicit etymologizing in the Hellenistic Greek and Roman poets that are signaled by the use of such words as ὄνομα / *nomen* and καλεῖν / *vocare.*

4. On the name Hippe, or Hippo ('Ιππώ), see *R-E* s.v. *Hippe* 1 and *Hippo* 2; Haupt, Ehwald, and Albrecht 1966, 128 and 131; and Moore-Blunt 1977, 138. On the name Melanippe, see Hyg. *Astr.* 2.18, Call. fr. 569, and Eur. *Melanippe.* At Ap. Rhod. 2. 966 a Melanippe is mentioned as the daughter of Ares. An Oceanid named Ὠκυρόη (Ocyroe) appears at Hom. *Hymn Dem.* 420; cf. also Hesiod *Theog.* 360 with the discussion of West 1966, 268 *ad loc.* Several recent studies have documented the subtlety of Ovidian reference in the tradition of Hellenistic allusion to variants: see Murgia 1984, 207-14; Knox 1985, 65-83; and Hinds 1987, Index of Subjects, s.v. "allusion."

5. Cf. Haupt, Ehwald, and Albrecht 1966, 131; Bömer 1969, 391; Moore-Blunt 1977, 138; and Hill 1985, 211.

6. Ovid's *doctrina* is abundantly clear to the modern reader, for this is the only occurrence of the name Ocyroe in extant Latin literature. In Greek literature too Melanippe (or Hippe) is the more frequent name of Chiron's daughter: see the references collected above, n. 4. It may be worth mentioning that the name of Ocyroe's mother, Chariclo, at *Met.* 2.636, is also unparalleled in Latin literature: see Bömer 1969, 391; Moore-Blunt 1977, 133; and Hill 1985, 211. In Greek literature, Chariclo appears at Pindar, *Pyth.* 4.103; cf. the scholia *ad* Pindar, *Pyth.* 4.103, and *ad* Ap. Rhod. 1.557, 554, and 4.813.

prophetic talents of the crow and raven, downplayed but nonetheless alluded to in the preceding episode. The Ovidian crow implicitly denies that she offers the raven a prophecy in her narrative when she calls her speech a warning (*mea poena volucres / admonuisse potest, ne voce pericula quaerant,* "my punishment can warn birds not to court danger with their talk," *Met.* 2.564-65), but Ovid alludes to the prophetic context of his literary model both in the inset narrative of the crow (*praesagia, Met.* 2.550) and in the raven's response to the crow (*Talia dicenti 'tibi' ait 'revocamina' corvus / 'sint precor ista malo: nos vanum spernimus omen,'* "As the crow was speaking, the raven said 'May your ominous reminiscences, a summons to return, bode you ill: we disdain your empty prophecy'," *Met.* 2.596-97). The understated allusions to the *Hecale* and especially to the relationship between the crow and the raven in their Callimachean context suggest that we should interpret Ovid's account of the metamorphosis of the raven at *Met.* 2.631-32 as the authentication of the prophecy contained in the literary model (*Hecale,* Hollis fr. 74.10-20). With its overtly prophetic stance, the story of Ocyroe, which centers upon Ocyroe's prophetic utterances, functions as a further and final allusion to the *Hecale* in the sequence of episodes at *Met.* 2.531-835.

Chiron's daughter is moved to utter her first prophecy upon looking at the infant Aesculapius.

> ergo ubi vaticinos concepit mente furores
> incaluitque deo, quem clausum pectore habebat,
> adspicit infantem 'toto' que 'salutifer orbi
> cresce puer' dixit....
>
> (*Met.* 2.640-43)

[And so when she conceived mantic frenzy in her mind and grew warm with the divine spirit, which she held within her breast, she looked upon the babe and said, "Health-bringer to the whole world, grow, child...."]

Inspired by the divine, Ocyroe proclaims that Aesculapius will be a supreme healer, calling him a "health-bringer," *salutifer,* and predicting that many will owe him their lives.

> ...dixit, 'tibi se mortalia saepe
> corpora debebunt; animas tibi reddere ademptas
> fas erit....
>
> (*Met.* 2.643-45)

[... she spoke: "often mortals will owe you their lives; it will be lawful for you to give back lives (already) cut off...."]

The reader encounters one such mortal in the final book of the *Metamorphoses*,[7] where Hippolytus explains to Egeria that but for Aesculapius' medical skill, Theseus' curse would have killed him.

> ... vidi quoque luce carentia regna
> et lacerum fovi Phlegethontide corpus in unda,
> nec nisi Apollineae valido medicamine prolis
> reddita vita foret....
>
> (*Met.* 15.531–34)

[... I saw the kingdom without sunlight and I bathed my wounded body in the water of Phlegethon. Nor would my life have been restored to me were it not for the powerful remedy of Apollo's son....]

Hippolytus explicitly attests to the ability of Aesculapius (identified in these lines as *Apollineae ... prolis*) to restore the dying to life, echoing Ocyroe's prophecy in Book 2 of the *Metamorphoses*. The verb *reddo*, "restore," appears in both passages with Aesculapius as the agent of restoration (*Met.* 2.644; *Met.* 15.534),[8] and *anima* (*Met.* 2.644) is used by many Latin poets as the equivalent of *vita* (*Met.* 15.534).[9] In this way Hippolytus' speech unobtrusively refers the reader back to Ocyroe's prophecy, allowing Ovid to substantiate late in the *Metamorphoses* the prophecy offered by Ocyroe early in the poem.[10]

In analyzing the tale of the raven's metamorphosis, we had occasion to examine two passages in the *Fasti* that function as cross-references

---

7. Cf. Hill 1985, 211 and Kenney 1986, 389.
8. For *reddo* in the sense "restore, give back," see *OLD* s.v. *reddo* 1.
9. Cf. Lucretius, *D.R.N.* 3.117, Virgil, *Geo.* 4.238, *Aen.* 4.385, *Aen.* 5.483, and Ovid, *Fasti* 1.380. See further *TLL* 2.70.59ff.; and cf. *OLD* s.v. *anima* 3b and 5.
10. This should give us pause in assuming that Ovid was running out of inventive powers and commitment towards the end of the *Metamorphoses* and in the concurrent *Fasti*, as some studies have suggested: see Fränkel 1945, 105–8; Wilkinson 1955, 225–26, 237–38, and 268–70; Segal 1969, 267 with n. 27; Otis 1970, 358–60; Johnson 1978; and Fantham 1983, 210–16. The evidence I consider in this chapter suggests, on the contrary, that Ovid's control of—and commitment to—the material of the *Metamorphoses* remained consistently high. For a similar view, see also Coleman 1971, 472; Galinsky 1975, 218; and Hinds 1987 *passim*.

to the *Metamorphoses*.¹¹ Let us consider another such cross-reference between the two poems, namely the account of Aesculapius' restoration of Hippolytus to life, which appears under the entry for the date of June 21 at *Fasti* 6.737-62. After briefly reviewing Phaedra's incestuous love for Hippolytus, Theseus' paternal curse, and Hippolytus' fatal meeting with the bull from the sea (*Fasti* 6.737-42), Ovid turns to the details of Hippolytus' contact with Aesculapius.

> exciderat curru, lorisque morantibus artus
>   Hippolytus lacero corpore raptus erat,
> reddideratque animam, multum indignante Diana.
>   'nulla' Coronides 'causa doloris' ait:
> 'namque pio iuveni vitam sine volnere reddam,
>   et cedent arti tristia fata meae.'

(*Fasti* 6.743-48)

[Hippolytus fell from his chariot; the reins entangled his limbs, his terribly wounded body was dragged along, and he gave up the ghost, though Diana was much aggrieved. "There is no cause for distress," Coronis' son said: "for I will restore his life to the devout youth, without a wound, and his sad destiny will yield to my skill."]

In the *Fasti*, Hippolytus "had given up the ghost," *reddideratque animam* (*Fasti* 6.745), in phrasing that recalls the diction of Ocyroe's prophecy and specifically her prediction that Aesculapius would "give back lives (already) given up," *animas tibi reddere ademptas* (*Met.* 2.644). It is an especially piquant touch to employ opposing meanings of the verb *reddo* in the two passages, and, indeed, the play occurs within the *Fasti* account: *reddideratque animam . . . vitam sine volnere reddam,* "he had given up the ghost . . . I shall restore his life without a wound" (*Fasti* 6.745, 747).¹² The parallelism of verb (forms of *reddo* at *Fasti* 6.745, 747, *Met.* 2.644 and 15.534) and object (forms of *anima* at *Fasti* 6.745 and *Met.* 2.644; forms of *vita* at *Fasti* 6.747 and *Met.* 15.534), in passages where the same story is told, constitutes a cross-reference between the poems.¹³ Even the matronymic *Coronides* (*Fasti* 6.746) may function as an allusion

---

11. For the contemporaneity of the *Metamorphoses* and the *Fasti,* see Chap. 2 n. 17.
12. For *reddo* as "give up," see *OLD* s.v. *reddo* 11a.
13. For another such cross-reference between the two poems in this sequence of episodes, see Chap. 2.

to Ocyroe's prophecies in the second book of the *Metamorphoses,* for the only extant account of Coronis' story in Latin literature is that given by Ovid in the second book of the *Metamorphoses.*[14]

The narrative concerning Hippolytus in the *Fasti* can also be related to Hippolytus' speech at *Met.* 15.497–546.

> ...vidi quoque luce carentia regna
> et lacerum fovi Phlegethontide corpus in unda,
> nec nisi Apollineae valido medicamine prolis
> reddita vita foret; quam postquam fortibus herbis
> atque ope Paeonia Dite indignante recepi....
>
> (*Met.* 15.531–35)

[...I saw the kingdom without sunlight and I bathed my wounded body in the water of Phlegethon. Nor would my life have been restored to me were it not for the powerful remedy of Apollo's son; and after I regained life through strong herbs and Apollo's aid, although Dis was aggrieved....]

In both poems, the adjective *lacer* describes Hippolytus' "mangled body" (*lacero corpore, Fasti* 6.744; *lacerum corpus, Met.* 15.532).[15] Moreover, Aesculapius asserts his powers of healing in the *Fasti.*

> 'nulla' Coronides 'causa doloris' ait:
> 'namque pio iuveni vitam sine volnere reddam,
>   et cedent arti tristia fata meae.'
>
> (*Fasti* 6.746–48)

["There is no cause for distress," Coronis' son said: "for I will restore his life to the devout youth, without a wound, and his sad destiny will yield to my skill."]

This assertion is confirmed in the *Metamorphoses* when Hippolytus avers that he owes his life to Aesculapius: *nec nisi Apollineae valido medicamine prolis / reddita vita foret* (*Met.* 15.533–34), "...nor would my life have been restored to me were it not for the powerful rem-

---

14. Cf. Bömer 1969, 373 and Hill 1985, 207.

15. The adjective occurs eleven times in the *Metamorphoses.* For its comparative rarity in Latin literature before Ovid, see *TLL* 7.2.820.11–821.65.

edy of Apollo's son." Both passages, *Fasti* 6.743-62 and *Met.* 15.531-35, attest to the fulfillment of Ocyroe's original prophecy at *Met.* 2.642-48.

Ocyroe's first words proclaim that the unnamed child in Chiron's care will be a savior for all of humanity, however, and not of Hippolytus alone.

> adspicit infantem 'toto' que 'salutifer orbi
> cresce puer' dixit, 'tibi se mortalia saepe
> corpora debebunt. . . .
>
> (*Met.* 2.642-44)

[she looked upon the child and said, "Health-bringer to the whole world, grow, child; often mortals will owe you their lives. . . ."]

Ocyroe's diction is echoed at the conclusion of another episode in Book 15 of the *Metamorphoses*, in which Ovid relates Aesculapius' removal to Rome in the guise of a snake.[16]

> huc se de Latia pinu Phoebeius anguis
> contulit et finem specie caeleste resumpta
> luctibus inposuit venitque salutifer urbi.
>
> (*Met.* 15.742-44)

[Here Phoebus' snake, Aesculapius, disembarked from the Roman ship; when he resumed his divine form he put an end to lamentation, and came as a health-bringer to the city.]

In this passage, Ovid echoes Ocyroe's prophecy of *Met.* 2.642-48 by repeating *-que salutifer* in the same metrical *sedes* (*Met.* 2.642; *Met.* 15.744), and through the similarity in sound of *orbi* and *urbi*.[17] The adjective *salutifer,* an Ovidian coinage, does not occur in the *Fasti,* and

---

16. Cf. Ludwig 1965, 70; Bömer 1969, 392-93; and Moore-Blunt 1977, 134.
17. For the repetition of *-que,* cf. *Met.* 1.456 and its relationship to *Amores* 1.1.5 and .24: see McKeown 1989, 26 and Moore-Blunt 1977, 12 on Ovid's idiosyncratic usage of *-que* connecting direct speech with what has preceded. See further the exhaustive discussion of this feature of Ovidian discourse by Avery (1937, 71-72 n. 1), and cf. Marouzeau 1958, 104-5.

within the *Metamorphoses* Ovid employs it exclusively of Aesculapius.[18] The alteration of Ocyroe's *orbi* to *urbi* is especially significant.[19] When Ocyroe delivers her prophecy in the second book of the *Metamorphoses* Rome has not yet become the world power that it is in Ovid's own day.[20] By Book 11 of the *Metamorphoses,* however, Ovid enters "historical" chronology, and he offers his own treatment of Aeneas' wanderings later in the poem, at *Metamorphoses* 13.623-14.608 (often referred to as Ovid's "Aeneid").[21] Moreover, in the final five hundred lines of Book 15 of the *Metamorphoses,* Ovid arrives at the period of Rome's recent history, treating even contemporary events. The city has become the center of the world, *orbis terrarum,* and it is unchallenged for supremacy within the Mediterranean: Rome is both *urbs* and *orbis.*

While punning wordplay on *urbs* and *orbis* in the oblique cases is perhaps best known now through its use by the Roman Catholic Church, there is ample evidence to show that the play predates the Church Fathers and was current among the writers of late Republican and Augustan Rome.[22] Propertius provides an example of the play that draws attention

---

18. On *salutifer* as an Ovidian coinage, see Linse 1891, 43, and Moore-Blunt 1977, 134. Ovid uses it of Aesculapius once in Ocyroe's prophecy at *Met.* 2.642, and twice in the final book of the poem (*Met.* 15.632, 744). *Salutifer* appears elsewhere in the Ovidian *oeuvre* only at *Her.* 21.174, of Apollo. It is worth noting, in addition, that Aesculapius pointedly recites "salubrious words" at *Fasti* 6.753: ... *ter verba salubria dixit.*

19. Predictably, *orbi* appears as a manuscript variant at *Met.* 15.744 (in *P*). There is, however, no manuscript disagreement at *Met.* 2.642, and the overwhelming consensus of the manuscripts in reading *urbi* at *Met.* 15.744 suggests that Ovid did indeed write two different words: *orbi* at *Met.* 2.642 and *urbi* at *Met.* 15.744.

20. Ovid mentions *Roma* by name in the *Metamorphoses* only at 15.431 and 15.597. The adjective *Romanus* occurs only once before the fourteenth book of the poem, at 1.201, *Romanum nomen;* in the last two books of the poem it occurs nine times (14.800, 809, 837, 849; 15.637, 654, 736, 826, and 877).

21. On "history" in the *Metamorphoses,* see Buchheit 1966; Ludwig 1965, 60-73; Segal 1969 *passim*; and Otis 1970, 316. Wiseman (1979, 143-54) has a valuable discussion concerning the fluidity of ancient distinctions between "mythical" and "historical."

22. See the discussion of Bréguet (1969, 140-41), which begins with the use made by the Church Fathers of this wordplay, the Papal "Urbi et Orbi." Our earliest examples of the play are from Cicero and span the years 63 to 46 B.C.; see *Cat.* 1.4.9, *Cat.* 4.6.11, *Pro. Mur.* 10.22, *Ad Fam.* 4.1.2, and *Parad. Stoic.* 2.18. Cicero's contemporaries Varro and Cornelius Nepos also provide evidence of the popularity of this play: see Nepos, *Att.* 3.3 and 20.5, and Varro, *L.L.* 5.143.

For modern discussion of the etymologies of *urbs* and *orbis,* which remain obscure, see Ernout-Meillet 466, s.v. *orbis,* and 754, s.v. *urbs*; Walde and Hofmann 1954, 219, s.v. *orbis,* and 838, s.v. *urbs*; P. Kretschmer, "Etym. *orbis, orbita,"* in *Zeitschrift für Vergleich. Sprachforschung* (Göttingen 1905), 128-37. F. Muller Izn defends Varro's etymology in *Altitalisches Wörterbuch* (Göttingen 1926) 306ff. Bréguet (1969) and Hardie (1986, 364-

Chiron's Daughter and the Art of Prophecy / 73

to the emergence of Rome as the foremost "world" power.[23]

> septem urbs alta iugis, toto quae praesidet orbi,
>   femineo timuit territa Marte minas.[24]
>
> (Prop. 3.11.57–58)

[The lofty city of seven hills, a city which presides over the whole of the world, was terrified at the prospect of war with a woman and feared her threats.]

Ovid too had already emphasized the connection between the two words in the *Ars Amatoria*.

> nempe ab utroque mari iuvenes, ab utroque puellae
>   venere, atque ingens orbis in Urbe fuit.[25]
>
> (*Ars Am.* 1.173–74)

[Indeed youths and girls came from either sea, and the vast world was in the city.]

There is another such pointed collocation of the two words in the *Fasti*.

> gentibus est aliis tellus data limite certo:
>   Romanae spatium est Urbis et orbis idem.[26]
>
> (*Fasti* 2.683–84)

[To other nations land has been granted with a fixed boundary: the expanse of the city of Rome is the same as the globe.]

In the *Metamorphoses,* the wordplay is explicitly activated at the begin-

---

66) collect the recent bibliography on the connection between *orbis* and *urbs* in the ancient world.

23. See Haupt, Ehwald, and Albrecht 1966, 129, *ad Met.* 2. 642. For contemporary Augustan examples of this wordplay, see (in addition to Prop. 3.11.57) Livy 1.16.6-7. As Galinsky (1975, 253, quoting Fränkel 1945, 103) remarks, "The underlying idea of the rather extensive account of the god's sojourn from the *omphalos* of Greece to Rome, is indeed, as Fränkel has observed, 'that Rome has become the center of the civilized world'."

24. All quotations from Propertius are from the 1984 Teubner edition of P. Fedeli.

25. On this collocation see Brandt 1902, *ad loc.,* and Hollis 1977, 64, *ad loc.*

26. Bréguet (1969, 144) argues convincingly for the tradition of *orbis/urbs* wordplay in both prose and poetry; cf. Bömer 1958, 131–32, *ad Fasti* 2.683ff., and 17 *ad Fasti* 1.85.

ning of Aesculapius' second appearance in the poem (*Met.* 15.622–744), thirteen books after Ocyroe's prophecy of his healing powers at *Met.* 2.642–48.

> ...mediamque tenentes
> orbis humum Delphos adeunt, oracula Phoebi,
> utque salutifera miseris succurrere rebus
> sorte velit tantaeque urbis mala finiat, orant.
>
> (*Met.* 15.630–33)

[...and they came to Delphi, which occupies the central point of the globe and is the seat of Apollo's oracle; and they begged the god to agree to come to their assistance in their wretched afflictions with his health-bearing lots and to end the ills of so great a city as theirs.]

It is clear, therefore, that Ovid makes use of the play, and there is no reason to suppose that he does not activate it at the close of the Aesculapius episode in Book 15 of the *Metamorphoses,* thereby fulfilling Ocyroe's early prophecy of Aesculapius' future importance to the world, *salutifer orbi* (*Met.* 2.642), with a punningly appropriate specificity at the end of the poem, *salutifer urbi* (*Met.* 15.744).

In tracing the fulfillment of Ocyroe's prophecy that specifies Aesculapius as savior of the dying (*Met.* 2.642–48) we have been examining three closely related passages in the *Metamorphoses* and the *Fasti* (*Met.* 15.531–35, *Fasti* 6.737–62, and *Met.* 15.622–744). There remains the question of Aesculapius' own death and divinity. Early in the *Metamorphoses,* Ocyroe predicts that Aesculapius, whom we meet as an immortal infant (*Met.* 2.629–42), will die and yet become a god again.

> ...idque semel dis indignantibus ausus
> posse dare hoc iterum flamma prohibebere avita
> eque deo corpus fies exsangue deusque,
> qui modo corpus eras, et bis tua fata novabis.
>
> (*Met.* 2.645–48)

[... and having dared this once against the will of the gods, you will be denied the power to grant this again by your grandsire's flame and from a god you will become a bloodless corpse; and as a god, though you were but recently mortal, you will twice renew your destiny.]

Aesculapius has already been saved from death by his father, at the very moment of his birth: *sed natum flammis uteroque parentis / eripuit,* "Phoebus snatched his child from his mother's womb and from the flames" (*Met.* 2.629-30). But Ocyroe prophesies a second renewal of Aesculapius' destiny, and her prophecy is fulfilled in passages of both the *Fasti* and the *Metamorphoses.* The death of Aesculapius is narrated in the *Fasti.*

> pectora ter tetigit, ter verba salubria dixit:
>   depositum terra sustulit ille caput.
> lucus eum nemorisque sui Dictynna recessu
>   celat: Aricino Virbius ille lacu.
> at Clymenus Clothoque dolent, haec fila teneri,
>   hic fieri regni iura minora sui.
> Iuppiter, exemplum veritus, derexit in ipsum
>   fulmina qui nimiae moverat artis opem.
>
> (*Fasti* 6.753-60)

[Thrice Aesculapius touched Hippolytus' breast, thrice spoke health-bearing words: the youth lifted his head laid low upon the earth. A grove received him, and Dictynna concealed him in a recess of her wood; he is Virbius of the Arician lake. But Clymenus and Clotho were grieved, she that her threads were checked, he that the rights of his kingdom were lessened. Jupiter, fearing his example, directed his thunderbolts at the one who had contributed the aid of too much skill.]

Ovid here explicitly ascribes Aesculapius' death to the displeasure of the gods (*Fasti* 6.757-60), and specifically to Jupiter (*Fasti* 6.759-60), echoing the substance of Ocyroe's prophecy in the *Metamorphoses* concerning the gods' righteous anger (*Met.* 2.645) and Jupiter's thunderbolt (*Met.* 2.646).[27] Ovid ends the account of Aesculapius in the *Fasti* with an ironic epigram.

---

27. On Zeus' role in the death of Aesculapius, cf. Hes. fr. 45c M-W, Pherekydes, *FGrH* 3 F 35a (Scholia Eur. *Alc.* 1), Diod. 4.71, and Apollodorus 3.122; a different version appears in Aes. *Ag.* 1022ff. See further the discussion of Bömer 1969, 393, *ad Met.* 2.646. It is worth noting also that two of the three passages that echo the diction of Ocyroe's prophecy at *Met.* 2.642-48 mention the righteous anger of the gods in an ablative absolute phrase with the verb *indignor* (*dis indignantibus, Met.* 2.645; *multum indignante Diana,*

76 / *The Play of Fictions*

> Phoebe, querebaris: deus est, placare parenti:
> propter te, fieri quod vetat, ipse facit.
>
> (*Fasti* 6.761-62)

[Phoebus, you complained: he is a god, be reconciled to your father: for your sake, he himself did what he forbids be done by others.]

This couplet fulfills with precision the enigmatic conclusion of Ocyroe's prophecy,

> eque deo corpus fies exsangue deusque,
> qui modo corpus eras, et bis tua fata novabis.
>
> (*Met.* 2.647-48)

[and from a god you will become a bloodless corpse, and as a god, though you were but recently mortal, you will twice renew your destiny.][28]

Although the death of Aesculapius is never mentioned in the *Metamorphoses* after Ocyroe's prophecy, Ovid narrates at some length the removal to Rome of the divine Aesculapius (identified both as *Coronides, Met.* 15.624, and as *Apolline nato, Met.* 15.639) in the guise of a snake at *Met.* 15.622-744.[29] The snake is referred to as *deus* no fewer than twelve times (*Met.* 15.646, 653, 663 [twice], 667, 670, 677 [twice], 683, 694, 697, and 720) in order to underscore the fact of the divine status finally achieved by Aesculapius.

After prophesying the fate of the infant Aesculapius, a prophecy that we have seen to be accurate, Ocyroe turns to consider what the future holds for her father Chiron.

Fasti 6.745; *Dite indignante, Met.* 15.535). Ocyroe's prophecy refers to gods in the plural (*Met.* 2.645), but in each of the two passages in which the story of Hippolytus' resurrection is narrated, a single divinity is described as righteously angry: in the *Fasti* the goddess Diana, and in the *Metamorphoses* the god Dis. Ocyroe's reference to gods in the plural is thus compendious, alluding to both accounts of Hippolytus' death.

28. Cf. Hyginus, *fab.* 251.2: *qui licentia Parcarum ab inferis redierunt... Asclepius, Apollinis et Coronidis filius,* "among those who returned from the underworld with the permission of the Parcae... is Asclepius, the son of Apollo and Coronis." In the next century *deus fieri* becomes a standard formula to express deification: see *TLL* 5.891.10-70.

29. On the connections between the Aesculapius episodes in Books 2 and 15 of the *Metamorphoses,* see also Davis 1980, 131.

> tu quoque, care pater, nunc inmortalis et aevis
> omnibus ut maneas nascendi lege creatus,
> posse mori cupies tum, cum cruciabere dirae
> sanguine serpentis per saucia membra recepto,
> teque ex aeterno patientem numina mortis
> efficient, triplicesque deae tua fila resolvent.
>
> (*Met.* 2.649-54)

[You too, dear father—though now immortal and destined by the law of birth to live through all ages—will wish you could die at the time when the blood of a dreadful serpent tortures you, penetrating your wounded limbs; the immortals will change you from an immortal being to one able to suffer death, and the three goddesses will release the threads of your life.]

Ovid does not narrate the tale of Chiron's death in the *Metamorphoses,* although the conclusion of the story offered a catasterism, and as such, an appropriate subject for the poem. We should be wary of concluding, however, that after tracing the fulfillment of Ocyroe's first prophecy with such care Ovid then lost interest in the rest of her speech. We have seen that Ovid includes in the *Fasti* a passage that complements, and comments on, his treatment of Aesculapius' story in the *Metamorphoses,* and he likewise narrates the Centaur's death and catasterism at *Fasti* 5.379-414, on the date of the third of May when the evening rising of one of the stars in the belly of the horse in the constellation *Centaurus* is visible at Rome.[30] In antiquity, the constellation *Centaurus* was associated with Chiron, the most famous centaur from myth, and it is therefore unexceptional for our poet to tell Chiron's story here.[31]

In both poems, Chiron dwells in a cave (*Chironis in antrum, Met.* 2.630; *saxo stant antra vetusto, Fasti* 5.383), where he acts as guardian and tutor, in the *Metamorphoses* to the infant Aesculapius (*Met.* 2.630-34), and in the *Fasti* to the young Achilles (*Fasti* 5.385-86, 390, 407-

---

30. See Frazer 1929, 4.30, and Bömer 1958, 313-15.
31. Similar accounts of Chiron's death and catasterism can be found in Eratosthenes, *Catáster.* 40; Hyginus, *Astr.* 2.38; and in the scholia to Caesar Germanicus, *ad Aratea* 417. An alternate version of the story, in which the centaur Pholus is wounded by Hercules' arrow, is told by Apollodorus at 2.5.4 and.11; cf. Diodorus Siculus, 4.12.8, Servius *ad* Virgil, *Aen.* 8.294, and Tzetzes, *Schol. on Lycophron* 670. See further Frazer 1929, 4.30, and Bömer 1958, 314.

12).³² Chiron is identified as *Philyreius heros* (*Met.* 2.676; *Fasti* 5.391) and *Centaurus* (*Met.* 2.636; *Fasti* 5.405), and is addressed by both Ocyroe (*Met.* 2.649) and Achilles (*Fasti* 5.412) as *care pater*.³³ There is, however, a notable discrepancy in the figure of Chiron as he is presented in the two poems. In the *Metamorphoses,* Ovid begins the Ocyroe episode with a description of Chiron's delight in his new charge.

> Semifer³⁴ interea divinae stirpis alumno
> laetus erat mixtoque oneri gaudebat honore.
>
> (*Met.* 2.633–34)

[Meanwhile the half-beast, Chiron, rejoiced in the care of a divine child and was gladdened by the prospect of honor along with the task.]

The opening lines of the passage in the *Fasti,* however, reveal a rather different aspect of Chiron.

> Nocte minus quarta promet sua sidera Chiron
> semivir et flavi corpore mixtus equi.
>
> (*Fasti* 5.379–80)

---

32. A cave is Chiron's usual abode: see Pindar, *Pyth.* 3.63, 4.102, 9.30, and Schol. Arat. 436. For Chiron as teacher of Aesculapius see Homer, *Il.* 4.219; Pindar, *Pyth.* 3.1–7 and 43–46, *Nem.* 3.43ff.; and Apollodorus 3.10.3. For Achilles' association with Chiron in the literary tradition, see Homer, *Il.* 11.832; Pindar, *Nem.* 3.43ff.; Ovid, *Ars* 1.17. On Chiron's teachings, see Χείρωνος ὑποθῆκαι (frs. 283–85 M-W), a poem ascribed in antiquity to Hesiod.

In the *Metamorphoses,* Chiron's functions as teacher and guardian are split: we see him as guardian of Aesculapius (*Met.* 2.630, 633–34) and teacher of Ocyroe (*non haec artes contenta paternas / edidicisse fuit,* "this child was not satisfied to have learned her father's skills," *Met.* 2.638–39). In the *Fasti,* however, Chiron acts as both guardian and tutor to Achilles: cf. *Fasti* 5.385–86 and 412.

33. Cf. *Phillyrides* of Chiron at *Fasti* 5.383. Frazer's discussion *ad loc.* (1929, 31), traces a poetic genealogy that shows how closely Ovid is working within the learned Alexandrian tradition: "Chiron is called Phillyrides by Hesiod (*Theog.* 1002), Pindar (*Pyth.* 3.1, 9.30), Apollonius Rhodius (1.554) and Ovid (*Ars* 1.11, and the present passage)," as well as by Virgil (*Geo.* 3.550) and Propertius (2.1.60). Cf. Bömer 1958, 313–14.

Dr. S.E. Hinds remarks (personal communication) that Achilles' use of the address *care pater* (*Fasti* 5.412) makes *pater* at *Fasti* 5.407 interestingly pointed. In terms of the *Fasti* itself, the use of *patrem* in the simile of *Fasti* 5.407 sets up the mention of Achilles' real father Peleus in the following line; but in terms of the cross-reference to the *Metamorphoses,* the poet's play with Chiron as a father-figure to Achilles evokes not Achilles' real father, but Chiron's real child.

34. The late tenth century manuscript *e* reads *semivir* at *Met.* 2.633. The rest of the manuscript evidence supports the reading *semifer* here.

[In less than four nights Chiron, half-man intermingled with the form of a golden horse, will show forth his stars.]

The poet's sophisticated play on the two "halves" of Chiron constitutes a subtle cross-reference between the two poems, the *Metamorphoses* and the *Fasti*.[35]

Chiron experiences the death prophesied by his daughter in the *Metamorphoses* (*Met.* 2.651-54) in the *Fasti*, where the suffering briefly suggested by Ocyroe (*cum cruciabere, Met.* 2.651) is dwelt on at length.

> dumque senex tractat squalentia tela venenis,
>   excidit et laevo fixa sagitta pede est.
> ingemuit Chiron, traxitque e corpore ferrum:
>   adgemit Alcides Haemoniusque puer.
> ipse tamen lectas Pagasaeis collibus herbas
>   temperat et varia volnera mulcet ope;
> virus edax superabat opem, penitusque recepta
>   ossibus et toto corpore pestis erat:
> sanguine Centauri Lernaeae sanguis echidnae
>   mixtus ad auxilium tempora nulla dabat.
>
> (*Fasti* 5.397-406)

[And while the old centaur was handling Hercules' weapons, which were covered with poison, an arrow fell out and stuck in his left foot. Chiron groaned, and drew the iron from his body: Hercules and

---

35. Ovid is fond of adjectives formed on numerical prefixes, among them *semi-*: see Haupt, Ehwald, and Albrecht 1966, 128; Bömer 1969, 391; Kenney 1973, 121-22; and Moore-Blunt 1977, 132-33. The play on *semi-* here suggested is not without parallel in the Ovidian corpus, for a notorious example of Ovidian wordplay with adjectives compounded with this very prefix occurs at *Ars* 2.24 (*semibovemque virum semivirumque bovem,* "half-bull man and half-man bull") and is the subject of a famous anecdote recounted by Seneca the Elder at *Contr.* 2.2.12.

Ovid may comment on this play across the *Fasti* and the *Metamorphoses* in Ocyroe's complaint about her transformation into a mare:

'... in equam cognataque corpora vertor.
tota tamen quare? pater est mihi nempe biformis.'

(*Met.* 2.663-64)

["... I am being turned into a kindred form, a mare. But why entirely equine? My father, after all, has a two-fold nature."]

Thessalian Achilles groaned too. But he himself blended herbs gathered on the hills of Pagasae and soothed the wounds with various resources; the greedy toxin overcame all efforts, the poison penetrated deep within his bones and spread through his whole body: the blood of the Lernaean hydra had been mixed with that of the Centaur and left no time for rescue.]

With Chiron's groan the poet begins an eight-line description of the centaur's pain and the attempts of Achilles and Hercules to help him, all to no avail: the pestilence invades Chiron's body (*Fasti* 5.403-4). At the climax of the episode, Ovid echoes a line from Ocyroe's prophecy in the *Metamorphoses*. Ocyroe mentions the blood of the Lernaean hydra, *sanguine serpentis* (*Met.* 2.652), while in the *Fasti*, Ovid begins a line with Chiron's blood, *sanguine Centauri,* and concludes it with the hydra's blood, *Lernaeae sanguis echidnae* (*Fasti* 5.405). Thus, the account of Chiron's death in the *Fasti* expands the compressed narrative of the *Metamorphoses*.

Ocyroe concludes her prophecy concerning her father Chiron's future without mentioning his catasterism after death. This catasterism Ovid himself narrates in the *Fasti*.

nona dies aderat, cum tu, iustissime Chiron,
    bis septem stellis corpora cinctus eras.

(*Fasti* 5.413-14)

[The ninth day was at hand when you, most righteous Chiron, girded your form with fourteen stars.]

In the *Metamorphoses*, however, our attention is drawn to the incompleteness of Ocyroe's prophecy: *restabat fatis aliquid,* "something remained to the fates" (*Met.* 2.655).[36] The poet hints that there is more to the story and sends us to the *Fasti* in search of the rest of the tale. We may thus understand the parallelism between the passages as the authentication in the *Fasti* of Ocyroe's second prophecy, delivered in the

---

36. Haupt, Ehwald, and Albrecht (1966, 130) and Hill (1985, 211) interpret these words as a reference to Chiron's catasterism. Melville (1986, 44) translates, "More prophecies remained...": for such an interpretation of the line, see my discussion below (pp. 89-90). Bömer (1969, 395) and Moore-Blunt (1977, 136) collect the lexical parallels.

Metamorphoses. There is no other extended treatment of the story of Chiron in the Ovidian corpus.

Ocyroe's prophetic prowess proves her undoing and her final words announce the impending loss of her faculty of speech. Chiron's daughter admits that the gift of prophecy was not worth risking the displeasure of the divine.

> atque ita 'praevertunt'[37] inquit 'me fata, vetorque
> plura loqui, vocisque meae praecluditur usus.
> non fuerant artes tanti, quae numinis iram
> contraxere mihi: mallem nescisse futura.
> iam mihi subduci facies humana videtur,
> iam cibus herba placet, iam latis currere campis
> impetus est: in equam cognataque corpora vertor.'
>
> (*Met.* 2.657-63)

[and so she spoke: "The fates forestall me, I am forbidden to say any more, and my faculty of speech is blocked. My skills were not worth so great a cost, skills which have brought upon me the anger of heaven: I would have preferred not to know the future. Now my human aspect seems to be disappearing, now the grass pleases me for food, now I feel an urge to run in the wide fields: I am being transformed into a mare, a kindred form."]

When she perceives the loss of her faculty of speech, Ocyroe denies that the skills (*artes, Met.* 2.638, 659) that had allowed her to reveal the secrets of the fates were worth the penalty. Chiron's daughter thereby implies that she loses her faculty of speech precisely because she has misused it, angering the gods by speaking.[38] Moreover, at the conclusion

---

37. Dr. S.E. Hinds suggests to me that there may be some Ovidian wordplay between *praevertunt* and a metamorphic *vertere*, here, and he compares Ocyroe's explicit statement of her transformation into a mare towards the close of her second speech, ... *in equam cognataque corpora vertor* (*Met.* 2.663).

38. Cf. Davis 1969, 29-30. Fredericks 1977, 355 explains Ocyroe's metamorphosis as the result of her "misuse of speech (her prophecy about Asclepius and Chiron)." Bernbeck (1967, 111) also draws attention to the paradoxical result of Ocyroe's abuse of her prophetic powers: "Ocyrhoe wird für den Mißbrauch ihrer Weissagungskunst bestraft und hätte sie daher lieber gar nicht erst besessen (II 660: *Mallem nescisse futura*)." For *usus* in the sense of "faculty" see *OLD* s.v. *usus* 3, and Lewis and Short s.v. *usus* IA1; for *usus* in the sense of "use," see *OLD* s.v. *usus* 12, and cf. *OLD* s.v. *usus* 11, and also Lewis and Short s.v. *usus* IIA. On internal narrators questioning the "utility" of story-telling, see Chap. 1. On Ovidian characters "misusing" the *vox*, see also Altieri 1973, 35 and Fredericks 1977, 244.

of the episode, we learn that Ocyroe is transformed into a mare as a result of having angered Jupiter in particular.

> Flebat opemque tuam frustra Philyreius heros,
> Delphice, poscebat. nam nec rescindere magni
> iussa Iovis poteras. . . .
>
> *(Met.* 2.676-78)

[The Philyreian hero wept and begged in vain for your aid, god of Delphi. For neither could you have revoked the commands of great Jove. . . .]

In this connection it is worth noting that, in drawing down divine anger upon herself (*Met.* 2.659-60), Ocyroe suffers a fate remarkably similar to that of Aesculapius, prophesied in the preceding speech by Ocyroe herself.

> . . . idque semel dis indignantibus ausus
> posse dare hoc iterum flamma prohibebere avita
>
> *(Met.* 2.645-46)

[and having dared this once against the will of the gods, you will be denied the power to grant this again by your grandsire's flame. . . .]

But when she denies that her skills were worth the cost of losing her faculty of speech, Ocyroe also resembles the Ovidian crow who called into question the utility of story-telling in her own narrative.[39]

For a prophetess, of course, the continuing unimpaired use of the *vox* is of the utmost importance. This is effectively illustrated later in the *Metamorphoses* when the Sibyl, a celebrated *vates,* claims that her *vox* will remain long after she has become invisible because of her great age.

---

39. Cf. especially the crow's statement at *Met.* 2.564-65: *mea poena volucres / admonuisse potest, ne voce pericula quaerant,* "my punishment can warn birds not to court danger with their talk."

tempus erit, cum de tanto me corpore parvam
longa dies faciet, consumptaque membra senecta
ad minimum redigentur onus....
. . . .
usque adeo mutata ferar nullique videnda,
voce tamen noscar, vocem mihi fata[40] relinquent.

(Met. 14.147-49, 152-53)

[There will come a time when a long span of days will render me, from so large a body, diminutive and my limbs, consumed with old age, will be reduced to the slightest weight... until, so transformed, I shall be borne aloft, unseen by anyone, and yet I shall be recognized by my voice, the fates will leave me my voice.]

Ovid's Sibyl asserts that her destiny will leave unchanged only her *vox*, and indeed in ancient discussions of the Sibyl her voice is often identified as her most important feature.[41] Ocyroe too emphasizes the importance

---

40. Ovid here situates *fata* in a context in which the etymological relationship between *fata* and *fari* is emphasized. The anaphora of *vox,* at line beginning and after the main caesura, may suggest that it is the Sibyl's "words," *fata,* which leave her "utterance," *vox,* to her. For a detailed analysis of Ovidian etymological play on *fata,* see the extensive discussion at the end of this chapter (pp. 87-92).

41. It is generally agreed that Ovid's Sibyl (*Met.* 14.101-54) is closely modelled on the Virgilian Sibyl: see Bömer 1986, 41-63 for thorough discussion and further bibliography. Ovid acknowledges his debt to the Virgilian portrayal of the Sibyl in typically Alexandrian fashion, for his Sibyl emphasizes the importance of her *vox* at the conclusion of her speech (*Met.* 14.152-53), while the *voces* of the Virgilian Sibyl coincide with her entrance into the *Aeneid*.

> Excisum Euboicae latus ingens rupis in antrum,
> quo lati ducunt aditus centum, ostia centum,
> unde ruunt totidem voces, responsa Sibyllae.
> ventum erat ad limen, cum virgo 'poscere fata
> tempus' ait; 'deus ecce deus!'...

(Aen. 6.42-46).

[There is a huge cave cut into the side of the Euboean rock where a hundred wide approaches lead, a hundred openings whence rush the same number of voices, the Sibyl's responses. They arrived at the threshold, when the virgin cried, "It is time to ask your destiny; behold the god himself!"...]

D.S. Potter reviews the evidence concerning what was known and believed about sibyls in antiquity, in the introduction to *An Historical Commentary on the Thirteenth Sibylline Oracle* (Oxford 1990). See also his review of *Sibyls and Sibylline Prophecy in Classical Antiquity* by H.W. Parke, ed. by B. McGing (London 1988), in *JRA* 3 (1990): 471-83.

of her *vox* (*Met.* 2.657-58), and this point of contact between Ocyroe and the Sibyl underscores Ocyroe's status as a *vates*. The account of Ocyroe's transformation that concludes this episode (*Met.* 2.665-75) further emphasizes the *vates'* professional reliance on the faculty of speech, for Ovid dwells at length upon the changes to Ocyroe's *vox* as her utterances, at first complaints (*querellae*), are transformed into the whinnies of a horse, *hinnitus*.[42]

> talia dicenti pars est extrema querellae
> intellecta parum, confusaque verba fuerunt;
> mox nec verba quidem nec equae sonus ille videtur,
> sed simulantis equam, parvoque in tempore certos
> edidit hinnitus et bracchia movit in herbas.
>
> (*Met.* 2.665-69)

[As she spoke the final part of her complaint could scarcely be understood and her words were confused; soon, indeed, they seemed neither words nor the sound of a mare, but of one imitating a mare, and in a short time she uttered definite neighs, as she stretched her limbs upon the grasses.]

Ovid's description of Ocyroe's metamorphosis includes many words for speech-acts (*dicenti, querellae, verba, sonus, hinnitus*), and underlines her reliance on the *usus vocis* for prophetic utterance. Although Ocyroe loses her voice (*vox*) in the process of her transformation into a mare, her words (*voces*) survive the loss of her voice, for the substance of her prophecies is fulfilled in passages in both the *Metamorphoses* and the *Fasti* that echo her words.[43] Thus despite Ocyroe's own denial of the power of her *vox*, Ovid attests to her prophetic ability through the subsequent reuse of his internal narrator's diction in both poems. He thereby implicitly denies that Ocyroe uttered her prophecies in vain.[44]

In the Ocyroe episode, then, Ovid introduces an internal narrator who raises the question of an appropriate use of her *vox*, an interest

---

42. Fredericks (1977, 244) observes that "Ovid's description of her [Ocyroe's] metamorphosis emphasises her loss of human speech." Cf. Solodow 1988, 187.

43. For *vox* in the sense of "words" see *OLD* s.v. *vox* 7; for *vox* in the sense of "voice" see *OLD* s.v. *vox* 1.

44. On the poet/narrator's quasi-divine power to confer narrative authority upon his characters, see Brenkman 1976, 299-303.

that we identified earlier in the embedded narrative of the crow. Another feature that distinguished the crow's narrative and that recurs throughout the Ocyroe episode is etymological wordplay. We have already had occasion to remark several examples of *lusus etymologici* in this episode: the opening word of the episode (*semifer, Met.* 2.633) participates in an elusive wordplay across our two poems; the two names of Chiron's daughter are glossed with Latin translations; and Ocyroe's prophecy of Aesculapius' health-bringing powers is echoed thirteen books later with a pointed pun which establishes that the city (*urbs*) of Rome has become the master of the world (*orbis*). These examples, however, by no means exhaust the poet's etymological invention in the Ocyroe episode.

Let us reexamine the opening lines of our passage.

> Semifer interea divinae stirpis alumno
> laetus erat mixtoque oneri gaudebat honore.
>
> (*Met.* 2.633–34)

[Meanwhile the half-beast, Chiron, rejoiced in the care of a divine child and was gladdened by the prospect of honor along with the task.]

D.E. Hill offers a translation faithful to Ovid's Latin pun with "so onerous an honour," but he denies any poetic significance to the collocation *oneri... honore,* merely remarking that it offers "another example of Ovidian word-play."[45] Yet, the close proximity of the two words is such as to suggest obliquely that their similarity in sound reflects a closer association in their meanings. The poet may even go so far as to imply that *honos* is contingent upon assuming the responsibilities that can be such a burden, *onus*. We know from Varro's discussion of the etymology of *honos* in *De Lingua Latina* that Roman poets had already explored the possibilities of a semantic connection between *honos* and *onus* through a proposed etymological association.

> Honos ab onere: itaque honestum dicitur quod oneratum, et dictum: onus est honos qui sustinet rem publicam.[46] (*L.L.* 5.73)

[*Honos,* "honor, office," is derived from *onus,* "burden": and so

---

45. Hill (1985, 211). The commentators otherwise ignore the play.
46. *Com. Rom. Frag.*, p. 147 Ribbeck³.

honestum, "that which is honorable," is said of that which is *oneratum,* "burdensome, onerous," and it has been said: "Full onerous is the honor which maintains the state."][47]

While modern scholars disagree concerning the etymology of *honos,* the Varronian material demonstrates that a postulated etymological link could be used by the *doctus poeta* to broaden the semantic range of the associated words.[48] Indeed, the ancient evidence suggests that we should not ignore the semantic significance of this type of wordplay in the Latin poets. It is well known that "etymology could be used by the poets as the basis for serious speculation; and in general terms it was the status of etymology in antiquity as a science which allowed poets to employ it freely as part of their intellectual substructure."[49] The Varronian evidence allows us to recognize this wordplay as an example of the etymological *doctrina* expected of the *doctus poeta.*

Another instance of such etymological erudition occurs in the poet's playful description of the metamorphosis of Ocyroe: *tum digiti coeunt et quinos adligat ungues / perpetuo cornu levis ungula...,* "then her fingers came together and a slender hoof bound the five nails in a single hoof of horn" (*Met.* 2.670–71). By exploiting the derivation of *ungula* from *unguis* in his deployment of these two words, Ovid documents with extraordinary effectiveness the fluidity and, indeed, the

---

47. I quote the translation of Kent 1938, 1:71.
48. See Ernout-Meillet 299 and Walde and Hofmann (1938), 655–56; on the etymology of *onus,* also unknown, see Ernout-Meillet 462 and Walde and Hofmann 1954, 210.
49. Cairns 1979b, 90, and, indeed, the critical assumptions outlined in his judicious discussion of etymologizing in Hellenistic (especially Tibullan) poetry underlie much of my discussion of etymological wordplay throughout this section: see Cairns 1979b, 92 and cf. Snyder 1980, 54–55, discussing Lucretian "wordplay," who notes that wordplay "is not intended merely to provide the reader with playful entertainment, but to reinforce the idea presented by finding an argument within the language itself." For modern discussion of ancient etymological theory see R. Schröter, *Studien zur varronsichen Etymologie* 1, Akad. der Wissenschaften und der Literatur: Abhandl. der Geistes- und Sozialwissenschaftlichen Klasse 1959, 12 (Wiesbaden 1959), 773ff.; H. Steinthal, *Geschichte der Sprachwissenschaft bei den Griechen und Römern mit besonderer Rücksicht auf die Logik* (Berlin 1890), 1:319ff.; *R-E* s.v. *Etymologika;* K. Barwick, *Probleme der stoischen Sprachlehre und Rhetorik,* Abhandl. der Sächsischen Akademie der Wissenschaften zu Leipzig Philol.-hist. Klasse 49, 3 (Berlin 1957); L.P. Rank, *Etymologiseering en verwante Verschijnselen bij Homerus* (Diss., Utrecht, 1951) 10ff.; Pfeiffer 1968, General Index s.v. "etymology"; Collart 1978; Snyder 1980, 11–30. On specifically Ovidian etymologizing, see Frécaut 1972, 39–42; André 1975; Ahl 1985; Knox 1986, Index Rerum s.v. "word-play"; and Hinds 1987, Index of Subjects s.v. "etymological word-play."

organic propriety of the metamorphosis.⁵⁰ Charisius attests to Varro's interest in the grammatical relationship between nouns and their derivatives, in a discussion that includes the relationship between *unguis* and *ungula*.

<h>ypocorismata semper generibus suis und<e oriuntur consonant, pauca dissonant, velut haec rana> hic ranunculus, hic ung<u>is haec ungula....⁵¹ (*L.L.* fr. 10)

[Diminutives always agree in gender with the words from which they derive; a few differ, as for example *rana* ("frog") is feminine but *ranunculus* ("a little frog, tad-pole") is masculine; *unguis* ("toe- or finger-nail") is masculine, but *ungula* ("hoof, talon") is feminine....]

Again, therefore, Ovid conforms to contemporary Roman etymological practice in the tradition of Hellenistic etymological investigation.

Ovid unites his complementary interests in the utility of story-telling and in wordplay through etymological exploration of the semantics of *fatum* within our passage. The etymological relationship between *fatum* and *fari* has long been recognized by modern philologists, and the link was also known, and widely discussed, in antiquity.⁵² Varro explains:

Fatur is qui primum homo significabilem ore mittit vocem. Ab eo, antequam ita faciant, pueri dicuntur infantes; cum id faciunt, iam fari; cum hoc vocabulum, <tum> a similitudine vocis pueri <fariolus> ac fatuus dictum. Ab hoc tempora quod tum pueris constituant Parcae fando, dictum fatum et res fatales. Ab hac eadem voce qui facile fantur facundi dicti, et qui futura praedivinando soleant fari

---

50. Cf. Moore-Blunt 1977, 138. *Ungula* is, of course, derived from *unguis*, and Ovid employs the play earlier in the *Metamorphoses* at 1.742. On the etymology of *unguis*, see Ernout-Meillet 747 and Walde and Hofmann 1954, 818-19.

51. Charisius, *Inst. Gram.* 1.37.13-18 Keil. Regarding the problems with the text here, Kent (1938, 2:606) reports "The right-hand edge of the manuscript is destroyed, but the restorations are made with certainty from almost verbatim repetitions Charisius i.90.10-12, 155.14-17, 535.21-25, 551.36-38 Keil, in which Varro is not mentioned as the source."

52. See Ernout-Meillet 220 s.v. *fatum. fata*, as Servius knew, is a passive participle from *for, fari*: see Servius *ad Aen.* 2.54; cf. *TLL* 6.355.12, and Ernout-Meillet 245 s.v. *for*. For further discussion and bibliography on this etymological connection, see Commager 1981.

88 / *The Play of Fictions*

fatidici; dicti idem vaticinari, quod vesana mente faciunt: sed de hoc post erit usurpandum, cum de poetis dicemus. (*L.L.* 6.52)⁵³

[He speaks, *fatur,* who first emits from his mouth a meaningful utterance. From that, before they do so, children are called infants (*infantes*), "nonspeaking"; when they do it they are now said to speak (*fari*); from this comes not only this word *fari* ("to speak"); then also, from the similarity to children's talk, come the words *fariolus* ("soothsayer") and *fatuus* ("prophetic speaker"). From this word, because the Parcae then set out the life-times for children by speaking (*fando*), come the words destiny (*fatum*) and fateful matters (*fatales*). From this same word, those who speak easily (*facile*) are called eloquent (*facundi*) and those who are accustomed to tell (*fari*) the future by prophesying are called fate-speakers (*fatidici*); likewise they are said to prophesy (*vaticinari*) because they do so with frenzied mind: but this matter will have to be taken up later, when we speak of the poets in my work *On Poets.*]

There are numerous examples of *lusus etymologici* on this association in the Roman poets. The phrase *fata fari* is quoted from the poetry of both Ennius and Caecilius, and Virgil's admirers, ancient and modern, have exhaustively catalogued the Virgilian contributions to the game.⁵⁴ Catullus and Horace too seem to have explored the possibilities of the etymology.⁵⁵ Indeed, it seems clear that this particular etymological play

---

53. In the following chapter (*L.L.* 6.53), Varro goes on to consider the etymological connection between *fari* and *fasti.*

54. On this play in early Roman poetry, see Ennius, *Alexander* 36 (Jocelyn) and Caecilius 279 (Warmington). For ancient discussion of Virgilian etymologizing on *fata* see, for example, Servius *ad Aen.* 2.54, Servius *auct. ad Aen.* 2.799, and Servius *auct. ad Aen.* 4.450. For modern discussion of this *lusus etymologicus* in Virgil see W.F. Jackson Knight, *CR* 48 (1934):124–25; *idem, Roman Virgil* (London 1944); Bartelink 1965; and Commager 1981. For bibliography after Bartelink, see O'Hara 1986, Appendix A.

55. There has been very little scholarly investigation of Catullan etymologizing: in general, see Cairns 1973, 18 and Thomas 1982, 144–54. Examples of Catullan etymological play on the *fas /fata /fari* nexus include Cat. 64.405, *fanda nefanda;* Cat. 64.325–27, where *veridicum oraclum* glosses *fata;* and Cat. 98.1–2, where *fatuis* is glossed by the preceding *dici, dicitur,* and *verbosis,* in order to emphasize the derivation of *fatuus* from *fari.*

Two examples of this *lusus etymologicus* in Horace's *Odes* are especially clear: *sed bellicosis fata Quiritibus / hac lege dico,* "On this condition do I tell the fates to the martial citizens of Rome" (*C.* 3.3.57–58); and *C.* 4.6.17–19, where *nefas* is implied to derive from *ne-* (*nescios*) + *fari.*

was of interest not only to Virgil and the antiquarian Varro, but to a large number of the Roman poets, and we should not be surprised to discover Ovid investigating the etymological possibilities offered by the relationship between *fari* and *fata*.

In his discussion of this play in Virgil, Commager cautions that "phrases such as *fata canere* or *dictu nefas* may be merely formulaic,"[56] and the Ovidian collocation *fatorum*...*canebat* at the outset of our passage (*Met.* 2.639) may therefore seem insignificant. Ovid goes on, however, to make the etymology of *fata* explicit in Ocyroe's second speech.

> restabat fatis aliquid: suspirat ab imis
> pectoribus, lacrimaeque genis labuntur obortae,
> atque ita 'praevertunt' inquit 'me fata, vetorque
> plura loqui, vocisque meae praecluditur usus.'
>
> (*Met.* 2.655-58)

[something remained to the fates: she drew breath from deep within her breast, tears welled up and rolled down her cheeks, and she spoke thus: "My destiny forestalls me, I am forbidden to say any more, and my faculty of speech is blocked."]

Ocyroe would admit, on one reading, that her "destiny," *fata* (*Met.* 2.657), prevents her from saying anything further.[57] But we have already noted that implicit in her words there lies the further disturbing suggestion that Ocyroe is denied the faculty of speech precisely because she angered the gods by speaking. The etymological derivation of *fata* from *fari*, glossed by our *doctus poeta* by the pointed collocation *loqui vocisque* at *Met.* 2.657-58, supports such an interpretation.[58] Ovid thus provides a context for *fata* at *Met.* 2.657-58 that underscores its etymological connection with *fari*.[59] The etymological play at *Met.* 2.657-

---

56. Commager 1981, 102.
57. For *fatum* in the sense of "fate," see *TLL* 6.357.14ff., and cf. *OLD* s.v. *fatum* 2c and 3.
58. On this type of etymological gloss, see Ross 1975, 62; Cairns 1979b, 93; and Hinds 1987, 142 n. 9.
59. It is worth remarking that the first meaning offered in the *OLD* for *fatum* is "prophecy"; see also *TLL* 6.356.24ff. This is another piquant touch in a passage in which Ocyroe loses the use of her *vox* specifically for having uttered prophecies against the wishes of the gods.

58 confirms the fleeting suggestion of a similar nuance felt in the line with which the quotation began: *restabat fatis aliquid* (*Met.* 2.655). The commentators interpret the words to mean "something remained of Chiron's fate." A recent translator, however, offers "More prophecies remained...," and Ocyroe's subsequent speech supports such an interpretation.[60] Ovid, as a *doctus poeta,* draws attention to the incompleteness of Ocyroe's prophecy of her father Chiron's destiny. With the sense of "fate" at *Met.* 2.655, *fatis* functions obliquely, and in typically sophisticated fashion, as a knowing comment that sends the reader to the *Fasti* for the rest of the story. But it is a short step from "prophecies remained" to "something remained for Ocyroe to say"; and we arrive again at the fleeting evocation of "words" in the poet's use of *fata.*[61]

In the light of all the etymological signposts surrounding *fatum* at the outset of Ocyroe's second speech, can the phrase *fatorum... canebat,* at the outset of her first speech (*Met.* 2.639), remain entirely innocent of this nuance? There is considerable evidence to support the suggestion of poetic etymologizing here, when we consider the context in which the phrase *fatorum... canebat* is situated. Ovid has pointedly drawn attention to the wordplay involving Ocyroe's name in the immediately preceding lines.

> fluminis in rapidi ripis enixa vocavit
> Ocyroen; non haec artes contenta paternas
> edidicisse fuit: fatorum arcana canebat.
>
> (*Met.* 2.637–39)

[Having brought her to birth on the banks of a swift river, Chariclo named her child Ocyroe, "Swift River"; this child was not satisfied to have learned her father's skills: she was versed in the secrets of destiny.]

Moreover, although none of the commentators remark upon the wordplay in *arcana canebat,* it is clear that such a prominent collocation of sound

---

60. Melville 1986, 44. Cf. the translation of F.J. Miller in the Loeb edition of the *Metamorphoses,* "still other fates remained to tell" (Goold [1977, 107]).

61. Cf. the conclusion of J. MacInnes ("The Conception of *Fata* in the *Aeneid,*" *CR* 24 (1910):169–74) reported by Commager 1981, 102: "MacInnes, in a survey of Virgil's various uses of *fatum / fata,* has estimated that out of 116 instances in the *Aeneid,* some 35 have the meaning of 'the spoken word'."

patterning is another example of Ovidian etymological wordplay. The commentators define *cano* here in the narrow sense of "prophesy," or "act as spokesman of the gods," and the collocation *arcana canebat* implies an etymology for *arcana,* derived from the verb *cano* itself. Thus we might understand *arcana* here to mean "hidden prophecies."[62]

Varro includes *vaticinari* in his discussion of the etymology of *fatum* at *L.L.* 6.52:

Ab hac eadem voce [i.e., fatur] qui facile fantur facundi dicti, et qui futura praedivinando soleant fari fatidici; dicti idem vaticinari....

[From this same word (*fatur*) those who speak easily (*facile*) are called eloquent (*facundi*), and those who are accustomed to tell (*fari*) the future by prophesying are called fate-speakers (*fatidici*); likewise they are said to prophesy (*vaticinari*)....]

R.G. Kent explains that *vaticinari* is included in Varro's discussion "as though *fati-;* but properly from the stems of *vates* 'bard' and *canere* 'to sing'."[63] In our passage, Ovid offers this very etymology for *vaticinos,* glossing it in the preceding line with *fatorum arcana canebat.*

fluminis in rapidi ripis enixa vocavit
Ocyroen; non haec artes contenta paternas

---

62. Moore-Blunt 1977, 133. Cf. *Schol. Virg. Veron. ad Aen.* 1.1: *canere quattuor significationes habet; ... ponitur pro praedicare ... ponitur pro vaticinari,* "The verb *canere* has four meanings: ... it is used for *praedicare* [to foretell] ... and it is used for *vaticinari,* [to prophesy]." Cf. *TLL* 3.264.29ff., and *OLD* s.v. *cano* 8.

No parallel from Varro's *De lingua latina* can be adduced for the Ovidian wordplay here; however, Cairns (1979b, 95) has forcefully argued that such documentation is, eventually, unnecessary: "The reader was not intended to recognise poetic etymologies by reference to a text-book of etymology. He was supposed instead to be engaged while reading in constant speculation about and discovery of etymological and other verbal complexes omnipresent in the text. Consequently the analysis of ... etymologies need not be confined to instances where independent etymological evidence is available from antiquity. Rather, all cases where verbal juxtapositions suggest etymology should be noticed."

The true etymology of the adjective *arcana* is revealed by its cognate *arca,* "chest, coffer," whose relationship to *arceo,* "to keep close, contain," was known in antiquity. Thus Varro explains, *Arca, quod arcebantur fures ab ea clausa,* "a strong-box is so-called, because thieves were 'kept away' [*arcebantur*] from it when it was locked" (*L.L.* 5.128); cf. *L.L.* 9.74. Modern etymological discussion agrees with Varro: see Ernout-Meillet 43, s.v. *arcana.*

63. Kent (1938,1:219 *ad L.L.* 6.52). See also Ernout-Meillet 93 s.v. *cano;* Ernout-Meillet 715 s.v. *vates;* and A. Ernout, *Philologica* (Paris 1940), 1.73ff.

>   edidicisse fuit: fatorum arcana[64] canebat.
>   ergo ubi vaticinos concepit mente furores
>
>   (*Met.* 2.637-40)

[Having brought her to birth on the banks of a swift river, Chariclo named her Ocyroe, "Swift River"; this child was not satisfied to have learned her father's skills: she was versed in the secrets of destiny. And so when she conceived prophetic inspiration in her soul....]

These four lines offer so dense a pattern of etymologizing that it becomes impossible to view the phrase *fatorum arcana canebat* as merely formulaic here.

The extraordinary density of etymological wordplay in the Ocyroe episode, and in particular that which explores the semantics of *fatum*, bears witness to the central theme of our passage, Ocyroe's illicit disclosure of destiny's secrets. It is unmistakably Ocyroe's misuse of her *vox* that causes her metamorphosis (*Met.* 2.657-63). Thus her transformation comes about as a punishment for the same verbal indiscretion as that which prompts the raven's metamorphosis. The raven's chattering tongue is explicitly identified as the cause of his metamorphosis (*Met.* 2.540-41) just as Ocyroe notes that her own words have drawn the wrath of heaven (*Met.* 2.659-60), and both the raven (*Met.* 2.545-47) and Ocyroe (*Met.* 2.639) reveal secrets.

The thematic continuity that links the two episodes is complemented by formal similarities in the structure of the narrative.[65] Both tales open with the reuse of figures from earlier episodes in the *Metamorphoses*: the account of the raven's metamorphosis begins with references to the translation of Argus' eyes to the peacock's tail and the metamorphosis of Cygnus into a swan, while the Ocyroe episode begins with Chiron rejoicing in his charge of Aesculapius, the infant entrusted to his keeping at the conclusion of the preceding episode. As befits the close thematic relationship between the two episodes, the second passage is generated from the immediately preceding episode, rather than from more distant episodes recounted earlier in the poem.

---

64. In the context of the extraordinary density of etymological play in these lines, it seems likely that Ovid also implies the etymological derivation of *arcana (Met.* 2.639) from *ars + cano,* with *artes* in the preceding line glossing *arcana,* together with the succeeding *canebat* (*Met.* 2.639).

65. There is some confusion about the thematic relationship between this episode and those that precede and follow it: see Galinsky 1975, 94, and Boillat 1976, 110.

Another structural parallel between the tales occurs in the treatment of the conclusion. Ovid closed his account of the raven's metamorphosis with a statement of the accomplishment of the metamorphosis (*Met.* 2.631-32) promised at the outset of the episode (*Met.* 2.540-41), and the Ocyroe episode also exhibits ring composition.

> Flebat opemque tuam frustra Philyreius heros,
> Delphice, poscebat. nam nec rescindere magni
> iussa Iovis poteras, nec, si rescindere posses,
> tunc aderas: Elim Messeniaque arva colebas.
>
> (*Met.* 2.676-79)

[The Philyreian hero wept and begged in vain for your aid, god of Delphi. For neither could you have revoked the commands of great Jove, nor, even if you could have revoked them, were you then at hand: you were dwelling in Elis and the land of Messenia.]

These four lines are often printed by modern editors as the opening of a new episode, the petrifaction of Battus (the subject of the next chapter of this study); yet the preceding analysis of narrative organization of our passage suggests that we should see in these lines not only the outset of a new episode but also the conclusion of the Ocyroe episode. The Ocyroe episode opens with Chiron's delighted fosterage of Aesculapius (*Met.* 2.633-34), and it closes with the centaur's emotions at the sight of another child, that is, his sadness over his daughter's transformation. Apollo returns to the narrative here from the conclusion of the preceding episode, reprising his role as the god of healing whose powers are useless (*Met.* 2.617-19; *Met.* 2.677-78).[66] We even receive a partial explanation for Ocyroe's metamorphosis in these lines, when the poet mentions that the orders were Jove's (*Met.* 2.678). An interpretation of these lines that sees in them the conclusion to the Ocyroe episode allows us to specify ring composition on the level of plot and character as an important element of narrative organization in this episode, as we saw it to be in the raven episode.

---

66. Cf. *Met.* 1.519-24.

Chapter 4

Battus and the Rewards for Telling Tales: *Met.* 2.676-707

ΒΑΤΤΟΣ Εἰπέ μοι, ὦ Κορύδων, τίνος αἱ βόες; ἦ ῥα Φιλώνδα;
ΚΟΡΥΔΩΝ οὔκ, ἀλλ' Αἴγωνος· βόσκειν δέ μοι αὐτὰς ἔδωκεν.
ΒΑ. ἦ πᾴ ψε κρύβδαν τὰ ποθέσπερα πάσας ἀμέλγες;
ΚΟ. ἀλλ' ὁ γέρων ὑφίητι τὰ μοσχία κἠμὲ φυλάσσει.
ΒΑ. αὐτὸς δ' ἐς τίν' ἄφαντος ὁ βουκόλος ᾤχετο χώραν;
—Theocritus, *Id.* 4.1-5

Following the account of Ocyroe's metamorphosis, and linked to it by a transition that has occasioned considerable critical confusion, comes the tale of the transformation of Battus into a rock upon his betrayal of Mercury's theft of Apollo's cattle (*Met.* 2.676-707).[1] It is, indeed, difficult on a first reading to see any connection between the tale of Battus, the rustic witness to Mercury's bovine theft, and the preceding story of Ocyroe. Nonetheless, we have seen that the poet collocatively juxtaposes the tales of Ocyroe, the raven, and the crow in an extended meditation on the theme of indiscreet loquacity, and it may therefore prove productive to examine the connections between the Battus episode and the preceding episodes while remaining alert to the possible recurrence of the thematic and formal structures that have organized the narrative up to this point.

Let us start by considering the troublesome transition from Ocyroe's metamorphosis into Mercury's theft of Apollo's cattle.

  illud erat tempus, quo te pastoria pellis
  texit onusque fuit baculum silvestre sinistrae,
  alterius dispar septenis fistula cannis;

---
1. See Little 1972, 98; Galinsky 1975, 94-95; and Boillat 1976, 110-11. Apollo's flocks are usually assumed to belong to Admetus: see Haupt, Ehwald, and Albrecht 1966, 131; Brown 1947, 146 n. 7; Bömer 1969, 399; Galinsky 1975, 94; and Hill 1985, 212.

dumque amor est curae, dum te tua fistula mulcet,
incustoditae Pylios memorantur in agros
processisse boves....

(*Met.* 2.680-85)

[That was the time when a herdsman's cloak clothed you, Apollo, you held a wooden staff in your left hand, and in the other, the shepherd's pipe unequal with its seven reeds; and while love was your concern, while your pipe soothed you, they say that your cows wandered, unattended, into the fields of Pylos....]

Like the accounts of the raven's metamorphosis and Ocyroe's transformation, the new episode opens with a temporal marker (*illud erat tempus*) that announces a change in narrative direction. In close conjunction with the chronological signpost we are told about the travels of the god Apollo, who has figured importantly in both the raven and Ocyroe episodes. Apollo appears as lover of Coronis and patron of the raven at the outset (*Met.* 2.543-45) and conclusion (*Met.* 2.598-632) of the raven episode, as well as in association with Chiron at the close of both the raven episode (*Met.* 2.628-30) and the Ocyroe episode (*Met.* 2.676-79). At the opening of the Battus episode Apollo is unavailable to help Ocyroe because he is absent in Elis, pursuing another love affair (*amor est curae, Met.* 2.683) after his disastrous infatuation with Coronis. Thus Apollo appears consistently at the beginning and end of the episodes in our passage, reprising his important role at the beginning and end of the first episode of Book 2 of the *Metamorphoses,* the account of the conflagration of the world instigated by Phaethon (*Met.* 2.1-400).[2] We have seen that, at the opening of both the raven and the Ocyroe episodes, the reappearance of characters whom we have already met in the world of the poem allows the poet to forge narrative connections with the preceding material, and in this respect, at least, the Battus episode is no different.

---

2. Book 2 opens with Phaethon's voyage to the Palace of the Sun in search of his father Sol (= Helios). Sol (named at *Met.* 2.1, 32, 154, 162, and 394; cf. the patronymic *Heliades* of Phaethon's sisters at *Met.* 2.340) is unambiguously assimilated to Apollo by the application of Apollo's epithet Phoebus to Sol at *Met.* 2.36, 110, and 399 (*contra* Fontenrose [1939, 439] and [1940]); cf. Hinds 1987, 144 n. 24. In our passage, the raven is identified from the start as the bird of Phoebus Apollo (*ales...Phoebeius, Met.* 2.544-45), while Apollo goes by the epithets Delphicus (*Met.* 2.543, 677) and Phoebus (*Met.* 2.608, 628).

The Battus episode begins with Mercury's theft of Apollo's unguarded cattle, a theft that is inadvertently witnessed by the old man.

> incustoditae Pylios memorantur in agros
> processisse boves. videt has Atlantide Maia
> natus et arte sua silvis occultat abactas.
> senserat hoc furtum nemo nisi notus in illo
> rure senex: Battum vicinia tota vocabant.
>
> (Met. 2.684-88)

[They say that your cows wandered, unattended, into the fields of Pylos. Maia's son Mercury saw them, and by his native craft drove them away and hid them in the woods. No one noticed this theft, except for an old man, well-known in that countryside: the whole neighborhood called him Battus.]

By observing Mercury's furtive theft Battus is implicated in a larger narrative pattern of concealment and illicit disclosure that recurs throughout the passage studied in this book, and that associates the old man with the daughters of Cecrops in the crow's narrative (*Met.* 2.552-61), the crow herself (*Met.* 2.549-68), the raven (*Met.* 2.540-49 and 596-632), and Ocyroe (*Met.* 2.640-60). We find the fullest expression within our passage of a narrative pattern of concealment and illicit disclosure in the crow's tale of the transgression of the Cecropids, where the constituent elements of this motif of violated prohibition are set out at some length.

> ... nam tempore quodam
> Pallas Erichthonium, prolem sine matre creatam,
> clauserat Actaeo texta de vimine cista
> virginibusque tribus gemino de Cecrope natis
> et legem dederat, sua ne secreta viderent.
> . . . .
> ... commissa duae sine fraude tuentur
> Pandrosos atque Herse; timidas vocat una sorores
> Aglauros nodosque manu diducit, et intus
> infantemque vident adporrectumque draconem.
>
> (Met. 2.552-56, 558-61)

> [... for once upon a time Pallas enclosed Erichthonius, child born without a mother, within a chest woven from Athenian osier, and gave to the three maiden daughters of biform Cecrops the injunction that they not look upon her secrets.... Two of the girls, Pandrosos and Herse, guarded their commission without deceit; one, Aglauros, called her sisters timid, unbound the fastenings with her hand, and within they saw the child and a serpent stretched out at his side.]

This act of opening the *cista* and looking upon the infant Erichthonius concealed within constitutes the transgression of the Cecropids. Pallas Athena's act of concealment, hiding the infant Erichthonius within the *cista,* is not, of course, illicit, unlike the furtive misdeeds of Mercury, Coronis, and the daughters of Cecrops. Moreover, it must also be noted that the Cecropids do not transgress inadvertently but, rather, purposefully, and in this respect too they must be distinguished from the other characters in our passage—the crow, the raven, Ocyroe, and Battus. Still, the discrete elements of the Cecropids' story, concealment and disclosure, combine to function collocatively as a paradigmatic framework, not only in the crow's narrative, but also in the surrounding first-layer Ovidian narrative that recounts the metamorphoses of the raven, Ocyroe, and Battus.[3]

The crow watches from a nearby tree as the Cecropids open the basket containing Erichthonius, and she involves herself in their transgression by reporting it to Athena: *abdita fronde levi densa speculabar ab ulmo, / quid facerent... acta deae refero,* "hidden in the thick foliage I watched what they did from a slender elm... and reported their actions to the goddess" (*Met.* 2.557-58, 562). The raven discovers Coronis' clandestine infidelity by chance (*Met.* 2.544-47), just as Battus inadvertently witnesses Mercury's cattle theft (*Met.* 2.685-90). Coronis' crime is hidden (*latentem... culpam, Met.* 2.545-46) and she thinks herself unobserved, while Mercury too acts stealthily in his theft of the cattle (*Met.* 2.686). The verb applied to Mercury's theft is *occultat,* a verb that explicitly denotes "concealment," and the noun *furtum,* used of the "theft" itself (*Met.* 2.687), also implies concealment.[4] The thematic similarities between Battus' story and that of the raven go beyond the mere verbal

---

3. Cf. Davis 1969, 26-28, who identifies this recurrent feature of the *indicium* paradigm as the "Discovery motif."

4. On *occulto* see *TLL* 9.2.376.64-72, and *OLD* s.v. *occulto* 1. On *furtum,* see *TLL* 6.1645.27-74, and *OLD* s.v. *furtum* 2.

repetition of *sentio* used of the discovery (*sensit, Met.* 2.545; *senserat, Met.* 2.687), for Battus, like the raven and the crow, is inadvertently a witness to clandestine crime.[5] Even the Ocyroe episode participates in this thematic continuum of illicit disclosure of secrets. Ocyroe's prophetic skills (the *artes* of *Met.* 2.638 and 659) allow her to observe and reveal the secrets of destiny (*fatorum arcana, Met.* 2.639), and her disclosure of these secrets prompts the gods to punish her by metamorphosis (*Met.* 2.659-60). In this sequence of episodes, therefore, we consistently find a character's inadvertent discovery of a secret leading inexorably to their purposeful narrative disclosure of the secret and subsequent punishment. The tales share a shifting pattern of associations that combine to assure the thematic coherence of our series of episodes.[6] Recurrent elements of plot configuration and theme were of central importance in the organization of the embedded narrative of the crow, and we can now begin to see the significance of that principle of narrative construction for our thematically related sequence of short episodes as well.

The preceding chapters have considered in some detail the interest evinced both in the embedded narrative of the crow and in the surrounding first-layer narrative (*Met.* 2.531-679) regarding verbal indiscretion, and in the rustic Battus we meet another example of the character of "tale-teller." The crow's narrative demonstrates unambiguously that she was punished for telling her divine patron Athena of what she saw (*Met.* 2.562-65), and it is the raven's insistence on telling Apollo of Coronis' infidelity that brings about his punishment by Apollo (*Met.* 2.598-99, 631-32). Even Ocyroe seems to claim that she loses her faculty of speech and is transformed into a mare because she has angered the gods by speaking (*Met.* 2.657-60). Battus too earns his metamorphosis as a result of telling a tale. Mercury specifically instructs the old man to deny having seen the stolen cattle, saying *si forte armenta requiret / haec aliquis, vidisse nega,* "if, by chance, anyone asks about these cattle, deny that you saw them" (*Met.* 2.692-93), and Battus explicitly promises Mercury his silence.

> ... [Battus] voces has reddidit: 'hospes,
> tutus eas! lapis iste prius tua furta loquetur,'
> et lapidem ostendit....
>
> (*Met.* 2.695-97)

---

5. For *senserat* used of uncovering a secret, see *OLD* s.v. *sentio* 2.
6. Chap. 1 argued that the technique of thematic patterning is characteristic of the construction of the crow's embedded narrative as well.

[... Battus responded with these words: "Stranger, you may go assured! This stone here will disclose your theft before I," and he pointed at a stone.]

When Mercury returns in disguise to test Battus' good faith by asking the whereabouts of the missing cattle, however, the rustic reveals all that he knows: *'sub illis / montibus' inquit 'erunt,' et erant sub montibus illis,* "'They will be at the foot of those mountains,' he said, and they were, indeed, at the foot of those mountains" (*Met.* 2.702-3). Battus' inopportune loquacity is the immediate cause of his metamorphosis, for his betrayal of Mercury's theft prompts the god to punish him by turning him to stone.

> risit Atlantiades et 'me mihi, perfide, prodis?
> me mihi prodis?' ait periuraque pectora vertit
> in durum silicem. . . .
>
> (*Met.* 2.704-6)

[Atlas' grandson laughed and said, "Do you betray me to myself, false friend? Me to myself, you betray?" And he transformed the faithless fellow into hard rock. . . .]

A subsequent reference to Battus' verbal indiscretion in the *Ibis,* a product of Ovid's exile, attests to the thematic relevance of the Battus episode in the context of Book 2 of the *Metamorphoses.*

> utve soror Pelopis, saxo dureris oborto,
>   ut laesus lingua Battus ab ipse sua.
>
> (*Ibis* 583-84)

[Or may you be hardened by growth of stone like Pelops' sister or like Battus, himself injured by his own tongue.]

The line in the *Ibis* recalls the poet's emphatic insistence on the raven's misuse of his tongue at the outset of our passage (*Met.* 2.540-41), and it confirms that the Battus episode is closely linked thematically to the tale-tellers of the preceding episodes. The episodes in this sequence consistently take as their focus the figure of a "tale-teller" who tells truths that would be more safely left untold.⁷

Ovid further underscores the thematic coherence of these episodes by emphasizing that Battus, the crow, and the raven are all motivated to speak out of greed. The raven's metamorphosis comes as an unexpected "reward" for his tale-bearing (*non falsae praemia linguae, Met.* 2.631), and the crow too had raised the question of just "recompense" for fidelity to her divine patron Athena (*gratia, Met.* 2.562; cf. *Met.* 2.589-90). Ocyroe, although not motivated by greed, nonetheless comes to regret the price she pays for her prophetic gifts, lamenting that her prophetic skills were not worth the cost: *non fuerant artes tanti, quae numinis iram / contraxere mihi,* "my skills, which have brought upon me the anger of the divine, were not worth so great a cost" (*Met.* 2.659-60). Battus' greed is clearly revealed by his promise of silence in return for Mercury's promise of a cow, in a passage in which the key words *gratia* and *praemia* reappear.

'... neu gratia facto
nulla rependatur, nitidam cape praemia vaccam,'
et dedit. accepta voces has reddidit. ...

(*Met.* 2.693-95)

["... and in order that your deed not go unrewarded, take this glossy cow as your price," and he gave it to Battus, who took it and replied with these words. ...]

When the disguised Mercury returns to test Battus' oath, offering a second animal and thus doubling the reward, Battus does not hesitate to tell all.

at senior, postquam est merces geminata,⁸ 'sub illis
montibus' inquit 'erunt,' et erant sub montibus illis.

(*Met.* 2.702-3)

---

7. Cf. Davis 1969, 18-39 and Fredericks 1977, 244-47.

8. Ovid playfully underscores the meaning of the verb *gemino* by doubling Battus' words in the *vox propria* of the omniscient narrator. Note the careful chiasmus effected by Ovid's restatement of Battus' words: *'sub illis / montibus' inquit 'erunt,' et erant sub montibus illis,* "'At the foot of those mountains the cattle will be found,' he said, and they were, indeed, at the foot of those mountains" (*Met.* 2.702-3). The end rhyme effected

[And the old man, after the payment was doubled, said, "The cows will be at the foot of those mountains," and they were, indeed, at the foot of those mountains.]

Thus Battus seems concerned with what is fundamentally an economic motivation for telling his tale.

Roland Barthes has pointed to this motivation of story-telling in observing: "pour se produire, le récit doit pouvoir *s'échanger,* s'assujettir à une économie."[9] Barthes formulates a theory of "narrative-contract" (*"récit-contrat"*) that is ultimately economic, and indeed, he explicitly poses the question of the "worth" of narrative.[10] Such a formulation of the problem of narrative utility or "worth" is unmistakably of immediate relevance to the discussion of this Ovidian narrative, since the crow, the raven, Battus, and even Ocyroe all come to question the "worth" of their tales. Ovid and his internal narrators constantly raise the issue of the "utility" of speech by explicitly formulating the question "what is

---

by the repetition of *illis* is also significant in this context. Moreover, Hermes, who doubles Battus' reward, also doubles his own speech: *risit Atlantiades et 'me mihi, perfide, prodis? / me mihi prodis?' ait,* "Mercury, the grandson of Atlas, laughed and said, 'Do you betray me to myself, false friend? Me to myself, you betray?'" (*Met.* 2.704-5). On *gemino,* see *TLL* 6.1737.84-1738.75, and cf. *OLD* s.v. *gemino* 2.

9. Barthes 1970, 95.

10. Barthes (1970, 95-97) uses the term "contract-narrative" ("le récit-contrat") in connection with "nested narratives" ("récits-gigognes"), i.e., embedded or inset narratives. His discussion is thus particularly relevant to this study of the sequence of episodes at *Met.* 2.531-835.

Le Récit: monnaie d'échange, objet de contrat, enjeu économique, en un mot *marchandise,* dont la transaction, qui peut aller . . . jusqu'au véritable marchandage, n'est plus limitée au cabinet de l'éditeur mais se représente elle-même, en abyme, dans la narration? . . . Voilà la question que pose peut-être tout récit. *Contre quoi échanger le récit? Que "vaut" le récit?* Ici [i.e., in Balzac's novella *Sarrasine*], le récit se donne en échange d'un corps (il s'agit d'un contrat de prostitution), ailleurs, il peut acheter la vie même (dans les *Mille et Une Nuits,* une histoire de Schéhérazade vaut pour un jour de survie); ailleurs enfin, chez Sade, le narrateur alterne systématiquement, comme dans un geste d'achat, une orgie contre une dissertation, c'est-à-dire du sens (la philosophie *vaut pour* le sexe, le boudoir): le récit est, par une astuce vertigineuse, la représentation du contrat qui le fonde: dans ces récits exemplaires, la narration est théorie (économique) de la narration: on ne raconte pas pour "distraire," pour "instruire" ou pour satisfaire un certain exercice anthropologique du sens; on raconte pour obtenir en échangeant; et c'est cet échange qui est figuré dans le récit lui-même: le récit est à la fois produit et production, marchandise et commerce, enjeu et porteur de cet enjeu. . . . (Barthes [1970, 95-96] all italics his)

Cf. Smith 1978, 83-106, on what she calls the "linguistic marketplace."

my story worth?" We saw in Chapter 1 that with her opening words the crow calls into question the practical utility of story-telling (*'non utile carpis... iter,'* Met. 2.549-50), and she makes her economic motivation in telling Pallas Athena quite clear.

> acta deae refero; pro quo mihi gratia[11] talis
> redditur, ut dicar tutela pulsa Minervae
> et ponar post noctis avem....
>
> *(Met. 2.562-64)*

[I reported their deeds to the goddess; for which my reward is such that I am reported to be banished from Minerva's protection and am esteemed after the owl, the bird of night....]

The crow has learned, however, from the outcome of the event, that her narrative was not "worth" the punishment, and she brings this knowledge to her encounter with the raven. Recognizing the implicitly economic motivation of the raven, the crow lays out the risks of telling stories for a price. She warns her interlocutor not only in order to instruct him (*Met.* 2.549-50, 564-65), but also because of her innate garrulity: the chattering crow just loves to talk.[12] Nor is Ocyroe motivated to prophesy out of greed; rather, she speaks in a frenzy of vatic inspiration (*Met.* 2.640-42). We must not, therefore, accept Barthes' formulation of an economic "narrative-contract" without further qualification, for our two internal narrators, the crow and Ocyroe, are not motivated to speech out of avarice, as are the raven, and Battus, and even the crow the first time she tells the story of the Cecropids' transgression (*Met.* 2.562). In this respect alone, Ovid's two internal narrators seem very similar to each other. By according these two characters the extended use of their *voces* in his own narrative, Ovid implicitly denies that his internal narrators, the crow and Ocyroe, "misuse" the faculty of speech.[13] This interpretation does not, of course, preclude such an assessment of the motivation of the raven or Battus (or still later, of Aglauros).

The poet underscores the theme of indiscreet loquacity, as in the preceding episodes, through etymological wordplay with verbs and nouns

---

11. For the financial connotations of *gratia,* see *TLL* 6.1.2228.26ff., and cf. *OLD* s.v. *gratia* 4.
12. For the proverbial garrulity of the crow in antiquity, see Chap. 1 n. 13.
13. *Pace* Fredericks 1977, 244.

of speaking. Ovid's etymological games begin with a carefully chosen name for the old man. Battus fits neatly into a sequence of episodes about chatterers, for his name itself means "chatterbox," and it thus characterizes him, like the raven and the crow, as garrulous by nature.[14] The thematic significance of the herdsman's name is emphasized by the introduction of his name in close conjunction with a verb of naming, which we saw in the preceding chapter is characteristic of the Alexandrian etymological gloss: . . . *Battum vicinia tota vocabant* (*Met.* 2.688).[15] It is a piquant touch in a "narrative about narratives" that the Chatterer should himself be the object of others' chatter.

The witty *lusus etymologicus* that dramatizes the meaning of Battus' name at the start of the episode ironically presages the outcome of the episode, where the chatterer is silenced but the neighborhood gossip continues. Although Battus is deprived of the power of speech as a result of his petrifaction, the stone continues to bear witness to his verbal indiscretion and is the subject of a tale that continues to be told in the surrounding countryside.

> risit Atlantiades et 'me mihi, perfide, prodis?
> me mihi prodis?'[16] ait periuraque pectora vertit
> in durum silicem, qui nunc quoque dicitur index,
> inque nihil merito vetus est infamia saxo.
>
> (*Met.* 2.704–7)

[Atlas' grandson laughed and said, "Do you betray me to myself, false friend? Me to myself, you betray?" And he transformed the faithless fellow into hard rock, a rock that is even now called "Informer," and on the undeserving rock the old infamy remains.]

The etymologies of *dicitur, index,* and *infamia* underline the point. We may begin by considering the etymological origins of *infamia*. Varro explains:

---

14. Cf. Bömer 1969, 402. For Battus as "Chatterbox" here, rather than "Stammerer," see LSJ 311 s.v. βαττολογία, with Holland 1926, 177–78, and Haupt, Ehwald, and Albrecht 1966, 132. For the ancient evidence of the garrulity of both the raven and the crow, see Chap. 1 n. 13 and Chap. 2 n. 14.

15. On the frequency of *voco* in etymologically charged contexts, see Chap. 3 n. 3.

16. I have retained the punctuation of Anderson 1977, despite Fränkel 1945, 215 n. 42.

Ab eodem verbo fari fabulae, ut tragoediae et comoediae, dictae. hinc fassi ac confessi, qui fati id quod ab [h]is quaesitum. hinc professi; hinc fama et famosi. (*L.L.* 6.55)

[From the same word "to speak" (*fari*) plays (*fabulae*), like tragedies and comedies, took their name. From this are derived the words for those who have admitted a thing (*fassi*), and those who have confessed it (*confessi*), since they have spoken (*fati*) that which was asked of them. From this comes the word for those who have affirmed a statement (*professi*); and from this word comes rumor (*fama*), and the word for those who are much talked of, "famous" (*famosi*).]

The etymology of *fatur* was the object of intense scrutiny in the preceding episode, and the recurrence in the Battus episode of *infamia,* whose etymological relationship with *fatur* was known to the ancient grammarians, fleetingly reprises that earlier discussion. Ovid offers an ironic commentary on the cause of Battus' metamorphosis by pointing out that the story, *fama* (cognate with Greek φήμη, "speech, story"), remains in the stone, *in saxo,* since the petrifaction of the herdsman will silence him forever.[17] On the other hand, *infamia* in this context may be more amenable to analysis as the combination of the negative prefix *in* and the noun *fama,* in order to bring out another irony in the poet's attribution of *infamia* to the newly metamorphosed rock: Battus the "Chatterer" now finds himself entirely without chatter.

In a semantically similar wordplay at *Met.* 2.706, *qui nunc quoque dicitur index,* Ovid juxtaposes the etymologically related *dicitur* and *index* so as to emphasize the herdsman's verbal indiscretion. The agent noun *index,* "informer" (literally, "one who shows by utterance") is formed on the Indo-European root **deik-,* "show," from which the Latin verb *dico,* "show by utterance," is also formed.[18] In the oblique cases of the noun (*indic-*) the etymological relationship between *dicitur* and *index* would be readily apparent, and we may assume that it was known to Varro:

---

17. For Ovid's awareness of the etymological possibilities of *fama,* see Chap. 3. For modern etymological discussion of the relationship between *fama* and *fari* (and φήμη), see Ernout-Meillet 214 s.v. *fari,* and cf. *TLL* s.v. *fama,* 6.206.63–69, and *TLL* 7.1.8.1337.29–30.

18. On *index* see *TLL* 7.1.1140.12–58, and *OLD* s.v. *index* 1. For the etymology of *-dex, -dicis,* and its relationship to *dico,* see Ernout-Meillet 172.

106 / *The Play of Fictions*

> dico originem habet Graecam, quod Graeci δεικνύω. hinc <etiam dicare, ut ait> Ennius: 'dico qui hunc dicare'; hinc iudicare, quod tunc ius dicatur; hinc iudex, quod iudicat accepta potestate, id est quibusdam verbis dicendo finit: sic enim aedis sacra a magistratu pontifice prae<e>unte dicendo dedicatur. hinc, ab dicendo, indicium.... (*L.L.* 6.61)

> [The verb "I speak" (*dico*) has a Greek origin, that which the Greeks call "I show" (*deiknúo*). Whence moreover comes "to show, dedicate" (*dicare*), as Ennius says: "I speak (*dico*), to indicate (*dicare*) this man"; from this is derived the verb "to judge" (*iudicare*), because at that time the law is spoken; from this comes "judge" (*iudex*), because he speaks the law (*iudicat*) after receiving the power to do so, that is, he finishes the matter by speaking (*dicendo*) with certain words: and thus a sacred temple is dedicated (*dedicatur*) by a magistrate by speaking (*dicendo*) the words after the Pontifex. Thence, from the verb to speak (*dicendo*) comes information (*indicium*)....]

Ovid's *figura etymologica* at *Met.* 2.706, *dicitur index,* playfully underlines the central theme of our passage, indiscreet loquacity, by documenting the transformation of the "informer" from a garrulous chatterer to the subject of other people's "talk."

In addition to its thematic and etymological point, moreover, the verb *dicitur* acts as an Alexandrian footnote, acknowledging the long literary tradition that lies behind this tale.[19] Ovid was by no means the first to narrate the story of Battus, and he gestures explicitly towards earlier accounts of the tale with another Alexandrian footnote at the outset of the episode. We have already noticed, in analyzing the episode of the raven and crow (*Met.* 2.531–632), that such references tend to cluster at beginning and end of the Ovidian narratives. Another Alexandrian footnote at the outset of the Battus episode complements that on *dicitur* at the close of the tale.

> illud erat tempus, quo te pastoria pellis
> texit onusque fuit baculum silvestre sinistrae,
> alterius dispar septenis fistula cannis;
> dumque amor est curae, dum te tua fistula mulcet,

---

19. On the Alexandrian "footnote," see Chap. 1 n. 60.

incustoditae Pylios memorantur in agros
processisse boves. . . .

(*Met.* 2.680-85)

[That was the time when a herdsman's cloak clothed you, Apollo, you held a wooden staff in your left hand, and in the other, the shepherd's pipe unequal with its seven reeds; and while love was your concern, while your pipe soothed you, they say that your cows wandered, unattended, into the fields of Pylos. . . .]

Both *memorantur* and *dicitur* obliquely evoke the numerous earlier accounts of Battus' transformation by Ovid's literary predecessors.

The earliest account of Hermes' theft of Apollo's cattle is that of the Homeric *Hymn to Hermes,* where the theft is witnessed by an unnamed old man.

An old man tilling his flowering vineyard saw the god hurrying along the plain through grassy Onchestus. The glorious son of Maia addressed him first. "Old man, cultivating your vines with curved shoulders, you will indeed have much wine when all these bear fruit if you [remember] not to have seen what you saw, and not to have heard what you heard, and to keep silent when nothing that is yours is harmed." So saying, he urged the stout cattle on together: glorious Hermes drove them on through many shady mountains, sounding glens, and flowering fields. (*h. Hermes* 87-96)[20]

Hermes extracts no promise from the old man and when Apollo, later in the hymn, asks this unnamed old man the whereabouts of his cattle (*h. Hermes* 190-200) the old man freely admits to having seen both the

---

20. I quote T.W. Allen's Oxford edition of the Homeric *Hymns* (Oxford 1946).

τὸν δὲ γέρων ἐνόησε δέμων ἀνθοῦσαν ἀλωὴν
ἱέμενον πεδίον δὲ δι' Ὀγχηστὸν λεχεποίην·
τὸν πρότερος προσέφη Μαίης ἐρικυδέος υἱός·
 ὦ γέρον ὅς τε φυτὰ σκάπτεις ἐπικαμπύλος ὤμους,
ἦ πολυοινήσεις εὖτ' ἂν τάδε πάντα φέρῃσι
καί τε ἰδὼν μὴ ἰδὼν εἶναι καὶ κωφὸς ἀκούσας,
καὶ σιγᾶν, ὅτε μή τι καταβλάπτῃ τὸ σὸν αὐτοῦ.
 Τόσσον φὰς συνέσευε βοῶν ἴφθιμα κάρηνα.
πολλὰ δ' ὄρη σκιόεντα καὶ αὐλῶνας κελαδεινοὺς
καὶ πεδί' ἀνθεμόεντα διήλασε κύδιμος Ἑρμῆς.

(*h. Hermes* 87-96)

cattle and their thief (*h. Hermes* 201-11). Apollo continues his search and learns the location of Hermes and the cattle by augury (*h. Hermes* 213-14).²¹ The old man thereafter disappears from the narrative. It is therefore generally agreed that Ovid's account, with its emphasis on Mercury's encounter with the old man, owes little to the Homeric hymn.²²

On the contrary, it is likewise generally agreed that Ovid's account resembles most closely a version that is preserved by Antoninus Liberalis in Chapter 23 of his *Metamorphoses*.²³ The manuscript containing the prose epitome of transformations ascribed to Antoninus Liberalis includes scholia with the names of the authors of earlier literary treatments of the stories.

> This tale is told by Nikander in the first book of the *Heteroioumena,* by Hesiod in the *Great Eoiai,* by Didymarchos in the third book of his *Metamorphoses,* by Antigonos in the *Alloioseis,* and by Apollonios the Rhodian in his Epigrams, according to Pamphilos in his first book.²⁴ (*scholium ad* Ant. Lib., *Met.* 23)

It has long been known that Nicander's Ἑτεροιούμενα, *Transformations,* were an important literary model for Ovid's own *Metamorphoses,* and the evidence of the scholia *ad* Ant. Lib. *Met.* 23 suggests that Nicander's account of Battus' metamorphosis is the principal model for Ovid's account at *Met.* 2.676-707.²⁵ The correspondences between the "Nican-

---

21. On the role of the unnamed old man in the Homeric *Hymn to Hermes,* see further Shelmerdine 1981, 119, *ad h. Hermes* 87-93.

22. See Haupt, Ehwald, and Albrecht 1966, 132-33; Holland 1926, 164; Brown 1947, 146-47; Bömer 1969, 398-405; Castellani 1980, 38; Shelmerdine 1981, 116-19, and Hill 1985, 211-12.

23. Haupt, Ehwald, and Albrecht 1966, 132-33; Holland 1926, 159-63; Brown 1947, 147; Bömer 1969, 401-2; Castellani 1980, 39-40; Shelmerdine 1981, 116; and Hill 1985, 212.

24. Ἱστορεῖ Νίκανδρος Ἑτεροιουμένων α΄ καὶ Ἡσίοδος ἐν Μεγάλαις Ἡοίαις καὶ Διδύμαρχος Μεταμορφώσεων γ΄ καὶ Ἀντίγονος ἐν ταῖς Ἀλλοιώσεσι καὶ Ἀπολλώνιος ὁ Ῥόδιος ἐν Ἐπιγράμμασιν, ὥς φησι Πάμφιλος ἐν α΄. (*scholium ad* Ant. Lib., *Met.* 23). For the status of the testimony of the scholia *ad* Ant. Lib. *Met.* 23, see C. Wendel, review of R. Sellheim, *De Parthenii et Antonini fontium indiculorum auctoribus,* Ph.D. diss., Halle, 1930, in *Gnomon* 8 (1929):148.

25. For general discussion of Nicandrian influence on Ovid's *Metamorphoses,* see Plaehn 1882; Bethe 1904; Lafaye 1904, 46-65; *R-E* 17.264.42-265.11; Gow and Scholfield 1953, 205-8; and Otis 1970, Appendix 1. Probus *ad* Virgil, *Geo.* 1.399 incidentally bears witness to Ovid's frequent use of Nicander: *Varia est opinio harum volucrum originis. Itaque in*

drian" narrative, as it is reported by Antoninus Liberalis at *Met.* 23, and Ovid's account in the second book of his *Metamorphoses* are noteworthy.

1 Magnes was the son of Argos, himself the son of Phrixos, and Perimele, the daughter of Admetos. This Magnes dwelt near Thessaly and men named this land Magnesia after him. To him was born a child famed for his beauty, Hymenaeus. 2 Apollo saw him and fell in love with the boy; and since he never left Magnes' dwelling, Hermes formed designs upon Apollo's herd of cattle that was pastured where Admetos' cattle were. First he cast drowsiness and dog-quinsy on the dogs that were guarding the herd, so that they forgot the cattle and neglected their guardianship. 3 Then he drove away from their pasturage twelve heifers, a hundred cows that had never felt the yoke, and a bull which had covered the cows. From their tails he hung on each a branch of wood, in order to obscure the tracks of the cattle, and he drove them through Pelasgia, Achaïa in Phthiotis, Lokris, Boeotia, Megaris, thence into the Peloponnese through Corinth and Larissa near Tegea, and thence he came up to Mount Lykaion, Maenalion, and the so-called Watch of Battus. 4 This Battus dwelt at the top of the watch. When he heard the sound of cattle being driven over the countryside he went out of his house and, recognizing that Hermes was driving stolen cattle, he demanded a bribe to reveal the stolen herd to no one. Hermes agreed to the bribe on Battus' conditions, and Battus swore an oath that he would tell no one about the cattle. 5 After Hermes had hidden the cattle, driving them into a cave on the headland alongside Coryphasion opposite Italy and Sicily, he immediately went back to Battus, having disguised himself, testing to see whether he would stand by his oath; giving Battus a cloak as a bribe, he asked him if he hadn't seen stolen cattle driven by. 6 Then Battus took the cloak and informed about the cattle. And Hermes, angered by his double-dealing, struck him with his wand and transformed him into a rock, which neither frost nor heat leaves. And to this day the place is called "Battus' Watch" by those who journey past. (Ant. Lib. *Met.* 23)[26]

---

altera sequitur Ovidius Nicandrum, in altera Theodorum, "Opinion is divided on the origin of these sea-birds [i.e., the halcyon], so Ovid follows Nicander in one place, Theodorus in another."

26. Ἄργου τοῦ Φρίξου καὶ Περιμήλης τῆς Ἀδμήτου θυγατρὸς ἐγένετο Μάγνης.

It is especially remarkable that the "Nicandrian" version reveals the same emphasis as we find in Ovid's account on Battus as witness to the theft, in addition to the question of payment for Battus' silence (Ant. Lib. *Met.* 23.4; *Met.* 2.687-88, 692-97). The "Nicandrian" account includes Hermes' return in disguise to test Battus by offering a second bribe (Ant. Lib. *Met.* 23.5), an element that we find also in Ovid's treatment (*Met.* 2.698-701). As in Ovid's *Metamorphoses* (2.702-3), the "Nicandrian" Battus accepts a second bribe and betrays Hermes' confidence, and both accounts conclude with Battus' petrifaction (Ant. Lib. *Met.* 23.6; *Met.* 2.705-7). The "Nicandrian" version is aetiologically motivated to account for the name applied to the stone, "Battus' Watch," Σκοπιαὶ Βάττου.[27] Ovid's translation of the Greek Σκοπιαὶ Βάττου into *index* allows him to retain the sense of "lookout," since *index* can signify "look-out man"; but *index* will also remind us of the rock's former existence as Battus the "informer," and thereby accord thematically with the sequence of episodes at *Met.* 2.531-835.[28]

To judge from Nicander's extant poems, the *Theriaca* and the *Alex-*

οὗτος ᾤκησεν ἐγγὺς Θεσσαλίας καὶ τὴν γῆν ταύτην ἀπ' αὐτοῦ Μαγνησίαν προσηγόρευσαν οἱ ἄνθρωποι. ἐγένετο δ' αὐτῷ παῖς περίβλεπτος τὴν ὄψιν Ὑμέναιος. 2 ἐπεὶ δὲ Ἀπόλλωνα ἰδόντα ἔρως ἔλαβε τοῦ παιδὸς καὶ οὐκ ἐξελίμπανε τὰ οἰκία τοῦ Μάγνητος, Ἑρμῆς ἐπιβουλεύει τῇ ἀγέλῃ τῶν βοῶν τοῦ Ἀπόλλωνος. αἱ δὲ ἐνέμοντο ἵναπερ ἦσαν αἱ Ἀδμήτου βόες. καὶ πρῶτα μὲν ἐμβάλλει ταῖς κυσίν, αἳ ἐφύλαττον αὐτάς, λήθαργον καὶ κυνάγχην, αἱ δὲ ἐξελάθοντο τῶν βοῶν καὶ τὴν φυλακὴν ἀπώλεσαν. 3 εἶτα δ' ἀπελαύνει πόρτιας δώδεκα καὶ ἑκατὸν βοῦς ἄζυγας καὶ ταῦρον, ὃς ταῖς βουσὶν ἐπέβαινεν. ἐξῆπτε δὲ ἐκ τῆς οὐρᾶς πρὸς ἕκαστον ὕλην, ὡς ἂν τὰ ἴχνη τῶν βοῶν ἀφανίσῃ, καὶ ἦγεν αὐτὰς ἐλαύνων διά τε Πελασγῶν καὶ δι' Ἀχαΐας τῆς Φθιώτιδος καὶ διὰ Λοκρίδος καὶ Βοιωτίας καὶ Μεγαρίδος καὶ ἐντεῦθεν εἰς Πελοπόννησον διὰ Κορίνθου καὶ Λαρίσσης ἄχρι Τεγέας καὶ ἐντεῦθεν παρὰ τὸ Λύκαιον ὄρος ἐπορεύετο καὶ παρὰ τὸ Μαινάλιον καὶ τὰς λεγομένας Βάττου Σκοπιάς. 4 ᾤκει δὲ ὁ Βάττος οὗτος ἐπ' ἄκρῳ τῷ σκοπέλῳ· καὶ ἐπεὶ τῆς φωνῆς ἤκουσε παρελαυνομένων τῶν μόσχων, προελθὼν ἐκ τῶν οἰκίων ἔγνω περὶ τῶν βοῶν, ὅτι κλοπιμαίας ἄγει, καὶ μισθὸν ᾔτησεν, ἵνα πρὸς μηδένα φράσῃ περὶ αὐτῶν. Ἑρμῆς δὲ δώσειν ἐπὶ τούτοις ὑπέσχετο καὶ ὁ Βάττος ὤμοσε περὶ τῶν βοῶν πρὸς μηδένα κατερεῖν. 5 ἐπεὶ δὲ αὐτὰς Ἑρμῆς ἔκρυψεν ἐν τῷ πρηῶνι παρὰ τὸ Κορυφάσιον εἰς τὸ σπήλαιον εἰσελάσας ἄντικρυς Ἰταλίας καὶ Σικελίας, αὖθις ἀφίκετο πρὸς τὸν Βάττον, ἀλλάξας ἑαυτὸν καὶ πειρώμενος, εἰ αὐτῷ συμμένειν ἐπὶ τοῖς ὁρκίοις ἐθέλει· διδοὺς δὲ μισθὸν χλαῖναν ἐπυνθάνετο παρ' αὐτοῦ, μὴ κλοπιμαίας βοῦς ἔγνω παρελασθείσας. 6 ὁ δὲ Βάττος ἔλαβε τὴν χλαμύδα καὶ ἐμήνυσε περὶ τῶν βοῶν. Ἑρμῆς δὲ χαλεπήνας, ὅτι διχόμυθος ἦν, ἐρράπισεν αὐτὸν τῇ ῥάβδῳ καὶ μετέβαλεν εἰς πέτρον· καὶ αὐτὸν οὐκ ἐκλείπει κρύος οὐδὲ καῦμα. λέγεται δὲ καὶ ὁ τόπος <ὑπὸ τῶν> παροδευόντων ἄχρι νῦν Σκοπιαὶ Βάττου. (Ant. Lib. *Met.* 23)

27. For σκοπιά as a "place whence one can look out, a look-out place," see LSJ s.v. σκοπιά 1.

28. For *index* in the sense of "look-out man," see *OLD* s.v. *index* 1c.

ipharmaca, he shared the taste of other Hellenistic poets for culling obscure and learned details from the poetry of Homer and Hesiod, and it is therefore not surprising to find that the scholia attribute the earliest account of the story of Battus to Hesiod in the Μεγάλαι 'Ηοῖαι, the *Great Catalog of Women* (Hes. fr. 256 M-W).²⁹ Although few modern scholars are prepared to accept Antoninus Liberalis' story of Battus (*Met.* 23) as authentically Hesiodic, it seems clear from the scholia that the story itself was attributed to Hesiod in antiquity.³⁰ Apollonius of Rhodes, in particular, is known to have written on questions of Hesiodic scholarship, and the report that he treated this story in his epigrams may therefore carry some weight in our assessment of the ancient attribution of Hesiodic authorship to the tale.³¹ We can even point to Ovid's deployment of specifically Hesiodic diction in his account of Battus' metamorphosis, for the Latin poet calls Mercury's mother *Atlantide Maia* (*Met.* 2.685), echoing Hesiod's reference to 'Ατλαντὶς Μαίη at *Theog.* 938.³² Unfortunately, the loss of both Hesiod's *Great Catalog of Women* and Nicander's *Transformations* severely limits our understanding of Ovid's use of his sources in this episode.³³

Although our inquiry into the Hesiodic background to the tale cannot

---

29. Nicander calls himself "Homeric Nicander," 'Ομηρείοιο ... Νικάνδροιο, at *Ther.* 957; see Gow and Scholfield 1953, 189 *ad loc.,* and H. White, *Studies in the Poetry of Nicander* (Amsterdam 1987), Select Index s.v. "Homeric rarities—reproduced by Hellenistic poets." For Nicander's use of Hesiod, see M. Geymonat, ed., *Scholia in Nicandri Alexipharmaca* (Milan 1974), 215, Index of "Auctores" s.v. 'Ησίοδος, and A. Crugnola, ed., *Scholia in Nicandri Theriaca* (Milan 1971), 325, Index of "Auctores" s.v. 'Ησίοδος. On Nicander's literary interests and style see *R-E* 17.260ff.; Gow and Scholfield 1953; H. Schneider, *Vergleichende Untersuchungen zur Sprachlichen Struktur der Beiden Erhaltenen Lehrgedichte des Nikander von Kolophon.* Klassisch-Philologische Studien Heft 24 (Wiesbaden 1962); Bulloch 1985, 602-4; and White, *op. cit.*

30. Thus Hesiod's Oxford editors comment (M-W p. 194), *quae sequuntur vix Hesiodea sunt.* Cf. Brown 1947, 141.

31. On Apollonios' scholarly interest in Hesiod, see Pfeiffer 1968, 144 and 177.

32. Cf. Holland 1926, 162, who also supposes that the accounts of both Nicander and Hesiod lie behind that of Ovid, and Moore-Blunt 1977, 140.

33. The loss of the Hesiodic Μεγάλαι 'Ηοῖαι is especially to be regretted, for Brown (1947, 144-47) has argued convincingly that the story of Battus was appended to that of the heroine Coronis in the Μεγάλαι 'Ηοῖαι. Although Brown does not consider the evidence of the Ovidian passage, his hypothesis would considerably advance our understanding of the allusive structure of *Met.* 2.531-835. Ovid's close juxtaposition of the stories of Coronis (*Met.* 2.596-632) and Battus (*Met.* 2.687-707), in a thematically connected sequence of episodes, may well owe something to the model of Hesiod's Μεγάλαι 'Ηοῖαι. On the importance of Hesiodic poetry in Ovid's *Metamorphoses*, see further Lafaye 1904, 76-80; Wilkinson 1955, 144; Ludwig 1965, 74-76 and the bibliography collected at 99 n. 89c; and Otis 1970, 318 and 358.

be pursued very far, the "Nicandrian" model points us towards another literary context in which to situate Battus, a context unmentioned in the scholia *ad* Ant. Lib. *Met.* 23. The scholia report that the transformation of Battus is narrated in the first book of Nicander's *Transformations,* and the evidence of the scholia regarding the provenance of the other Nicandrian episodes recounted by Antoninus Liberalis suggests that the tales of the first book shared a bucolic setting. The metamorphoses of Cragaleus (Ant. Lib. *Met.* 4), Cerambos (Ant. Lib. *Met.* 22), Battus (Ant. Lib. *Met.* 23), Dryope (Ant. Lib. *Met.* 32), and Lykos (Ant. Lib. *Met.* 38) are explicitly cited as episodes from the first book of Nicander's *Transformations,* and all these characters are identified as shepherds or cowherds whose transformations occur in a bucolic landscape.[34] The episodes reportedly occurring in the second, third, and fourth books of Nicander's *Transformations,* however, display no such consistently pastoral setting.

Now pastoral poetry itself offers a generically appropriate context for the rustic Battus, since a certain Battus is one of two rustic speakers in Theocritus' *Fourth Idyll.*[35] Ovid playfully alludes to the generic propriety of Battus' presence in a bucolic countryside: *notus in illo / rure senex,* "an old man, well-known in that countryside" (*Met.* 2.687-88). Ovid draws heavily upon elements of pastoral poetry in his scene-setting at the outset of the episode.

> illud erat tempus, quo te pastoria pellis
> texit onusque fuit baculum silvestre sinistrae,

---

34. Cragaleus is described as an aged cowherd who is so well-respected among the country folk of Ambracia that Apollo, Artemis, and Herakles apply to him (as he is pasturing his herd) to judge the ownership of Epirote Ambracia. Cerambos is a bucolic poet, inventor of the shepherd's pipe and the first mortal to play the lyre. He is transformed into a long-horned beetle after insulting the rural nymphs and disregarding Pan's advice that he take his flocks to their winter pasturage. Cf. Ovid's account at *Met.* 7.353-56. Dryope is Cragaleus' sister (Ant. Lib. *Met.* 4.1), the daughter of a certain Dryops. She is a shepherdess and companion of the country nymphs, and is metamorphosed into a tree. Cf. Ovid's account at *Met.* 9.329-93. Even the transformation of the wolf, Lykos, occurs in a rustic context after he attacks Peleus' unattended flocks. For the importance of Peleus' flocks to the tale, cf. Ovid's account of the episode at *Met.* 11. 266-409. The evidence would seem to support the suggestion, therefore, that the metamorphoses recounted in the first book of Nicander's Ἑτεροιούμενα were linked by their shared bucolic context. For this reason I think it possible that the transformation of the cowherds narrated at Ant. Lib. *Met.* 35, and ascribed by the scholia to Nicander's *Transformations* without specific provenance, occured in the first book.

35. For Battus in bucolic poetry see Theocr. *Id.* 4., with Gow 1952, 2:87 *ad* 4.41, and cf. Segal 1968, 17.

alterius dispar septenis fistula cannis;
dumque amor est curae, dum te tua fistula mulcet,
incustoditae Pylios memorantur in agros
processisse boves....

(*Met.* 2.680-85)

[That was the time when a herdsman's cloak clothed you, Apollo, you held a wooden staff in your left hand, and in the other, the shepherd's pipe unequal with its seven reeds; and while love was your concern, while your pipe soothed you, they say that your cows wandered, unattended, into the fields of Pylos....]

Apollo's accoutrements and pursuits in these lines are typical of the pastoral world. The Ovidian coinage *pastoria,* "of or connected with herdsmen" (*Met.* 2.680), evokes the Theocritean ποιμενικός, "belonging to the shepherds" (*Id.* 1.23).[36] The phrase *baculum silvestre sinistrae* ("his left hand held a wooden staff") recalls Theocritus' description of the goatherd Lycidas at *Id.* 7.18-19, ῥοικὰν δ' ἔχεν ἀγριελαίῳ / δεξιτερᾷ κορύναν, "in his right hand he grasped a crooked club of wild olive."[37] The shepherd's reed-pipe, whether the Latin *fistula* (*Met.* 2.682, 683) or the Greek σῦριγξ, is a familiar item in both Theocritean bucolic (e.g., *Id.* 1.129, 4.28, 8.18-24) and Virgilian pastoral poetry (e.g., *Ecl.* 2.37, *Ecl.* 3.22, 25, *Ecl.* 10.34).[38] *Amor* too (*Met.* 2.683) is a frequent subject of pastoral poetry, and both Theocritus and Virgil often combine the themes of music and love (e.g., Theocr. *Id.* 11, Virg. *Ecl.* 2 and 10, *passim*).[39]

In this context it is worth considering more closely the opening lines of the Theocritean idyll in which Battus appears, and their relationship to the Ovidian passage.[40]

> *Battos:* Tell me, Korydon, whose cattle are these? Are they Philondas'?
> *Korydon:* No, they belong to Aegon. He gave them to me to pasture.

---

36. On the adjective *pastorius* (*Met.* 2.680) as an Ovidian coinage, see Linse 1891, 34 and Bömer 1969, 400.
37. Cf. Moore-Blunt 1977, 139.
38. Cf. Bömer 1969, 400 and Moore-Blunt 1977, 140.
39. Cf. Bömer 1969, 400-1 and Moore-Blunt 1977, 140.
40. I owe the following observations to Dr. S.E. Hinds (personal communication).

Ba.: And are you milking them all secretly in the evening?
Ko.: The old guy puts calves under the mothers and he watches me.
Ba.: But the cowherd himself, to what country has he gone and disappeared?[41]

If the name Battus is already attached by the Hellenistic period to the old man in our myth, as seems likely from the scholiasts' report that Apollonius the Rhodian recounted the tale, the Theocritean Battus' opening question, "Whose cattle are these?" (τίνος αἱ βόες; *Id.* 4.1), may slyly allude to the stolen cattle.[42] This might then be further underscored in the development of the notion of furtive misappropriation at *Id.* 4.3 (κρύβδαν τὰ ποθέσπερα πάσας ἀμέλγες, "And are you milking them all secretly in the evening?"), and the rustic's question about the location of the herd's rightful owner at *Id.* 4.5 (αὐτὸς δ' ἐς τίν' ἄφαντος ὁ βουκόλος ᾤχετο χώραν, "But the cowherd himself, to what country has he gone and disappeared?"). If the Theocritean lines do indeed refer to the other account of Battus, then Ovid's bucolic *color* at *Met.* 2.680-85 would reveal our poet's understanding of Theocritus' mythological reference at *Id.* 4.1-3. If, however, the name Battus as yet had no connection with the myth of Hermes' theft, the thematic parallelism of the Theocritean lines is insignificant—until a poet later in the tradition, whether Nicander or Ovid, activates the parallel.

The Battus episode closes as it began, with a geographical transition as Mercury flies away from Pylos towards Attica.

    Hinc se sustulerat paribus Caducifer alis
Munychiosque volans agros gratamque Minervae
despectabat humum cultique arbusta Lycei.

(*Met.* 2.708-10)

[The Caduceus-bearer had taken himself hence, borne aloft on bal-

---

41. ΒΑΤΤΟΣ   Εἰπέ μοι, ὦ Κορύδων, τίνος αἱ βόες; ἦ ῥα Φιλώνδα;
    ΚΟΡΥΔΩΝ   οὔκ, ἀλλ' Αἴγωνος· βόσκειν δέ μοι αὐτὰς ἔδωκεν.
    ΒΑ.   ἦ πά ψε κρύβδαν τὰ ποθέσπερα πάσας ἀμέλγες;
    ΚΟ.   ἀλλ' ὁ γέρων ὑφίητι τὰ μοσχία κἠμὲ φυλάσσει.
    ΒΑ.   αὐτὸς δ' ἐς τίν' ἄφαντος ὁ βουκόλος ᾤχετο χώραν;

(*Id.* 4.1-5)

42. Gow (1952, 2:87, *ad* Theocr. *Id.* 4.41) countenances the idea that the name Battus comes from our myth.

anced wings, and in his flight he caught sight of the Munychian fields, a land in which Minerva delights, and the groves of the cultivated Lyceum.]

Mercury, the figure of divine retribution in Battus' tale, will go on to play an important role in the subsequent episode that concludes with Mercury punishing Aglauros with the same type of metamorphosis, petrifaction (*Met.* 2.830-34), as that meted out to Battus (*Met.* 2.705-7).

In the episodes of the crow, the raven, and Ocyroe, we have traced a recurrent pattern of inquiry into the rewards of speech and storytelling, a theme that reappears in the Battus episode. Recurrent characters (Apollo and the chattering tale-teller) reenact a now-familiar plot of indiscreet loquacity, which results in the punishment of the tattle-tale by metamorphosis. The Battus episode even recasts specific features of individual tales that precede it in this sequence. Battus' role as an informer (*index, Met.* 2.706) recalls the introduction of the raven as the unwavering witness to Coronis' adultery (*non exorabilis index, Met.* 2.546).[43] Like the raven (*Met.* 2.535, 540) and the crow (*Met.* 2.547), Battus is a garrulous chatterer by nature, while like Ocyroe, Battus is punished for his speech with silence. Finally, both the Ocyroe and Battus episodes explore the etymological implications of *fari,* and such recurrent etymological speculation contributes to the thematic coherence of the narrative sequence.

---

43. On the raven's predilection for acting as an informer, or *index,* see Labate 1986, 137-44.

Chapter 5

The Petrifaction of Aglauros: *Met.* 2.708–835

The general critical confusion regarding the relationship of the Battus episode to the preceding narrative is paralleled in the scholarly literature concerning the Aglauros episode, the episode that concludes the focus of this study.[1] N.G.G. Davis alone has interpreted the tale of Aglauros' envy and consequent petrifaction as an integral part of the sequence of *indicium* episodes that begins at *Met.* 2.531, regarding it as "the climax" of the sequence.[2] His study, although very different in scope and focus from this one, has shown conclusively that the Aglauros episode must be read in close conjunction with the preceding episodes in order to be understood fully. We may therefore proceed to a detailed analysis of the Aglauros episode in the expectation that it will reveal narrative concerns substantially similar to those elucidated in the preceding episodes (*Met.* 2.531–707), which as we have seen are thematically linked in an exploration of the use, or rather abuse, of the *vox*.

The transition from the story of Battus into the Aglauros episode has been described as "legerdemain," and if we compare this transition with that from the Callisto episode into the tale of the raven (*Met.* 2.531–40), we may be able to see in it a similar concern for achieving narrative cohesion.[3] Indeed, such a concern has been shown to characterize each tale in the sequence of episodes inaugurated by the account of the raven's

---

[1]. For critical discussion of the Aglauros episode, see Wimmel 1962; Galinsky 1975, 164–68; Fredericks 1977; and Henrichs 1983; in addition to the commentaries.

[2]. Davis 1969, 18–39.

[3]. I quote "legerdemain" from Galinsky 1975, 164, at the beginning of his sensitive discussion of the humor of the Aglauros episode (1975, 164–68). Cf. my discussion in Chap. 2 of the transition into the account of the raven's metamorphosis.

118 / *The Play of Fictions*

transformation, and it will prove relevant to the transition into the tale of Aglauros' petrifaction that succeeds Battus' metamorphosis (*Met.* 2.708-832). Flying away from Pylos, Mercury arrives over Athens and the narrative returns to the Attic setting that was also the scene of the first story related in the embedded narrative of the crow.

> illa forte die castae de more puellae
> vertice subposito festas in Palladis arces
> pura coronatis portabant sacra canistris.
> (*Met.* 2.711-13)

[By chance that was the day on which chaste maidens traditionally carried hallowed objects in garland-wreathed baskets on their heads to the festive citadel of Pallas.]

As with every transition we have considered in this study, the opening of the Aglauros episode is strongly marked by a temporal referent, *illa . . . die.* In addition to Mercury, who acts as the linking figure from the conclusion of the Battus episode to the new episode, other characters from the preceding sequence of episodes reappear in the new tale. Minerva was a figure of central importance in the crow's narrative, and she reappears in the new episode (named at *Met.* 2.709, 712) surrounded by maidens tending sacred baskets.

Moreover, at least one of these *virgines* is familiar to us from an earlier episode.

> quanto splendidior quam cetera sidera fulget
> Lucifer et quanto quam Lucifer aurea Phoebe,
> tanto virginibus praestantior omnibus Herse
> ibat eratque decus pompae comitumque suarum.
> (*Met.* 2.722-25)

[as much more brilliant as Lucifer shines than all the remaining stars; and as much more brilliant as golden Phoebe shines than Lucifer; so much more beautiful was Herse than all the maidens as she went: she was the glory of the procession and her companions.]

We first glimpsed Herse, along with her sisters Aglauros and Pandrosos, in the embedded narrative of the *cornix,* where she was also engaged in the performance of ritual service to the goddess Athena.[4]

> ... nam tempore quodam
> Pallas Erichthonium, prolem sine matre creatam,
> clauserat Actaeo texta de vimine cista
> virginibusque tribus gemino de Cecrope natis
> et legem dederat, sua ne secreta viderent.
>
> (*Met.* 2.552-56)

[For once upon a time Pallas enclosed Ericthonius, child born without a mother, within a chest woven from Athenian osier, and gave to the three maiden daughters of biform Cecrops the injunction that they not look upon her secrets.]

After Battus' petrifaction, we find the Cecropids once again in the context of ritual service to Athena. In both episodes, therefore, the goddess Pallas Athena (*Met.* 2.553; *Met.* 2.712) is served by *virgines* (*Met.* 2.555; *Met.* 2.711, 724-25) carrying sacred baskets (*Met.* 2.554, 560; *Met.* 2.713). These lexical reminiscences of the crow's account of the Cecropids at the outset of the Ovidian first-layer narrative of Aglauros' metamorphosis reveal the poet alluding straightforwardly to the crow's narrative. Indeed the crow's narrative provides the key to interpretation of the poet's subsequent account of Aglauros' petrifaction.

Aglauros is reintroduced to the narrative with the pointed reuse of several motifs from the crow's embedded narrative.

> pars secreta domus ebore et testudine cultos
> tris habuit thalamos, quorum tu, Pandrose, dextrum,
> Aglauros laevum, medium possederat Herse.
> quae tenuit laevum, venientem prima notavit
> Mercurium nomenque dei scitarier ausa est
> et causam adventus....
>
> (*Met.* 2.737-42)

[A recessed part of the house held three bedchambers decorated with ivory and tortoise-shell; yours, Pandrosus, was the right, Aglauros

---

[4]. On the aetiological nature of this myth in Athenian ritual, see Burkert 1985, 228-29.

possessed the left, and Herse the middle. She who dwelt on the left was the first to see Mercury when he came, and she dared to inquire of the god his name and the reason for his visit....]

Aglauros' inquiry into the purpose of the god's visit at *Met.* 2.741-42 recalls the question that the garrulous crow puts to the raven.

> ... quem garrula motis
> consequitur pennis, scitetur ut omnia, cornix
> auditaque viae causa....
>
> (*Met.* 2.547-49)

[... the chattering crow followed the raven on her swift wings, in order to learn all the gossip, but when she heard the reason for his journey....]

Just as the crow's curiosity brought about her downfall, so too will Aglauros' curiosity result in disaster.

> adspicit hunc oculis isdem, quibus abdita nuper
> viderat Aglauros flavae secreta Minervae.
>
> (*Met.* 2.748-49)

[Aglauros caught sight of this god with the same eyes that had recently looked upon the hidden secrets of blond Minerva.]

These lines recall not only Aglauros' earlier disdainful disobedience of the goddess' instructions, but also the crow's observation of the Cecropids' transgression.

> abdita fronde levi densa speculabar ab ulmo,
> quid facerent: commissa duae sine fraude tuentur
> Pandrosos atque Herse; timidas vocat una sorores
> Aglauros nodosque manu diducit, et intus
> infantemque vident adporrectumque draconem.
>
> (*Met.* 2.557-61)

[Hidden in thick foliage I watched what they did from a slender elm: two of the girls, Pandrosos and Herse, guarded their commission without deceit; one, Aglauros, called her sisters timid, unbound the fastenings with her hand, and within they saw the child and a serpent stretched out at his side.]

It is the crow who is "hidden" (*abdita, Met.* 2.557) in her own narrative, but Ovid echoes the adjective in his later account of Aglauros' petrifaction to characterize the contents of the basket Athena had entrusted to the Cecropidae (*abdita...secreta, Met.* 2.748-49; cf. *secreta, Met.* 2.556). The verbal reminiscence underlines the close thematic relationship between the crow's autobiographical account of how she witnessed the transgression of the Cecropids (*Met.* 2.549-62) and Ovid's first-layer narrative of Aglauros' discovery of Mercury's passion for her sister Herse (*Met.* 2.741-51).[5]

Thus, the setting of the crow's first story recurs in the first-layer narrative of Aglauros' petrifaction.[6] Moreover, Ovid includes a simile, at the outset of the Aglauros episode, that suggests another level of engagement with the embedded narrative of the crow. The crow's story of the Cecropids is told to another bird, the raven (*Met.* 2.547-67), in a passage that is conditioned in part by Callimachus' *Hecale* (Hollis frr. 70-74), the source for the Ovidian crow's narrative. But the transition into that sequence of stories (*Met.* 2.531-40) begins with a bird that exists already in the world of the *Metamorphoses* (the peacock, *pavo,* created at *Met.* 1.720-23), and concludes with three other birds (doves, geese, and swans).[7]

> tam nuper pictis caeso pavonibus Argo,
> quam tu nuper eras, cum candidus ante fuisses,
> corve loquax, subito nigrantes versus in alas.
> nam fuit haec quondam niveis argentea pennis
> ales, ut aequaret totas sine labe columbas
> nec servaturis vigili Capitolia voce
> cederat anseribus nec amanti flumina cygno.
>
> (*Met.* 2.533-39)

[As recently as the peacock was bedecked with the eyes of dead Argus,

---

5. Cf. Fränkel 1945, 221 n. 77 and Davis 1969, 35.
6. On Ovid's "appropriation" of literary models provided both by his own earlier poetry and by that of his poetic predecessors, see Seneca the Elder, *Suas.* 3.7, and cf. Chap. 1 n. 60.
7. See Chap. 2.

so recently were you, chattering raven, though earlier you had been white, transformed suddenly into black wings. For at one time this bird was silver-hued with white feathers, so that it could equal doves entirely without stain, nor would it yield to geese, birds who would prove saviors of the Capitoline with their watchful cry, nor to the river-loving swan.]

Ovid's reintroduction of the Cecropids begins with a bird simile.

> inde revertentes deus adspicit ales iterque
> non agit in rectum, sed in orbem curvat eundem
> ut volucris visis rapidissima milvus extis,
> dum timet et densi circumstant sacra ministri,
> flectitur in gyrum nec longius audet abire
> spemque suam motis avidus circumvolat alis:
> sic super Actaeas avidus Cyllenius arces[8]
> inclinat cursus et easdem circinat auras....
>
> (*Met.* 2.714–21)

[The winged god caught sight of them returning from there, and instead of carrying on his appointed route, he bent into the same curve as when a bird, say a very swift kite, spying entrails—though it knows fear and the attendants stand closely round the sacrificial victim—turns its course into a circle, nor does it dare to go further away, and it greedily flies round its hoped-for prey on swiftly moving wings: so Cyllenian Mercury greedily bent his course above the citadel of Athens, and circled round through the same breezes....]

The poet thus playfully adapts the ornithological introduction to the crow's embedded narrative at the opening of the Aglauros episode, contextualizing the later episode by reference to the earlier. In these thematically associated episodes, the temporal referents, the reappearance of the same characters (Athena, *virgines,* the Cecropids) and the same setting (Athens), the sacred baskets, and even the reuse of bird similes,

---

8. Ovid reworks a simile from *Aen.* 4.252–55, where the winged figure of Mercury is explicitly compared to a bird. Ovid may even imply a punning derivation of *avidus* from *aves* in this line, with the collocation *avidus circumvolat alis,* applied to a bird (*milvus, Met.* 2.716).

all combine to comment upon the close connection between the Aglauros episode and the embedded narrative of the crow two hundred lines earlier.

On the chronological level, the embedded narrative of the crow might be said to function as the aetiological motivation for the religious ritual in which Herse is engaged upon the reintroduction of the Cecropids.[9] But the account of Aglauros' punishment for impeding Mercury's access to Herse (*Met.* 2.708-832) addresses one of the problems that was isolated earlier in our discussion of the crow's narrative (*Met.* 2.549-62), viz., that the crow's narrative implies that the Cecropids go unpunished for their transgression.[10] Ovid addresses this problem explicitly when he reintroduces the goddess Athena.

> vertit ad hanc torvi dea bellica luminis orbem
> et tanto penitus traxit suspiria motu,
> ut pariter pectus positamque in pectore forti
> aegida concuteret. subit hanc arcana profana
> detexisse manu tum, cum sine matre creatam
> Lemnicolae stirpem contra data foedera vidit,
> et gratamque deo fore iam gratamque sorori
> et ditem sumpto, quod avara poposcerat, auro.
>
> (*Met.* 2.752-59)

[The warrior goddess turned her pitiless eyes toward this girl and drew sighs from deep within, in so much agitation that both breast and the aegis on her stalwart breast, shook alike. She recalled that this girl had uncovered the holy secrets with her own hand at the time when, contrary to the instructions she had been given, she looked upon the child of Lemnian Vulcan, born without a mother; and she saw that the girl would please the god now, then her sister, and be rich too upon receipt of the gold that she had demanded.]

Ovid's second Cecropid episode, like the preceding episodes of this sequence, is thus generated by the existing material world of the *Metamorphoses*, which includes the stories told by characters within the poem.

Beyond the world of the *Metamorphoses*, however, the crow's narrative

---

9. For possible ritual connections between the Arrephoria and Panathenaia, see Burkert 1985, 232-33.

10. Cf. Fränkel 1945, 221 n. 77; Wimmel 1962, 329; Davis 1969, 34; and Henrichs 1983, 41.

124 / *The Play of Fictions*

engages in literary reminiscence of Callimachus' *Hecale,* and the new Cecropid episode also seems to rework a specifically Callimachean model, as a recently reedited papyrus from Herculaneum testifies.

[.....]Καλλιμ[α-
[....].υφους, Πάν-
[δρο]σον δὲ καὶ λί-
[θο]ν, διότι τὴν ἀ-
[δελ]φὴν {π} Ἕρσην
[οὐ] προήκατ' αὐτῷ.

(*PHerc.* 243 II.1-6)[11]

[...Callimachus..., Pandrosos and a stone, because she did not surrender to him her sister Herse.]

This papyrus fragment refers to Hermes' love for Herse as told by a certain Callimachus, in an account that coincides with Ovid's in broad outline.[12] In both versions one of Herse's sisters obstructs the god's access to his beloved (*PHerc.* 243 II.4-6; *Met.* 2.748-51, 814-17) and she is therefore punished by being turned into a rock (*PHerc.* 243 II.2-4; *Met.* 2.818-32). The evidence provided by *PHerc.* 243 II suggests that Ovid did not invent the story of the Cecropid Aglauros' petrifaction, but rather that he remodeled an already existing story.[13]

In Chapter 1, the Callimachean model for the crow's narrative was considered as a prelude to analysis of the Ovidian crow's engagement with the *Hecale* (Hollis frr. 70-74). A similar investigation cannot be pursued at this point because of our loss of the Callimachean account of this story. Indeed, we do not even know precisely where Callimachus told this story.[14] The loss of the Callimachean model may be felt particularly when we turn to consider the lengthy excursus on *Invidia,* and

---

11. I quote from the text of Henrichs 1983, 37. For the most recent text and discussion see Henrichs 1983 and Luppe 1984. Lloyd-Jones and Parsons (1983, 142-43) reprint the outdated conjectures of Gomperz and Schober at *SH* 307.

12. This Callimachus is generally agreed to be the Hellenistic poet from Cyrene: see Henrichs 1983, 37-39; Lloyd-Jones and Parsons 1983, 142-43; and Hollis 1990, 230-31.

13. See Haupt, Ehwald, and Albrecht 1966, 134. Henrichs (1983, 42-43) discusses the many compositional subtleties of the Ovidian passage.

14. The fragmentary text of the *Hecale* is an obvious possibility for the location of this tale in Callimachus' *oeuvre*: see Henrichs 1983, 42; Lloyd-Jones and Parsons 1983, 142-43; and Hollis 1990, 230-31.

the meaning of her role in the episode and in the greater context of this sequence of episodes. It is clear that the figure of personified *Invidia* (*Met.* 2.760-805) is important to Aglauros' motivation for denying Mercury access to her sister Herse (*Met.* 2.805-15).[15] But *invidia* may earlier have played a role in the crow's narrative, in the crow's hostile references to Nyctimene (*Met.* 2.589-95); in prompting the raven to tell Apollo about Coronis' infidelity (*Met.* 2.543-47, 596-99); and even, perhaps, in Apollo's murderous anger at Coronis, his response to the raven's report.[16] Indeed, *invidia* may be said to dominate the psychology of the crow and the raven, as well as that of Aglauros. *Invidia* thus motivates much of the action in this sequence of episodes long before she openly arrives in the narrative.

Davis' discussion of the *indicium* tales in the *Metamorphoses* includes a similar interpretation of Aglauros' *invidia*. In an analysis of the narrative elements that recur in episodes centering upon an *index*-figure, he shows that such episodes often include "the visual discovery of a secret and illicit erotic intrigue," and we have already had occasion to remark upon this plot pattern in our sequence of episodes.[17] Aglauros' two transgressions involve her illicit discovery of a secret concealed from view, and both moments of discovery are announced by a verb of seeing (*video* of looking into the chest at *Met.* 2.556, 561; *adspicio* and *video* of watching Mercury's illicit affair at *Met.* 2.748-49, 812). In his discussion of another *index*-figure (Clytie, *Met.* 4.234-70), Davis notes that

> the relative frequency of the colorless word *videre* as the signal of the Discovery motif enables the narrator to make a characteristic etymological word-play with the compound *in-videre*... "to look with hostile intent," and it is this primary signification as well as the derived

---

15. On envy as the motivation for an *index*-figure, see Davis 1969, 26-28. Henrichs (1983, 43) suggests that Pandrosos was motivated by extreme avarice in the Hellenistic version of this myth.

16. Labate (1986, 140) even suggests that Apollo kills Coronis because he is overcome by envy, "sconvolto dalla gelosia." In this connection, it is notable that Horace *Epist.* 1.17.50-51 associates the raven's garrulity and begging with *invidia: sed tacitus pasci si posset corvus, haberet / plus dapis et rixae multo minus invidiaeque,* "but if the raven could feed in silence, he would have more dinner and much less quarreling and envy."

17. Davis 1969, 35. Cf. my discussion in Chap. 4. Davis (1969, 21-23 and 35) shows that of the raven, the crow, Ocyroe, Battus, and Aglauros (those whose stories are told at *Met.* 2.531-835), Battus alone does not bear witness to an erotic intrigue.

one ("to envy") that Ovid injects into the tale of Clytie: *invidit Clytie*... (*Met.* 4.234).[18]

Davis' discussion of the envy aroused in Clytie (by her discovery that the Sun loves not herself but Leucothoe) foreshadows his insightful interpretation of Aglauros' *invidia*, for it is, after all, Aglauros' discovery of Mercury's interest in a clandestine romance with Herse that causes her *invidia*. In the following discussion I summarize Davis' findings.[19]

He begins by drawing attention to the emphatic juxtaposition of the two moments of seeing that inaugurate Aglauros' illicit discoveries of the secrets of Minerva and Mercury:

adspicit hunc oculis isdem, quibus abdita nuper
viderat Aglauros flavae secreta Minervae

(*Met.* 2.748-49)

[Aglauros caught sight of Mercury with the same eyes that had just recently looked upon the hidden secrets of blond Minerva.]

Minerva reacts angrily to Aglauros' second discovery: *vertit ad hanc torvi dea bellica luminis orbem,* "the warrior goddess turned towards this girl the orb of her pitiless eyes" (*Met.* 2.752). The goddess' slantwise glance dramatizes her burgeoning envy of "the gratitude and material recompense which will accrue to the treacherous Aglauros" (*Met.* 2.758-59).[20] Thus the emphasis on the manner in which both goddess and maiden visually follow events foreshadows the skewed "eyeing" personified in the figure of *Invidia*. Moreover, when Minerva visits *Invidia,* she finds herself unable to look directly at her. Instead she must avert her gaze.

... videt intus edentem
vipereas carnes, vitiorum alimenta suorum,
Invidiam, visaque oculos avertit. ...

(*Met.* 2.768-70)

---

18. Davis 1969, 28. The etymological relationship between *invideo* and *video* is discussed by Varro at *L.L.* 6.80.
19. Davis 1969, 37-39.
20. Davis 1969, 38.

[Minerva saw Envy within, eating snakes' flesh, the proper food for her faults, and upon seeing her, she turned her eyes away....]

As Davis suggests, the etymological play foregrounded by the collocation *Invidiam visaque oculos* vividly documents the action of "looking aslant," which is the primary meaning of *invidere*. Indeed, the wordplay seems to be prompted by the skewed vision that is the subject of the narrative. *Invidia*'s emphatic arrival in the narrative makes literal the recurrent thematic pattern of visual discovery of a secret and the envious disclosure to which such discoveries inevitably lead in this sequence of episodes.

There may also be a broader literary significance in the poet's personification of *Invidia*. Envy's long and illustrious literary history provides a context for the Ovidian *Invidia* that cannot be ignored when we come to assess her function in *Met.* 2.531–835. *Invidia,* and her synonyms φθόνος, βασκανία, and *livor,* are used by many ancient poets in metaphorical expositions of their poetics. As a literary construct both "envy," φθόνος, and "the envious," φθονεροί, make frequent appearances in Pindar's poetry.[21] It has been suggested that "the frequency in Pindar's poetry of the theme of envy and ingratitude is to be accounted for by the requirements of the religion in which he and his audiences believed."[22] Such Pindaric passages, however, were interpreted in the Hellenistic period as Pindaric polemic against specific poets, and it is clear that, at least on occasion, Pindar's statements were intended as metaphorical assertions of the poet's art.[23] Nor is Pindar alone in his use of φθόνος as a metaphorical vehicle for assertions of his poetic principles: the dithyrambic poet Timotheus concluded his lyric nome *Persae* with a request to Apollo to defend the poet against the criticism, μῶμος, which his new style of poetry might engender.[24] The lives of the ancient poets bring this poetic metaphor to life. In one of the Euripidean *Vitae,* for example, Euripides is said to have left Athens not only because audiences preferred Sophocles but also "because the comic poets tore

---

21. For φθόνος see, e.g., *Ol.* 8.55, *Pyth.* 1.85, *Pyth.* 7.19, and *Isth.* 7.39; for φθονερός see, e.g., *Ol.* 1.47, *Pyth.* 2.90, *Pyth.* 11.54, *Nem.* 8.21, *Pyth.* 10.20, *Isth.* 1.44, and *Isth.* 2.43.

22. H. Lloyd-Jones, "Modern Interpretation of Pindar: The Second Pythian and Seventh Nemean Odes," *JHS* 93 (1973):136.

23. See Hopkinson 1988, 88–89, on the reception of such Pindaric statements in Hellenistic poetry. Cf. Lefkowitz 1980, 4–5; 1981, 57; and 1981, 121 on *Pyth.* 1.81–86.

24. For μῶμος, cf. Pindar, *Pyth.* 1.82.

128 / *The Play of Fictions*

him to pieces in their *envy*."²⁵ Inheriting this literary tradition, the Alexandrian scholar-poet Callimachus employs both φθόνος and βασκανία in metaphorical statements of his polemical poetics. Callimachus personifies Envy, Φθόνος, together with Blame, Μῶμος, in the programmatic conclusion of the Hymn to Apollo.

> Envy spoke secretly in Apollo's ears: "I do not admire the singer who sings not even as much as the sea." Apollo struck Envy with his foot and spoke thus in reply: "Great is the flow of the Assyrian river, but it draws much filth from land and refuse on its water. The bees do not carry water to Deo from every source but from the spring which, pure and undefiled, bubbles up from a holy font, a small spring, the choicest of its kind."
> Farewell, lord. And may Blame go where Envy is. (Call. *Hymn* 2.105-13)²⁶

The Hymn's most recent commentator has called this passage a "literary *apologia*."²⁷ For our purposes, it is sufficient to note that the context in which Φθόνος and Μῶμος are introduced is an explicit statement of poetic program in which the poet metaphorically expresses his poetic principles, using the conventional language of his literary predecessors.

In the Latin literary tradition, Virgil translates the Callimachean φθόνος and βασκανία into Latin as *invidia* in a programmatically charged context at the conclusion of the proem to *Georgica* 3.

---

25. Lefkowitz 1981, 96, italics mine. In the ancient Life of Sophocles, the dramatist is said to have quarrelled with one son, Iophon, who is envious (φθονοῦντα) of a half-brother, also named Sophocles: see *Vita Sophoclis* (13), ed. Radt (1977).

26. ὁ Φθόνος Ἀπόλλωνος ἐπ' οὔατα λάθριος εἶπεν·
'οὐκ ἄγαμαι τὸν ἀοιδὸν ὃς οὐδ' ὅσα πόντος ἀείδει.'
τὸν Φθόνον ὡπόλλων ποδί τ' ἤλασεν ὧδέ τ' ἔειπεν·
"Ἀσσυρίου ποταμοῖο μέγας ῥόος, ἀλλὰ τὰ πολλὰ
λύματα γῆς καὶ πολλὸν ἐφ' ὕδατι συρφετὸν ἕλκει.
Δηοῖ δ' οὐκ ἀπὸ παντὸς ὕδωρ φορέουσι μέλισσαι,
ἀλλ' ἥτις καθαρή τε καὶ ἀχράαντος ἀνέρπει
πίδακος ἐξ ἱερῆς ὀλίγη λιβάς, ἄκρον ἄωτον.'
χαῖρε, ἄναξ· ὁ δὲ Μῶμος, ἵν' ὁ Φθόνος, ἔνθα νέοιτο.
(Call. *Hymn* 2.105-13)

Cf. βασκανίη in the *Aetia* Prologue, fr. 1.17 (Pf.), and *Epigr.* 21.4. (Pf.).

27. F. Williams 1978, 86. Cf. also Bulloch 1985, 560, who calls the poem "a vehement statement of literary principles."

stabunt et Parii lapides, spirantia signa,
Assaraci proles demissaeque ab Iove gentis
nomina, Trosque parens et Troiae Cynthius auctor.
Invidia infelix Furias amnemque severum
Cocyti metuet tortosque Ixionis anguis
immanemque rotam et non exsuperabile saxum.

(*Geo.* 3.34-39)

[Parian marble will stand forever, lifelike statues of Assaracris' offspring, and the names of the race descended of Jove, father Tros, and Apollo Cynthius, founder of Troy. Ill-omened Envy will fear the Furies and the dread stream of Cocytus, Ixion's twisting snakes and immense wheel, and the unconquerable stone.]

L.P. Wilkinson has suggested that the personified figure of *Invidia* here refers "to the envy that Virgil's poetic triumph will arouse, in other poets especially," in addition to "envy of Octavian's successes and supremacy," as has been more generally supposed.[28] There are good reasons for understanding a specifically literary claim to Virgil's stance here, since Virgil has a predilection for setting his most explicit statements of literary program at the center of a work, and the proem in which these lines occur has been called "Virgil's most extensive statement of literary purpose."[29]

Ovid, never one to leave a Callimachean or Virgilian motif untested, seems to have been intrigued by the programmatic potential of Envy as a literary construct from the outset of his career, and he adopts such a programmatic stance in the final poem of the first book of the *Amores*, where he is concerned to articulate a specifically literary challenge to Envy.

Quid mihi, Livor edax, ignavos obicis annos
 ingeniique vocas carmen inertis opus

---

28. Wilkinson 1969, 170: see the bibliography collected there in support of this view, and now also Thomas 1983, 99-100 and 1985, 68-71. This view is rejected by F. Klingner, *Virgils Georgica* (Zurich 1963), 136ff., 252, and ignored by Dickie 1983. Thomas (1988, 2:46-47) rejects a reference to specifically Pindaric envy in favor of Callimachean reference, noting that envy is a standard feature of Callimachean programmatic poetry; cf. Wilkinson 1969, 171; Thomas 1983, 99-100; and Ross 1987, 184. For *invidia* in another Augustan programmatic context, cf. Horace, *Sat.* 1.4 with Dickie 1981, 185-93.
29. Thomas 1983, 92. On *Ecl.* 6 and *Aen.* 7.37-45, see also Thomas 1985.

> . . . .
> pascitur in vivis Livor; post fata quiescit,
>   cum suus ex merito quemque tuetur honos.
>
>   (*Am.* 1.15.1–2, 39–40)

[Why, carping Envy, do you cast my idle years up to me in reproach, and call my poetry the product of an artless wit. . . . Envy feeds on the living but grows quiet after death, when each man's dignity protects him as he deserves.]

The challenge frames a catalog of admired poets of Greece and Rome, and thus it functions as an assertion on Ovid's part both of his understanding of the literary tradition in which he writes and also of his right to inclusion within it. Elsewhere in his oeuvre, he makes similar assertions of his poetic genius.[30] Moreover, even within the *Metamorphoses,* Ovid uses both *livor* and *invidia* in contexts of the public reception of artistic endeavor. Arachne's skill in weaving, for example, is such that even Envy could not disparage it: *non illud carpere Livor / possit opus,* "not even Envy could find fault with that masterpiece" (*Met.* 6.129–30).[31]

Considered against this literary background, Ovid's ekphrasis on personified *Invidia* assumes a programmatic significance.[32] Ancient poets could characterize the public reception of their artistic production as one of envy: Hesiod was the first, but by no means the last, to point out that even poets may respond to one another's work enviously.[33] It has often been noted that the literary inspiration for the Ovidian personification of *Invidia* is Virgil's description of personified *Fama* at *Aen.* 4.173–97.[34] Thus, one way to interpret the relationship of the Ovidian reference to the

---

30. See, for example, *Rem.* 365 (*ingenium magni livor detractat Homeri,* "Envy disparages the genius of great Homer"), *Rem.* 389 (*rumpere, Livor edax,* "rupture yourself, greedy Envy"), and *Rem.* 397 (*hactenus invidiae respondimus,* "up to this point we have simply responded to Envy"), which concludes an excursus on literature prompted by the poet's reference to envy, *livor,* at *Rem.* 365. For *invidia* applied to artistic integrity, cf. *Tr.* 3.4.43, 4.4.26, and 5.8.24.

31. On the programmatic undertones in this passage, see Anderson 1968, 103 and Hofmann 1985, 233–34.

32. Cf. Hofmann 1985, 233–34.

33. Hesiod, *Erga* 25–26, καὶ κεραμεὺς κεραμεῖ κοτέει καὶ τέκτονι τέκτων, / καὶ πτωχὸς πτωχῷ φθονέει καὶ ἀοιδὸς ἀοιδῷ, "potter bears a grudge towards potter, carpenter towards carpenter, beggar feels envy towards beggar, and bard towards bard."

34. Bömer 1969, 417; Otis 1970, 120; Hill 1985, 214; and Kenney 1986, 390. The Virgilian figure of Allecto (*Aen.* 7.324–562) is also an important model for the Ovidian *Invidia*.

Virgilian model here is, quite literally, as literary *aemulatio*.[35] Virgil's *Fama* could thus be read as the focus of Ovid's *Invidia*. In this respect it seems significant that the final allegorical figure described at length in the *Metamorphoses* is *Fama* herself (*Met.* 12.39-63), as though Ovid's own aspirations to literary glory can be articulated only after he has documented *invidia*. Such an interpretation of the passage complements the explicit subject of the narrative in this sequence of episodes, for in accordance with the theme of indiscreet loquacity that links the episodes in an exploration of the utility of speech and story-telling, the appearance of *Invidia* here self-consciously reflects—and reflects upon—Ovid's undertaking. Poetic production had enjoyed a long history of attracting the attention of the "envious," and it is typical of Ovid's literary sophistication to consider the specifically literary nature of "Envy" in a passage that explores the risks and rewards of story-telling.

Indeed, the theme of the abuse of the *usus vocis,* which we have traced in the preceding episodes, dominates the conclusion of the Aglauros episode. Although Aglauros does not disclose her secret, the poet emphasizes her desire to do so.

> saepe mori voluit, ne quicquam tale videret,
> saepe velut crimen rigido narrare parenti....
>
> (*Met.* 2.812-13)

[Often she wished she could die so that she might see no such happiness, and often she wanted to tell her strict father, as though it were a crime....]

Ovid depicts Aglauros wrestling with her desire to disclose the secret she has discovered, and her impulse to inform aligns her with the other tale tellers in this sequence of episodes. Moreover, as with the characters of the preceding episodes, Aglauros' metamorphosis finally comes about as the direct result of her abuse of the *usus vocis*.

> denique in adverso venientem limine sedit
> exclusura deum; cui blandimenta precesque
> verbaque iactanti mitissima 'desine' dixit,
> 'hinc ego me non sum nisi te motura repulso.'

---

35. On *aemulatio* see Williams 1983, 230; Conte 1986; and Thomas 1986.

132 / *The Play of Fictions*

> 'stemus' ait 'pacto' velox Cyllenius 'isto.'
> . . . .
> Has ubi verborum poenas mentisque profanae
> cepit Atlantiades. . . .
>
> (*Met.* 2.814-18, 833-34)

[Finally she took her place at the threshold opposite, to refuse the god admittance when he came; and as he tossed out inducements, entreaties, and wheedling words, she said, "Enough! I will not move from this spot until I send you away!" Swiftly the Cyllenian god said, "Let us stand by this new compact!" . . . When the grandson of Atlas had inflicted this penalty for her words and impious spirit. . . .]

Mercury punishes Aglauros for her words with the literal accomplishment of those very words, just as he punishes Battus at *Met.* 2.705-7 by metamorphosing him into a rock and thereby fulfilling the substance of Battus' assurance that a rock would betray the cattle theft before he would (*Met.* 2.695-97).[36]

The hardening of Aglauros' vocal passages is reserved for the climactic conclusion of her petrifaction.

> nec conata loqui est nec, si conata fuisset,
> vocis habebat iter; saxum iam colla tenebat,
> oraque duruerant, signumque exsangue sedebat;
> nec lapis albus erat: sua mens infecerat illam.
>
> (*Met.* 2.829-32)

[She did not try to speak, nor—if she had tried—did she have a passage for her voice; now rock constricted her throat, her face grew hard, and she sat a bloodless statue; nor was the stone white: her personality had stained it.]

Aglauros is forever deprived of the *usus vocis* (*nec . . . vocis habebat iter*, *Met.* 2.829-30), because she has misused her faculty of speech. The collocation *vocis . . . iter* recalls not only the crow's warning to the raven (*'non utile carpis'* / *inquit 'iter: ne sperne meae praesagia linguae,* "'You undertake a useless journey,' she said: 'do not disdain my tongue's pro-

---

36. Cf. Fredericks 1977, 246.

phetic warnings'," *Met.* 2.549–50), but also Ocyroe's metamorphosis, which begins with the loss of her *vocis . . . usus* (*Met.* 2.658). And indeed, Ovid depicts the consequences of Aglauros' misuse of speech in such a way as to show that the Aglauros episode shares the same concern with the *vocis usus* that is emphasized in the preceding episodes of Ocyroe, the raven, and the crow.[37] The Aglauros episode invites interpretation as the culmination of this sequence of thematically linked episodes. With Davis, then, we may characterize Aglauros as "a frustrated *index* who is finally rendered mute."[38]

Ovid marks the formal conclusion of the *indicium* sequence by the familiar structural technique of ring composition, for the phrase *vocis . . . iter* at the close of the Aglauros episode (*Met.* 2.830) echoes the opening words of the crow to the raven: *'non utile carpis'* / *inquit 'iter: ne sperne meae praesagia linguae.* As Mercury flies away from Athens after his abortive affair with Herse, his father, Jupiter, commands his assistance in arranging what will prove to be a briefly told affair with Europa.

> sevocat hunc genitor nec causam fassus amoris
> 'fide minister' ait 'iussorum, nate, meorum,
> pelle moram solitoque celer delabere cursu,
> quaeque tuam matrem tellus a parte sinistra
> suspicit (indigenae Sidonida nomine dicunt),
> hanc pete, quodque procul montano gramine pasci
> armentum regale vides, ad litora verte.'
>
> (*Met.* 2.836–42)

[His father summoned him, and without admitting that his reason was love, said, "Loyal minister of my commands, son, brook no delay: glide swiftly in your customary flight, and seek out the land that looks up to your mother from the left (the inhabitants call it Sidon by name); and when you see the royal herd pasturing far away on the mountain grasses, drive it towards the shore."]

The narrative moves thence, away from the *indicium* sequence of *Met.* 2.531–835 and its concern with story-telling, into a Theban cycle (*Met.*

---
37. Cf. Fredericks 1977, 244–46.
38. Davis 1969, 36.

2.836-4.603). Thus Jupiter's affairs with Callisto (*Met.* 2.401-530) and Europa (*Met.* 2.836-3.2) frame the sequence of *indicium* episodes in the second half of Book 2 of the *Metamorphoses,* setting it off as a narrative unit from what precedes and follows.

Epilogue

Each of the episodes at *Met.* 2.531–835 contains a basic plot of divine punishment for mortal speech and reveals a recurrent concern with the issue of an "appropriate" use of the voice. The raven and the crow (at least in her first account of the Cecropids' transgression) are prompted by *fides* to tell stories to their divine patrons: both birds are punished rather than rewarded. Ocyroe, in a mantic frenzy, prophesies the fates of Aesculapius and her own father Chiron, and she is punished for doing so against the will of the gods (*Met.* 2.659–60, 677–78). Battus and Aglauros both refuse to comply with promises they have made to Mercury, and the god then takes advantage of their "careless use of language" to turn them into stones.[1] Although the motives that prompt the characters to speak vary from one episode to the next, the outcome is invariably divine punishment. In the end, the stance taken by Ovid's crow, who tells her story to the raven in order to warn him away from speech altogether, seems to represent the only practical use of storytelling in the world of the *Metamorphoses*.

The historical context in which Ovid wrote may illuminate this conspicuous theme. It has been remarked that under Augustus "free speech, at least among the upper classes, was confined within increasingly narrow limits."[2] Nor were the poets of the Augustan Age unaware of governmental pressures to produce material favorable to the new regime.[3] It is naive to assume that Ovid did not recognize the political stakes. In the *Ars Amatoria* he affirms the propriety of the poem in terms that very

---

1. Cf. Fredericks 1977, 246.
2. Kenney 1982a, 297. Wallace-Hadrill (1982, 38) remarks that "since the execution of Cicero, no man had been free to speak against the dynast with power of life and death, except to the extent that he permitted it." Cf. A.J. Boyle, *Ramus* 16 (1987):1–3.
3. For imperial pressure on Virgil and Horace, see Suetonius *De poetis*.

precisely call that propriety into question (*Ars Am.* 1.31-34, 2.597-600, 3.611-16; cf. *Tr.* 2.246-56), and it has recently been suggested that the *Fasti* explore the limits of speech under tyranny.[4] Ovid's relegation to Tomis in A.D. 8, caused by his *carmen et error* (*Tr.* 2.207) can only have confirmed the essential nature of the Principate.[5]

Four years after Ovid's relegation to Tomis, the Senate ordered that the books of the historian and orator Labienus be burnt, a then-unprecedented event.

> In hoc primum excogitata est nova poena; effectum est enim per inimicos ut omnes eius libri comburerentur: res nova et invisitata supplicium de studiis sumi.... Facem studiis subdere et in monumenta disciplinarum animadvertere quanta et quam non contenta cetera materia saevitia est!... Eius qui hanc inscripta Labieni sententiam dixerat postea viventis adhuc scripta conbusta sunt: iam non malo exemplo quia suo. (Sen. *Contr.* 10. *pr.* 5.4, 7.1, 3)

> [In the (matter of T. Labienus) a new penalty was first devised; for his enemies brought about the burning of all his books: it was a new and unheard of matter for punishment to be exacted from literature.... How great—and how ill-contented with the rest of its powers—is the savagery that puts a torch to literature and directs its attention to monuments of learning!... But the writings of the senator who had proposed the burning of Labienus' books were themselves put to the torch later in his life: now not a bad example since it was his.]

The first century of the Principate was to see even more severe penalties applied in an effort to restrict free speech.[6]

---

4. D.C. Feeney, in correspondence, noting the Varronian derivation of *fas* and *fasti* from *for* / *fari* (*L.L.* 6.53).

5. There is a striking correspondence between Ovid's own fate as he reports it in the exile poetry (see, e.g., *Tr.* 2.103-6 and 3.5.49), and the doom of those who saw and told in the sequence of episodes at *Met.* 2.531-835. See further the observations of L. Cahoon, "The Parrot and the Poet: the Function of Ovid's Funeral Elegies," *CJ* 80 (1984):34, who connects Ovid's remarks in the exile poetry about his own inopportune loquacity with the *garrulitas* of the *psittacus* whose death is the focus of *Amores* 2.6.

6. See Tac. *Dial.* 2, *Agr.* 2-3, *Ann.* 4.34ff. and 15.49; Dio 47.22.5; and Phaedrus, *Fabulae* 3, Prol. 41ff.

Appendix 1

Swans in *Metamorphoses* 2

In antiquity, the song of the dying swan was regarded as especially beautiful, and the literary tradition in which Ovid wrote had, therefore, long associated the swan in its musical aspect first with the god Apollo, and then with poetry.[1] Ovid's immediate predecessors had gone still further in self-consciously identifying the songs of the swan with the compositions of the poet. Nisbet and Hubbard, commenting on Horace *C.* 2.20 (itself a remarkable "literalization" of the metaphor of the poet as swan), point out that the swan's connection with poetry was felt to be so close that "poets and other literary men are often compared or identified with swans."[2] The *Thesaurus Linguae Latinae* offers abundant evidence for this connection in the poetry of the earlier Augustan poets.[3]

Ovid too associates the song of the swan with the poet's literary production of song: indeed, examination of the occurrences of the swan's song in the Ovidian corpus suggests in each case the subtle evocation of song of a literary nature.[4] It has been suggested, therefore, that Ovid implies a connection between the swan's *carmina* and a poet's literary *carmina* with his first reference to the bird in the *Metamorphoses*.[5]

---

1. On the song of the dying swan, see Thompson 1936, 179-86, s.v. ΚΥΚΝΟΣ, and Arnott 1977. On the association between swans' songs and poetry, see Nisbet and Hubbard 1978, 333-34, *ad* Hor. *C.* 2.20, and Ahl 1982, 373-77.

2. Nisbet and Hubbard 1978, 342, *ad* Hor. *C.* 2.20.10.

3. On *cycnus,* see *TLL* 4.1585.16ff., and cf. *OLD* s.v. *cycnus* b. On *olor,* see *TLL* 9.2.572.15ff., and cf. *OLD* s.v. *olor* a. For the association in the Augustan poets see Virg. *Ecl.* 8.55, 9.29 (with Coleman 1977 *ad loc.*), and 9.36; Prop. 2.34.84; and Hor. *C.* 1.6 (with H. Jacobson, "Horace's Maeonian Song," *AJP* 108 [1987]:648), 4.2.25, and 4.3.20. Lucretius had already exploited the connection at *D.R.N.* 3.7, 4.181, and 4.910.

4. See *Her.* 7.1-2; *Met.* 5.386-87 with Hinds 1987, 44-48; *Met.* 14.429-30; *Fasti* 2.108-10; and *Tr.* 5.1.11-12. My examples do not include the three references to the swan in *Met.* 2 (252-53, 367-80, 539), since they are the focus of the following discussion.

5. Hinds 1987, 47, with full discussion at 149 n. 65. I have recapitulated and expanded

> et quae Maeonias celebrabant carmine ripas
> flumineae volucres, medio caluere Caystro.
>
> (*Met.* 2.252-53)

[And the water birds who filled up the Maeonian banks with song grew warm in the middle of the Caÿster.]

The *flumineae volucres* of this passage have been shown to enjoy an illustrious literary background. Ovid provides specific geographical information (*Maeonias... ripas /... medio... Caystro*) that allows the *doctus lector* to identify these unnamed river birds as swans. There is a great deal of literary evidence for the association of the swan with this part of Asia, and as early as the *Iliad* we find swans floating and singing on the river Caÿster.

> As the many nations of winged birds, geese or cranes or long-throated swans in the Asian meadow around the streams of the Caÿster, fly here and there delighting in their wings, then as they settle with a din the meadow resounds with them.... (*Iliad* 2.459-63)[6]

Ovid's unnamed river birds, then, bear an obvious affinity to the swans of the *Iliad*. The literary implications of Ovid's presentation of the "swans" at *Met.* 2.252-53 are further illuminated when placed in context against two lines from Lucretius' *De Rerum Natura*.

> et variae volucres, laetantia quae loca aquarum
> concelebrant circum ripas fontisque lacusque....
>
> (*D.R.N.* 2.344-45)

---

many of his arguments in order to prepare the ground for my reading of *Met.* 2.367-80, the passage in which Cygnus is transformed into the first swan.

6. ...ὥς τ' ὀρνίθων πετεηνῶν ἔθνεα πολλά,
χηνῶν ἢ γεράνων ἢ κύκνων δουλιχοδείρων,
Ἀσίῳ ἐν λειμῶνι, Καϋστρίου ἀμφὶ ῥέεθρα,
ἔνθα καὶ ἔνθα ποτῶνται ἀγαλλόμενα πτερύγεσσι,
κλαγγηδὸν προκαθιζόντων, σμαραγεῖ δέ τε λειμών.

(*Il.* 2.459-63)

On the association see in addition Strabo, *Geog.* 13.14.12; Virg. *Geo.* 1.383-84; Ovid, *Met.* 5.386-87 and *Tr.* 5.1.11-12; and Mart. 1.53.7-8.

[And the many-colored birds, which throng the delightful regions of water around river-banks, springs, and lakes. . . .]

The Lucretian lines point up the much more open signification of the Ovidian echo. Ovid's unnamed *flumineae volucres* are almost, but not quite, as general as Lucretius' unspecified *variae volucres*. For in two significant ways the Ovidian lines admit potential ambiguities that are inadmissible in the Lucretian passage. Our poet employs the simplex *celebro,* a verb frequently used by poets of poetic composition, rather than Lucretius' compound verb *concelebro,* and Ovid introduces a further undertone of literary composition with *carmine* (*Met.* 2.252). *Carmen* is normally understood to mean "bird-song" here; and *celebro* too, it is often assumed, retains the sense of "thronging" of Lucretius' compound verb *concelebro*.[7] However, the collocation *celebrabant carmine* (*Met.* 2.252) opens up the possibility that the poet may here activate another meaning, that the swans "make the Maeonian banks famous through their song."[8] Ovid's lines would thus go far beyond the Lucretian passage, with their suggestion that, in celebrating the Maeonian banks in their song, the swans are indulging in artistic production of a literary nature.[9]

Thus, at *Met.* 2.252-53 Ovid allusively suggests artistic production on the part of the swans, and he may complement this with a pointed reference to his own artistic production here. Our *doctus poeta* flirts in this passage with the possibility of an "error." F. Bömer, for example, takes Ovid to task for introducing swans at this point in the poem: "Die Schwäne am Kaystros sind ein 'poetischer Anachronismus': Erst II 373ff. wird Cycnus in einen Schwan verwandelt."[10] But we might, rather, credit

---

7. For *celebro* in the sense of fame accruing to the poet's literary composition, see *TLL* 3.746.52ff.; cf. *OLD* s.v. *celebro* 6. These undertones do not seem to be present in *concelebro*: see *TLL* 4.1.18.48ff. For *carmen* used of literary composition, see *TLL* 3.463.46ff. and 3.468.61ff.; cf. *OLD* s.v. *carmen* 2 and 3. For *carmen* of "bird-song," see *TLL* 3.469.12ff., and *OLD* s.v. *carmen* 4. Cf. Hinds 1987, 149 n. 65.

8. Hinds 1987, 149 n. 65.

9. Ovid modifies both the Lucretian passage (*D.R.N.* 2.344-45) and his own echo of it at *Met.* 2.252-53 later in the poem. In language that recalls the unspecified birds of Book 2 of the *Metamorphoses,* he mentions swans specifically: . . . *non illo plura Caystros / carmina cygnorum labentibus edit in undis,* "the river Caÿster does not produce more swans' songs in its waves than that lake" (*Met.* 5.386-87). Here an argument for the evocation of literary production also seems compelling: see the stimulating discussion of the poetic associations of these Ovidian swans by Hinds 1987, 44-48.

10. Bömer 1969, 306.

Ovid with great ingenuity at this point. He characterizes these birds as swans in every way except one: they are not so named (*flumineae volucres, Met.* 2.253). Thus Ovid creates the potential for error, Bömer's "poetischer Anachronismus," but then neatly sidesteps the error. Ovid playfully declines to call the birds swans at *Met.* 2.253 because swans do not yet exist in the world of the *Metamorphoses*. Cygnus will not be transformed into the first swan until the end of the story of Phaethon, one hundred lines later (*Met.* 2.367-80). Moreover, when our poet does narrate the (first) metamorphosis of Cygnus, he pointedly asserts that this is a new bird: *fit nova Cygnus avis*, "Cygnus became a new bird" (*Met.* 2.377).[11]

Thus in his first reference to swans in the *Metamorphoses*, Ovid playfully explores the possibilities of artistic self-definition that had already been exploited in the poetry of his predecessors, and the subsequent metamorphosis of the Ligurian prince Cygnus offers a second opportunity to reflect on the artistic process.[12]

> ... ille relicto
> (nam Ligurum populos et magnas rexerat urbes)
> imperio ripas virides amnemque querellis
> Eridanum inplerat silvamque sororibus auctam,
> cum vox est tenuata viro canaeque capillos
> dissimulant plumae.... (*Met.* 2.369-74)

[... Cygnus, abandoning his kingdom (for he had ruled over the peoples and great cities of the Ligurians), filled the green river-banks and the stream, the Eridanos, with plaintive songs, as well as the forest created by Phaethon's transformed sisters, when his voice grew thin and white feathers hid his hair....]

Cygnus' metamorphosis begins with the transformation of his *vox*, which is thinned or attenuated (*tenuata*) in the process. The adjective *tenuis*, along with its related forms, is one of the Latin translations of the Greek λεπτός, a word that had acquired a precise literary-critical sense in

---

11. There are, as is well known, three metamorphoses into swans in the course of the poem: the first (which I discuss here) occurs at *Met.* 2.367-80; the second at *Met.* 7.371-81; and the third at *Met.* 12.71-167.

12. The story of Phaethon's death and the metamorphosis of his lover Cygnus enjoyed considerable popularity with the Hellenistic poets and historians. See Wiseman 1979, 163 for a summary of the development of the story.

Callimachean poetics.[13] The Callimachean concept, which characterizes the "lightness" and "delicacy" of the poetic touch, was taken up by Catullus and remained an important and well-known concept in Augustan literary criticism.[14] Ovid here attributes to the swan a poetic quality of the foremost importance to the Augustan heirs of Callimachus' poetics, a *vox tenuis,* and in this way our poet may obliquely evoke the swan's poetic powers.

Can we go further in our analysis and identify the specific genre with which the swan is implicitly associated by Ovid? The programmatically

---

13. For *tenuis* = λεπτός, see Hor. *Epist.* 2.1.225; Virgil *Geo.* 4.6 with Thomas 1985, 70, and *Aen.* 7.14 with Thomas 1985, 66; and Ovid, *Tr.* 2.327. The most prominent programmatic occurrence of λεπτός (or rather, of a related form) in Callimachus' poetry occurs in the *Aetia* Prologue:

καὶ γὰρ ὅτε πρώτιστον ἐμοῖς ἐπὶ δέλτον ἔθηκα
γούνασι, Ἀπόλλων εἶπεν ὅ μοι Λύκιος·
"..........] ἀοιδέ, τὸ μὲν θύος ὅττι πάχιστον
θρέψαι, τὴ]ν Μοῦσαν δ' ὠγαθὲ λεπταλέην·"

(fr. 1.21-24 Pf.)

[For when I first set my writing-tablet upon my knees, Lycian Apollo said to me: "poet, feed the sacrificial victim so that it may be as fat as possible, but the Muse, my good fellow, keep her slender."]

Another such programmatic usage of the word by Callimachus occurs at *Epigr.* 27.3 (Pf.) in praise of Aratus: χαίρετε λεπταί / ῥήσιες, Ἀρήτου σύμβολον ἀγρυπνίης, "hail subtle discourses, token of Aratus' sleeplessness." Cf. also frs. 228.14, 1.11 (Pf.), and *Hymn* 3.243. For modern discussion of λεπτός as a Callimachean literary critical term, see Reitzenstein 1931; Jacques 1960, 48-61; and Pfeiffer 1968, 137.

14. Catullus' generation of Latin poets took a renewed interest in this critical debate, as is clear from a bilingual pun at the beginning of Catullus' dedicatory poem: *Cui dono lepidum novum libellum,* "to whom do I give this newly polished witty little book of mine?" (Cat. 1.1). Wiseman (1979, 169-70, and 1985, 183 n. 2, with the bibliography collected there) has shown that *lepidum* is here equivalent to λεπτός. For the relevance of λεπτός to the literary critical debate of the "neoteric" and Augustan Latin poets see Wimmel 1960; Clausen 1964, 193-95; Latta 1972, 204 and 210-13; Ross 1975, 26-30; and Thomas 1983, 107. For bibliography on this nexus of Augustan literary critical terms and for discussion of their significance in the literary climate of the day, see Wimmel 1960, and, more recently, Hinds 1987, 21-22, with 141 n. 58 and the references collected there.

There is a striking parallel for the implicit generic classification which, it has been suggested, can be understood at *Met.* 2.367-80, later in the poem at *Met.* 5.320. There the Pierids, in poetic competition with the Muses, are reported to have offered a song in which they denigrate the deeds of the gods: ... *extenuat magnorum facta deorum,* "she belittled the deeds of the great gods" (*Met.* 5.320). Hinds suggests that a wordplay on the verb *extenuat* may raise the possibility that the Pierid's song was rather more successful than the Muse who reports it allows: see Hinds 1987, 166 n. 40 (*contra* Hofmann 1985, 228).

suggestive *tenuata* (*Met.* 2.373) points to one of the "slighter" genres of Augustan literary output (i.e., lyric or elegy rather than epos and tragedy),[15] and the context of Cygnus' transformation provides a second important clue. Cygnus' metamorphosis occurs as he laments the death of his kinsman Phaethon, and the genre that is most closely and most frequently associated with mourning in the ancient literary tradition is the "humble" genre of elegy.[16] This association is frequently alluded to in the poetry of the Roman elegists.[17] In the *Ars Poetica,* Horace too points explicitly to the connection: *versibus impariter iunctis querimonia primum,* "in verses joined unequally elegiac lamentations were first composed" (*Ars Poetica* 75).

---

15. On the place of tragedy in Callimachus' poetics, see Thomas 1979.

16. The association is made as early as the end of the fifth century B.C. (see Eur. *Hel.* 184ff., and Ar. *Av.* 218) and arose from the ancient etymologies that derived elegy, the Greek ἐλεγία, from ἔλεος or ἒ ἒ λέγειν: see, for example, the *Et. Mag.* 326.48ff. Cf. Varro's discussion of ἐλεγία in *De poematis* (*GRF* fr. 303):

nam et elegia extrema mortuo accinebatur sicuti nenia, ideoque ab eadem elogium videtur tractum cognominari, quod mortuis vel morituris ascribitur novissimum....

[for an elegy, like a dirge, is sung at the last to the dead; and therefore the word *elogium* ("epitaph") seems to have been derived from the same root, because it is written at the last for the dead or those about to die....]

The true etymology of ἐλεγία remains obscure: see Frisk 486 and Chantraine 334. For modern discussion of the origins of elegy and its associations with mourning see D. Page, *Greek Poetry and Life* (Oxford 1936), 206–30; *R-E* 5.2261ff. For the exploitation of this etymological connection in the poetry of the Augustan poets (especially Horace) see Nisbet and Hubbard 1970, 371 *ad* Hor. *C.* 1.33.2; Brink 1971, 165–67, on Hor. *Ars Poetica* 75–78; and, in Ovid, Hinds 1987, 103–4.

17. See, for example, Cat. 65.12 with Wiseman 1969, 14–18, Prop. 1.5, 1.6, 1.22, and 3.25; cf. also Hor. *Epod.* 11.12, *C.* 1.33.1–4, 2.9.17, and 3.11.52. It has been plausibly suggested that Propertius' fascination with death can be read, on one level, in terms of this etymologically derived association of the genre. Ovid himself explicitly alludes to the association of elegy as a song of lament most notably at the beginning of his elegy on Tibullus' death, especially, *flebilis indignos, Elegia, solve capillos,* "Elegy, accompanied by tears, untie your undeserving hair" (*Am.* 3.9.3). These are also the terms in which Domitius Marsus describes Tibullus as an elegiac poet, one "who bewailed tender loves in his elegies" (*elegis molles qui fleret amores,* fr. 9 M). Cf. also Fedeli 1981, 229–30 and 240 n. 12.

Erotic elegy was not the only arena in which the Latin poets gestured towards the supposed origins of the genre, as the examples from Horace collected just above demonstrate. Conte has suggested that Virgil too takes part in the discussion at *Geo.* 4.525–27: see Conte 1986, 137 n. 8. Cf. also *Her.* 15.7 which, although not Ovidian as Tarrant (1981) has shown, also acknowledges the association.

The lexical choices of our poet, himself a distinguished writer of elegiac poetry, suggest that Ovid may here implicitly characterize the swan as an elegiac poet. Cygnus wanders aimlessly lamenting Phaethon's death: *ille... ripas virides amnemque querellis / Eridanum inplerat...*, "he filled up the green river-banks and stream, the Eridanus, with plaintive songs" (*Met.* 2.369–72).[18] The noun *querella* can designate funereal plaint as well as simple complaint, and it is also frequently used by both Propertius and Ovid to evoke the plaintive tone of elegiac poetry.[19] It is tempting, therefore, to understand in *querella* an allusive evocation of the genre of elegy. Moreover, the syntax here suggestively parallels that of the earlier passage in which we saw the (unnamed) swans celebrate the Caÿster in song (*Met.* 2.252–53). Once again Ovid employs a noun in the ablative that is evocative of poetic composition (*querellis, Met.* 2.371; cf. *carmine, Met.* 2.252), and he employs as the direct object a river and its environs already associated in the literary tradition with musical swans (*amnem... Eridanum, Met.* 2.371–72; cf. *Maeonias... ripas /... medio... Caystro, Met.* 2.252–53).[20] Finally, Ovid may even have chosen the verb *elegit* (*Met.* 2.380) to close his description of Cygnus' metamorphosis, in order to suggest a punning reference to the swan's powers of poetic, and specifically elegiac, composition.[21]

stagna petit patulosque lacus ignemque perosus,
quae colat, elegit contraria flumina flammis.

(*Met.* 2.379–80)

---

18. I note in passing the identical phraseology with which Ovid describes Ceres lamenting Proserpina at *Fasti* 4.481-82:... *miseris loca cuncta querellis / implet,* "she filled up all the places with woeful plaints." See Hinds 1987, 105, 119–20, and 162–63 n. 10, where he demonstrates the generic self-consciousness of the context in which these lines occur in the *Fasti.*

There is considerable humor as well, in having the newly created swan—whose musical *forte* was considered by the ancients to be the song sung at the moment of his own imminent death (whence our "swan-song")—offer a "swan-song" whose subject is Phaethon's recent death.

19. See Saylor 1967, who shows that Propertius uses *querela* in the technical sense of "elegy"; on which see also Fedeli 1981, 229–30, with 240 n. 12, and 232–33. For *querela* in Ovid see the assessment of the specifically elegiac force of *querela* in *Her.* 1 by Baca 1969, and, in the *Heroides* as a collection, by Anderson 1973, 69, with n. 11 and p. 82. Cf. also Conte 1986, 100–29, and 137 n. 8.

20. For the association of the Caÿster with musical swans, see above n. 6. For musical swans on the Eridanus, see Virg. *Aen.* 11.457–58, and Wiseman 1979, 163.

21. The difference in the quantities of the vowels is unimportant in ancient etymologizing: see Chap. 3 n. 2.

[He seeks pools and open lakes, and hating fire he chose rivers, the opposite of flames, to make his home in.]

Virgil too, in his treatment of Cygnus' metamorphosis, had already played overtly with the figure of the swan as poet, and Virgil's characterization of Cygnus is, like Ovid's, as an elegiac poet.

Non ego te, Ligurum ductor fortissime bello,
transierim, Cunare, et paucis comitate Cupavo,
cuius olorinae surgunt de vertice pennae
(crimen, Amor, vestrum) formaeque insigne paternae.
namque ferunt luctu Cycnum Phaethontis amati,
populeas inter frondes umbramque sororum
dum canit et maestum Musa solatur amorem,
canentem molli pluma duxisse senectam
linquentem terras et sidera voce sequentem.

(*Aen.* 10.185–93)

[I could not pass over you, Cunarus, bravest captain of the Ligurians in pitched battle, and, accompanied by few companions, you, Cupavo, from whose crest rise swan's feathers (a reproach to you, Amor), the mark of his father's form. For they say that while Cycnus sang in grief for his beloved Phaethon, amid the leafy poplars in the shade cast by his sisters, and while he solaced his unhappy love with song, there stole over him white-haired old age in soft plumage, and he left the earth, pursuing the stars with his song.]

Virgil's Cygnus is provoked to song, *canit et... Musa solatur amorem* (*Aen.* 10.191), in his grief after the death of Phaethon, *luctu Cycnum Phaethontis amati* (*Aen.* 10.189). Virgil, however, has followed a version of the myth in which Phaethon and Cygnus are lovers, and we may note also the learned footnote *ferunt,* at *Aen.* 10.189.[22] This allows Virgil to overdetermine the elegiac quality of Cygnus' song by combining the elegiac motifs of love and mourning, for the motifs occur together twice in this passage (*luctu... amati, Aen.* 10.189; *maestum... amorem, Aen.* 10.191). Moreover, Virgil's parenthetical address to Love, *crimen, Amor, vestrum,* conjures up an Amor strikingly similar to the god of the elegiac

---

22. On this version see Wiseman 1979, 163.

poets.²³ Finally, Virgil's account connects the whiteness of Cygnus' new feathers to his singing via a contrametrical pun on *cano*, "sing," and *caneo*, "become white," in the phrase *canentem molli pluma ... senectam* (*Aen.* 10.192).²⁴ Ovid's characterization of Cygnus, then, follows Virgil's in making Cygnus an elegiac poet, and in offering a contrametrical pun that alludes to the connection between the swan's song and the poet's composition of poetry.

However this final suggestion is viewed, it seems clear that Ovid has taken great care not only to cross-reference his descriptions of the swan in their first two appearances in the second book of the *Metamorphoses,* but also to evoke the swan's powers of literary production in both passages. Each of the two passages assumes a greater significance when read against the other, and the third and final appearance of the swan in this book of the *Metamorphoses* glances briefly backwards to the earlier swans.

nam fuit haec quondam niveis argentea pennis
ales [i.e., corvus], ut aequaret totas sine labe columbas
nec servaturis vigili Capitolia voce
cederet anseribus nec amanti flumina cygno.
(*Met.* 2.536-39)

[For at one time this bird, the raven, was silver-hued with white feathers, so that it could equal doves entirely without stain, nor would it yield to geese, birds who would prove saviors of the Capitoline with their watchful cry, nor to the river-loving swan.]

Ovid is careful, in his comparison of the raven to the swan, to allude to that feature of the swan's character with which he had concluded the metamorphosis of Cygnus. Thus *amanti flumina cygno* (*Met.* 2.539) pointedly refers the reader to the closing lines of Cygnus' metamorphosis (*elegit contraria flumina flammis, Met.* 2.380), as well as to the first reference to "swans" as *flumineae volucres* (*Met.* 2.253). The poet's playful connections between swans gently articulate the movement of the second book of the poem, distinguishing the Phaethon episode (*Met.*

---

23. Cf. Prop. 1.1.4, 17, 34 and 1.7.25-26; Ovid, *Am.* 1.1.3-4 and 2.8.
24. On *cano*, "sing," see *TLL* 3.263.79ff.; on *caneo*, "become white," see *TLL* 3.249.12ff. Cf. Ahl 1985, 33.

2.1–366) from the Callisto episode (*Met.* 2.401–530), and the Callisto episode from the final sequence of stories (*Met.* 2.535–835). The swans thus provide the second book of the *Metamorphoses* itself with its own internal narrative rhythm.

Appendix 2

The Cercopes

Striking correspondences in subject matter between the first and fifteenth books of the *Metamorphoses* have long been recognized,[1] but recent discussions of the organization of the poem as a whole have begun to suggest that such ring compositional structures pervade the poem, rather than being restricted to the opening and closing books. Thus Davis has documented several points of contact between Books 1 and 2 and Book 15, while Crabbe, in addition to noting correspondences between the first and fifteenth books, discusses the concentric thematic structuration of Book 7 and Book 9 around the central Book 8.[2] This study of the sequence of episodes at *Met.* 2.531-835 has contributed to an understanding of the overall ring structure of the poem in two ways: first, by analyzing the links between Ocyroe's prophecy in Book 2 and its fulfillment in Book 15 (though without reference to ring composition, since this is well discussed by Davis); and second, by noting Ocyroe's close resemblance to the Sibyl in Book 14.[3] There remains, of course, considerable work to be done in this area, but this Appendix is restricted to a discussion of some points of contact between the sequence of episodes at *Met.* 2.531-835 and the brief account of the Cercopes narrated at *Met.* 14.82-100, in order to bring out a further link between Books 2 and 14.

After a mere four-line reference to the Trojan stay at Carthage (*Met.* 14.78-81), Ovid charts Aeneas' course up the coast of Italy towards

---

1. On ring composition in the *Metamorphoses,* see Fränkel 1945, 109-10; Wilkinson 1955, 147-48 and 223-24; Ludwig 1965, 32-83; Otis 1970, 34-90 and 357-61; and Coleman 1971, 462 and 476. See now also Feeney 1991.
2. See Davis 1980 and Crabbe 1983.
3. See Chap. 3, and cf. Davis 1980, 131.

147

Cumae and the Cumaean Sibyl (*Met.* 14.82-103). En route, Aeneas skirts the island of Pithecusae, which, we are told, takes its name from the apes (Greek πίθηκοι) said to inhabit it. Ancient tradition explained that these apes were originally a race of men, the Cercopes, who had been transformed into monkeys in punishment for their acts of verbal deception.

In the 'Kerkopes' ascribed to Homer, it is related that the Kerkopes were deceivers and liars. Xenagoras says that they were transformed into apes and the Ape-Islands, 'Pithecusae,' took their name from them. Aeschines the Sardian recorded their names as Andoulos and Atlantos in his iambic verses.[4]

Ovid's brief account of the Cercopes' transformation at *Met.* 14.82-100 accords very closely with Harpocration's notice.

>   ... orbataque praeside pinus
> Inarimen Prochytenque legit sterilique locatas
> colle Pithecusas habitantum nomine dictas.
> quippe deum genitor fraudem et periuria quondam
> Cercopum exosus gentisque admissa dolosae
> in deforme viros animal mutavit, ut idem
> dissimiles homini possent similesque videri,
> membraque contraxit naresque a fronte resimas
> contudit et rugis peraravit anilibus ora
> totaque velatos flaventi corpora villo
> misit in has sedes nec non prius abstulit usum
> verborum et natae dira in periuria linguae:
> posse queri tantum rauco stridore reliquit.
>
> (*Met.* 14.88-100)

[... the pine-built ship, deprived of its pilot, sailed close past the islands of Inarime and Prochyte, and Pithecusae situated on a barren

---

4. ἐν τοῖς εἰς Ὅμηρον ἀναφερομένοις Κέρκωψιν δηλοῦται ὡς ἐξαπατητῆρές τε ἦσαν καὶ ψεῦσται οἱ Κέρκωπες. Ξεναγόρας δὲ εἰς πιθήκους αὐτοὺς μεταβαλεῖν φησί, καὶ τὰς Πιθηκούσσας νήσους ἀπ' αὐτῶν κληθῆναι. Αἰσχίνης δ' ὁ Σαρδιανὸς ἐν τοῖς ἰάμβοις καὶ τὰ ὀνόματα αὐτῶν ἀναγράφει, Ἄνδουλον καὶ Ἄτλαντον (Harp. 1, p. 174 Dindorf, s.v. Κέρκωψ). Other accounts connect the Kerkopes with Herakles: see Plut. *Mor.* 60B (and cf. *SH* 17) and Diotimus Adramyttenus Ἡρακλέους Ἆθλα (= *SH* 394).

hill and named after its inhabitants. For once the father of the gods, hating the deceit and lies of the Cercopes, and all the crimes of that treacherous race, transformed them into a misshapen animal so that they might seem at the same time like and unlike men. He shortened their limbs, crushed their noses until they were turned up, marked their faces with the wrinkles typical of an old woman, and sent them covered in yellow fur to this island; but first he deprived them of the use of words and their tongues designed for dreadful perjury: he left them able to utter only harsh shrieks in complaint.]

Specifying the Cercopes' faults as deceit and lies (*Met.* 14.91), Ovid concludes with the moral that abuse of the *usus vocis* resulted in their punishment by transformation into apes. Now the cause of the Cercopes' punishment is remarkably similar to those of each of the characters in the sequence of episodes at *Met.* 2.531-835. The crow is punished because of her misuse of speech; the raven's tongue brings about his metamorphosis from white to black; Ocyroe's misuse of her prophetic gifts angers the gods and prompts her transformation into a mare; Battus' verbal indiscretion results in his petrifaction; and the Cecropid Aglauros' abusive words to Mercury are the immediate cause of her own transformation to stone. There is, of course, a significant difference between the characters of *Met.* 2.531-835, who are punished for their illicit but truthful disclosure of secrets, and the Cercopes in Book 14 of the *Metamorphoses*, who are explicitly characterized as liars. Nonetheless, abuse of the *usus vocis* is an infrequent charge in the *Metamorphoses*, and the brief thematic recapitulation of the close of Book 2 at the opening of Book 14 thus contributes significantly to the ring structure of the poem as a whole.[5]

Even more striking, perhaps, than the thematic correspondence between the two passages is the verbal correspondence of syllabic recapitulation. For the Cercopes (*Met.* 14.92), after all, have a name that is remarkably close to that of Cecrops, whose daughters, the Cecropids—Aglauros, Pandrosos, and Herse—play such a prominent role in both

---

5. The motif of the misused *vox* is not a constant structural characteristic in the *indicium* paradigm analyzed by Davis (1969, 18-63), for it does not recur outside the sequence of episodes at *Met.* 2.531-835. The only other example of perjury in the poem is Laomedon's *perfidiae cumulum, falsis periuria verbis* (*Met.* 11.206), a story that is narrated fully at *Met.* 11.194-220. There the theme is inherited from the literary tradition, and it is deployed at the start of the Trojan narrative as the poem's strict chronological sequentiality demands.

the opening and closing episodes of the sequence of tales at *Met.* 2.531–835. Moreover, that sequence of episodes has an unusually large cast of characters whose names participate in syllabic play around the consonantal configuration c—r: the raven *corvus* (*Met.* 2.535, 596, 632), the crow *cornix* (*Met.* 2.548), Apollo's beloved Coronis (*Met.* 2.542, 599), the daughters of Cecrops (*Met.* 2.555, 784, 797, 806), the daughter of Coroneus (*Met.* 2.569, whether her name is the Greek word for crow, Corone/κορώνη or the patronymic Coronis), the centaur Chiron (*Met.* 2.630), his wife Chariclo (*Met.* 2.636), and his daughter Ocyroe (*Met.* 2.638).[6] This suggestion need not be rejected out of hand because Battus' name cannot be inserted neatly into the paradigm, for the very fluidity of the shifting associations, thematic and syllabic, among the sequence of episodes at *Met.* 2.531–835 is appropriate in a poem whose fundamental subject is change. Rather, the recognition of thematic and syllabic recapitulation of *Met.* 2.531–835 at *Met.* 14.82–100 can enrich our understanding of how Ovid weaves poetic order out of narrative disorder and an aesthetically satisfying continuity out of the discontinuity of episodic narrative in the *Metamorphoses*.

---

6. On variation in syllabic vowel and vowel quantity in ancient wordplay, see Chap. 3 n. 2.

Appendix 3
Text of Callimachus' *Hecale*
(Hollis frr. 70-74)

5 μέσφ' ὅτε Κεκροπίδ[η]σιν επ......κατρλ.αν
   λάθριον ἄρρητον, γενεῇ δ' ὅθεν οὔτε νιν ἔγνων
   οὔτ' ἐδάην φ.........ωγαγιρυσε....υται
   οἰωνούς, ὡς δῆθεν ὑφ' Ἡφαίστῳ τέκε Γαῖα.
   τουτάκι δ' ἡ μὲν ἑῆς ἔρυμα χθονὸς ὄφρα βάλοιτο,
10 τήν ῥα νέον ψήφῳ τε Διὸς δυοκαίδεκά τ'ἄλλων
   ἀθανάτων ὄφιός τε κατέλλαβε μαρτυρίῃσιν,
   Πελλήνην ἐφίκανεν Ἀχαιΐδα· τόφρα δὲ κοῦραι
   αἱ φυλακοὶ κακὸν ἔργον ἐπεφράσσαντο τελέσσαι
   κ.ιστη....[.].....ακαδ......ανεισαι
           (Hollis fr. 70.5-14; = *SH* 288.19-29; 260.19-29 Pf.)

   ἡ μὲν ἀερτάζουσα μέγα τρύφος Ὑψιζώρου
   ἄστυρον εἰσανέβαινεν, ἐγὼ δ' ἤντησα Λυκείου
   καλὸν ἀεὶ λιπόωντα κατὰ δρόμον Ἀπόλλωνος
           (Hollis fr. 71; = *SH* 289; 261 Pf.)

   ἡ δὲ πελιδνωθεῖσα καὶ ὄμμασι λοξὸν ὑποδράξ
   ὀσσομένη
           (Hollis fr. 72; = 374 Pf.)

5 ....ν.ς
   ......ουναι δὲ παραπ.......κορῶναι
   δ.......ου γὰρ ἔγωγε τεόν ποτε πότνια θυμόν
   ....πολλὰ παραίσια μήπο[τ]' ἐλαφροί
   ......οἰωνοί, τότε δ' ὤφελον ε............

10 .υτω.[..].τερην μὲ[ν] ἀπε...ευ......
    ἡμετερ[..] ἐκλειν..ε....λλ..ε.οι
    μηδ[έ] ποτ' ἐκ θυμοῖο· βαρὺς χόλος αἰὲν Ἀθήνης.
    αὐτὰρ ἐγὼ τυτθὸς παρέῃ[ν] γόνο[ς· ὀ]γδ[ο]άτ[η] γάρ
    ἤδη μοι γενεὴ π...δε..[..]ευ..... .
15   ]...ε.
        (Hollis fr. 73; = SH 288.30-43A; 260.30-43 Pf.)

    γαστέρι μ[ο]ῦνον ἔ]χοιμι κ[ακῆς ἀλκτήρια λιμοῦ
    .]δουμεχ[..... .]έχειδο[
    ἀ]λλ' Ἐκάλ[η..].ε λιτὸν εδ.[
    ...ακ[..... .]νον παγ.[
 5 καὶ κ[ρῖμν]ο[ν] κυκεῶνος ἀπ[ο]στάξαντος ἔραζε
    ..].μησ[....]. οὔτις ἐπέσσεται[
    ...]θων[....]γ[ι] κακάγγελον· εἴθε γὰρ [εἴης
    κεῖν[ον ἔτι] ζώουσα κατὰ χρόνον, ὄφρα τ[....]ης
    ὣς Θρ[ιαὶ τὴν] ἐπιπνείουσι κορών[ην.
10 ναὶ μὰ τ[όν]—οὐ γάρ [π]ω πάντ' ἤματα—ναὶ [μ]ὰ τὸ ῥικνόν
    σῦφαρ ἐμόν, ναὶ το[ῦτ]ο τὸ δένδρ[ε]ον αὖον ἐόν περ—
    οὐκ ἤδη ῥυμόν τε κ[α]ὶ ἄξονα καυάξαντες
    ἠέλιοι δυ[σ]μέων εἴσω πόδα πάντες ἔχουσι,
    δ]<ε>ίελος ἀλλ' ἢ νὺξ ἢ ἔνδιος ἢ ἔσετ' ἠώς
15 εὖτε κόραξ, ὅς νῦν γε καὶ ἂν κύκνοισιν ἐρίζοι
    καὶ γάλακι χροιὴν καὶ κύματος ἄκρωι ἀώτωι,
    κυάνεον φὴ πίσσαν ἐπὶ πτερὸν οὐλοὸν ἕξει,
    ἀγγελίης ἐπίχειρα τά οἵ ποτε Φοῖβος ὀπάσσει
    ὁππότε κεν Φλεγύαο Κορωνίδος ἀμφὶ θυγατρός
20 Ἰσχυϊ πληξίππῳ σπομένης μιαρόν τι πύθηται."
    τὴν μὲν ἄρ' ὣς φαμένην ὕπνος λάβε, τὴν δ' ἀΐουσαν.
        (Hollis fr. 74.1-21; = SH 288.43B-62; 346, 260.44-62, 351 Pf.)

At fr. 73.13, ὀ]γδ[ο]άτ[η] is the reconstruction of Gomperz. Hollis follows Lloyd-Jones and Parsons 1983, 132 in reading γόνο[ς.] .δ[.]...γάρ, and he includes their comment (p. 133) 42 *fin. vestigia minima*. Both Lloyd-Jones and Parsons 1983 and Hollis 1990, 242 find Gomperz' suggestion attractive.

Bibliography

Ahl, F. 1982. "Amber, Avallon, and Apollo's Singing Swan." *AJP* 103:373-411.
———. 1985. *Metaformations: Soundplay and Wordplay in Ovid and Other Classical Poets.* Ithaca, N.Y.
Altieri, C. 1973. "Ovid and the New Mythologists." *Novel* 7:31-40
Alton, E.H., D.E.W. Wormell, and E. Courtney, eds. 1978. *Ovidius, Fasti.* Leipzig.
Anderson, W.S. 1963. "Multiple Change in the *Metamorphoses.*" *TAPA* 94:1-27.
———. 1968. Review of *Ovid as an Epic Poet,* by B. Otis. *AJP* 89:93-104.
———. 1969. Review of *Beobachtungen zur Darstellungsart in Ovids Metamorphosen,* by E.J. Bernbeck. *AJP* 90:352-55.
———. 1971. Review of *Landscape in Ovid's Metamorphoses,* by C.P. Segal. *AJP* 92:685-92.
———. 1973. "The *Heroides.*" In *Ovid,* ed. J.W. Binns. Greek and Latin Studies: Classical Literature and Its Influence. London.
———, ed. 1977. *Ovidius, Metamorphoses.* Leipzig.
André, J. 1975. "Ovide helléniste et linguiste." *Rev. Phil.* 49:191-95.
Arnott, W.G. 1977. "Swan Songs." *Greece and Rome* 24:149-53.
Auerbach, E. 1953. *Mimesis.* Trans. W.R. Trask. Princeton. Originally published as *Mimesis.* Berne, 1946.
Avery, M.M. 1937. *The Use of Direct Speech in Ovid's Metamorphoses.* Chicago.
Baca, A.R. 1969. "Ovid's Claim to Originality and *Heroides* I." *TAPA* 100:1-10.
Bakhtin, M.M. 1981. *The Dialogic Imagination.* Trans. C. Emerson and M. Holquist, Austin. Originally published as *Voprosy literatury i estetiki.* Moscow, 1975.
Bal, M. 1985. *Narratology, Introduction to the Theory of Narrative.* Trans. C. van Boheemen, Toronto. Originally published as *De theorie van vertellen en verhalen.* Muiderberg, 1980.
Barchiesi, A. 1989. "Voci e istanze narrative nelle Metamorfosi di Ovidio." *MD* 23:55-97.
Barigazzi, A. 1954. "Sull' Ecale di Callimaco." *Hermes* 82:308-30.

Barsby, J.A. 1978. *Ovid.* Greece and Rome New Surveys in the Classics 12. Oxford.
Bartelink, G.J.M. 1965. *Eymologisering Bij Virgilius.* Mededelingen der Kon. Neder. Akad. van Wetenschappen, Deel 28, no. 3. Amsterdam.
Barthes, R. 1970. *S/Z.* Paris.
———. 1977. "Introduction to the Structural Analysis of Narratives." In *Image-Music-Text.* Trans. S. Heath. New York.
Bernbeck, E.J. 1967. *Beobachtungen zur Darstellungsart in Ovids Metamorphosen.* Zetemata 43. Munich.
Bethe, E. 1904. "Ovid und Nikander." *Hermes* 39:1-14.
Boillat, M. 1976. *Les Métamorphoses d'Ovide: Thèmes majeurs et problèmes de composition.* Bern and Frankfurt.
Bömer, F., ed. 1957-58. *P. Ovidius Naso, die Fasten.* Wissenschaftliche Kommentare zu lateinischen und griechischen Schriftstellern. 2 vols. Heidelberg.
———. 1968. "Ovid und die Sprache Virgils." In *Ovid.* See von Albrecht and Zinn 1968.
———. 1969-86. *P. Ovidius Naso, Metamorphosen.* Wissenschaftliche Kommentare zu griechischen und lateinischen Schriftstellern. 7 vols. Heidelberg.
Brandt, P., ed. 1902. *P. Ovidi Nasonis, De Arte Amatoria Libri Tres.* Leipzig.
Bréguet, E. 1969. *"Urbi et Orbi." Hommages à Marcel Renard,* Collection Latomus 101:141-52. Brussels.
Brenkman, J. 1976. "Narcissus in the Text." *Georgia Review* 30:293-327.
Brink, C.O., ed. 1971. *Horace on Poetry: The "Ars Poetica."* Cambridge.
Brown, N.O. 1947. *Hermes the Thief.* Madison.
Buchheit, V. 1966. "Mythos und Geschichte in Ovids Metamorphosen I." *Hermes* 94:80-108.
Bulloch, A.W. 1985. "Hellenistic Poetry." In *Greek Literature,* edited by P.E. Easterling and B.M.W. Knox. The Cambridge History of Classical Literature 1. Cambridge.
Burkert, W. 1983. *Homo Necans.* Trans. P. Bing. Berkeley and Los Angeles.
———. 1985. *Greek Religion.* Trans. J. Raffan. Cambridge, Mass.
Cairns, F. 1973. "Catullus' *Basia* Poems (5, 7, 48)." *Mnemosyne* 26:15-22.
———. 1979a. "Self-Imitation within a Generic Framework: Ovid, *Amores* 2.9 and 3.11 and the *renuntiatio amoris."* In *Creative Imitation and Latin Literature,* edited by D.A. West and A.J. Woodman. Cambridge.
———. 1979b. *Tibullus: A Hellenistic Poet at Rome.* Cambridge.
Cameron, A. 1968. "The First Edition of Ovid's *Amores." CQ* n.s. 18:320-33.
Castellani, V. 1980. "Two Divine Scandals: Ovid *Met.* 2.680 ff. and 4.171 ff. and His Sources." *TAPA* 110:37-50.
Castiglioni, L. 1906. *Studi intorno alle fonti e alla composizione delle Metamorfosi de Ovidio.* Pisa.
Cazzaniga, I., ed. 1962. *Antoninus Liberalis, Metamorphoseon Synagoge.* Milan.
Clausen, W.V. 1964. "Callimachus and Latin Poetry." *GRBS* 5:181-96.
Clayman, D.L. 1980. *Callimachus' Iambi.* Leiden.
Coleman, R.G.G. 1971. "Structure and Intention in the *Metamorphoses." CQ* n.s. 21:461-77.

———, ed. 1977. *The Eclogues of Virgil*. Cambridge.
Collart, J., ed. 1978. *Varron, Grammaire Antique et Stylistique Latine*. Paris.
Commager, S. 1981. "Fateful Words: Some Conversations in *Aeneid* 4." *Arethusa* 14:101-14.
Conte, G.B. 1986. *The Rhetoric of Imitation: Genre and Poetic Memory in Virgil and Other Latin Poets*. Cornell Studies in Classical Philology 44. Ithaca, N.Y.
Crabbe, A. 1983. "Structure and Content in Ovid's *Metamorphoses*." In *Aufstieg und Niedergang der römischen Welt*, edited by H. Temporini and W. Haase. Band II.31.4:2274-2327. Berlin.
Crump, M.M. 1931. *The Epyllion from Theocritus to Ovid*. Oxford.
Davis, N.G.G. 1969. *Studies in the Narrative Economy of Ovid's Metamorphoses*. Ph.D. diss., University of California, Berkeley.
———. 1980. "The Problem of Closure in a *Carmen Perpetuum*. Aspects of Thematic Recapitulation in Ovid *Met*. 15." *Grazer Beiträge* 9:123-32.
———. 1983. *The Death of Procris: "Amor" and the Hunt in Ovid's Metamorphoses*. Rome.
de Cola, M. 1937. *Callimaco e Ovidio*. Palermo.
de Jong. I.J.F. 1987. *Narrators and Focalizers. The Presentation of the Story in the Iliad*. Amsterdam.
de Saint-Denis, E. 1940. "La génie d'Ovid d'après le livre XV des Métamorphoses." *REL* 18:111-40.
Dickie, M.W. 1975. "Ovid, *Metamorphoses* 2.760-764." *AJP* 96:378-90.
———. 1981. "The Disavowal of *Invidia* in Roman Iamb and Satire." *PLLS* 3:183-208.
———. 1983. "*Invidia infelix:* Virgil, *Georgics* 3.37-39." *ICS* 8:65-79.
Döpp, S. 1968. *Virgilischer Einfluß im Werk Ovids*. Munich.
Due, O.S. 1974. *Changing Forms: Studies in the Metamorphoses of Ovid*. Classica et Mediaevalia: Dissertationes 10. Copenhagen.
Evans, H.B. 1983. *Publica Carmina: Ovid's Books from Exile*. Lincoln and London.
Fantham, R.E. 1983. "Sexual Comedy in Ovid's *Fasti*: Sources and Motivation." *HSCP* 87:185-216.
———. 1985. "Ovid, Germanicus and the Composition of the *Fasti*." *PLLS* 5:243-81.
Fedeli, P. 1981. "Elegy and Literary Polemic in Propertius' *Monobiblos*." *PLLS* 3:227-42.
———, ed. 1984. *Sexti Properti Elegiarum Libri IV.* Stuttgart.
Feeney, D.C. 1991. *The Gods in Epic*. Oxford.
Fontenrose, J.E. 1939. "Apollo and Sol in the Latin Poets of the First Century B.C." *TAPA* 70:439-55.
———. 1940. "Apollo and the Sun-god in Ovid." *AJP* 61:429-44.
Fowler, D.P. 1989. "First Thoughts on Closure: Problems and Prospects." *MD* 22:75-122.
Fränkel, H. 1945. *Ovid: A Poet between Two Worlds*. Sather Classical Lectures 18. Berkeley and Los Angeles.

———, ed. 1961. *Apollonii Rhodii, Argonautica*. Oxford.
Frazer, J.G., ed. 1898. *Pausanias' Description of Greece*. 6 vols. London.
———, ed. 1921. *Apollodorus, the Library*. The Loeb Classical Library. 2 vols. London and Cambridge, Mass.
———, ed. 1929. *The Fasti of Ovid*. 5 vols. London.
Frécaut, J.M. 1968. "Les transitions dans les Métamorphoses d'Ovide." *REL* 47:247–63.
———. 1972. *L'esprit et l'humeur chez Ovide*. Grenoble.
Fredericks, B.R. 1977. "Divine Wit vs. Divine Folly: Mercury and Apollo in Metamorphoses 1–2." *CJ* 72:244–49.
Galinsky, G.K. 1975. *Ovid's Metamorphoses: An Introduction to the Basic Aspects*. Berkeley and Los Angeles.
Genette, G. 1972. *Figures III*. Collection Poétique. Paris.
———. 1980. *Narrative Discourse*. Trans. J.E. Lewin, Oxford. (= Genette [1972] 65–282.)
Gildersleeve, B.L., ed. 1885. *Pindar, The Olympian and Pythian Odes*. New York.
Goold, G.P., ed. 1977. *Ovid III, Metamorphoses I*. 3d ed. Trans. F.J. Miller. The Loeb Classical Library. London and Cambridge, Mass.
Gow, A.S.F., ed. 1952. *Theocritus*. 2d ed. 2 vols. Cambridge.
Gow, A.S.F., and A.F. Scholfield, eds. 1953. *Nicander, the Poems and Poetical Fragments*. Cambridge.
Gutzwiller, K.J. 1981. *Studies in the Hellenistic Epyllion*. Beitr. zur Klass. Philol. 114. Königstein.
Hardie, P. 1986. *Virgil's Aeneid: Cosmos and Imperium*. Oxford.
Haupt, M., R. Ehwald, and M. von Albrecht, eds. 1966. *P. Ovidius Naso Metamorphosen, Erster Band: Buch I–VII*. Zurich and Dublin.
Haupt, M., O. Korn, R. Ehwald, and M. von Albrecht, eds. 1966. *P. Ovidius Naso Metamorphosen, Zweiter Band: Buch VIII–XV*. Zurich and Dublin.
Heinze, R. 1919. *Ovids elegische Erzählung*. Berichte der Sachsischen Akademie zu Leipzig. Philologisch-historische Klasse 71.7. Leipzig. (= Heinze [1960] 308–403.)
———. 1960. *Vom Geist des Römertums*. 3d ed., ed. E. Burck. Stuttgart.
Henrichs, A. 1983. "Die Kekropidensage Im P.Herc. 243: Von Kallimachos zu Ovid." *Cronache Ercolanesi: bollettino del centro internazionale per lo studio dei papiri ercolanesi* 13:33–43.
Herescu, N.I., ed. 1958. *Ovidiana. Recherches sur Ovide, publiées à l'occasion du bimillénaire de la naissance du poète*. Paris.
Herter, H. 1948. "Ovids Kunstprinzip in den Metamorphosen." In *Ovid*. See von Albrecht and Zinn 1968. First published in *AJP* 69:129–48.
Hill, D.E., ed. 1985. *Ovid, Metamorphoses I–IV*. Oak Park, Ill.
Hinds, S.E. 1982. "An Allusion in the Literary Tradition of the Proserpina Myth." *CQ* n.s. 32:476–78.
———. 1987. *The Metamorphosis of Persephone: Ovid and the Self-conscious Muse*. Cambridge.

Hofmann, H. 1985. "Ovid's *Metamorphoses: Carmen Perpetuum, Carmen Deductum.*" *PLLS* 5:223-42.
Holland, R. 1926. "Battos." *RhM* 75:156-83.
Hollander, J. 1981. *The Figure of Echo.* Berkeley.
Hollis, A.S., ed. 1977. *Ovid, Ars Amatoria Book I.* Oxford.
———. 1982. "Notes on Callimachus, *Hecale.*" *CQ* n.s. 32:469-73.
———, ed. 1990. *Callimachus, Hecale.* Oxford.
Hopkinson, N. 1988. *A Hellenistic Anthology.* Cambridge.
Hunter, R.L., ed. 1989. *Apollonius of Rhodes: Argonautica III.* Cambridge.
Hutchinson, G.O. 1988. *Hellenistic Poetry.* Oxford.
Jacques, J. M. 1960. "Sur un acrostiche d'Aratos." *REA* 62:48-61.
Johnson, W.R. 1978. "The Desolation of the *Fasti.*" *CJ* 74:7-18.
Kenney, E.J., ed. 1961. *P. Ovidi Nasonis Amores, Medicamina Faciei Femineae, Ars Amatoria, Remedia Amoris.* Oxford.
———. 1970. Review of *Landscape in Ovid's Metamorphoses*, by C.P. Segal. *Gnomon* 42:418-19.
———. 1972. Review of *Metamorphosen I-III*, by F. Bömer. *CR* n.s. 22:38-42.
———. 1973. "The Style of the *Metamorphoses.*" In *Ovid*, edited by J.W. Binns. Greek and Latin Studies: Classical Literature and Its Influence. London.
———. 1976. "*Ovidius prooemians.*" *PCPS* n.s. 22:46-53.
———. 1982a. "Ovid." In *Latin Literature,* edited by E.J. Kenney. The Cambridge History of Classical Literature Volume 2. Cambridge.
———. 1982b. "Books and Readers in the Roman world." In *Latin Literature,* edited by E.J. Kenney. The Cambridge History of Classical Literature Volume 2. Cambridge.
———, ed. 1982c. *Latin Literature.* The Cambridge History of Classical Literature Volume 2. Cambridge.
———. 1986. Introduction and Notes to *Ovid, Metamorphoses.* Trans. A.D. Melville. Oxford.
Kent, R.G. 1938. *Varro, 'De Lingua Latina.'* 2 vols. The Loeb Classical Library. London and Cambridge, Mass.
Kermode, F. 1966. *The Sense of an Ending.* Oxford.
———. 1983. *The Art of Telling.* Cambridge, Mass.
Klimmer, W. 1932. *Die Anordnung des Stoffes in den ersten vier Buchern der Metamorphosen.* Ph.D. diss., Erlangen.
Knox, P.E. 1986. *Ovid's Metamorphoses and the Traditions of Augustan Poetry.* Cambridge Philological Society Supplementary Volume 11. Cambridge.
Labate, M. 1986. "Di nuovo sulla poetica dei nomi in Petronio: Corax 'il delatore'?" *MD* 16:135-46.
Lafaye, G. 1904. *Les Métamorphoses d'Ovide et leurs modèles grecs.* Paris.
Lamacchia, R. 1960. "Ovidio interprete di Virgilio." *Maia* 12:310-30.
———. 1969. "Precisazioni su alcuni aspetti dell'epica Ovidiana." *Atene e Roma* n.s. 14 (2):1-20.
Lateiner, D. 1984. "Mythic and Non-mythic Artists in Ovid's *Metamorphoses.*" *Ramus* 13:1-30

Latta, B. 1972. "Zu Catulls Carmen I." *Mus. Helv.* 29:201-13.
Leach, E.W. 1974. "Ekphrasis and the Theme of Artistic Failure in Ovid's *Metamorphoses.*" *Ramus* 3:102-42.
Lefèvre, E. 1976. "Die Lehre von der Entstehung der Tieropfer in Ovids Fasten I, 335-456." *RhM* 119:39-64.
Lefkowitz, M.R. 1980. "The Quarrel between Callimachus and Apollonios." *ZPE* 40:1-20.
———. 1981. *The Lives of the Greek Poets.* Baltimore.
Lenz, F.W. 1967. "Betrachtungen zu einer neuen Untersuchung über die Struktur und Einheit der Metamorphosen Ovids." *Helikon* 7:493-506.
Linse, E. 1891. *De P. Ovidio Nasone vocabulorum inventore.* Diss., Dortmund.
Little, D.A. 1970. "Richard Heinze: Ovids elegische Erzählung." In *Ovids Ars amatoria und Remedia amoris: Untersuchungen zum Aufbau,* edited by E. Zinn. Stuttgart.
———. 1972. *The Structural Character of Ovid's Metamorphoses.* Ph.D. diss., University of Texas at Austin.
Lloyd-Jones, H., and P. Parsons, eds. 1983. *Supplementum Hellenisticum.* Berlin.
Lloyd-Jones, H., and J. Rea. 1968. "Callimachus, Fragments 260-261." *HSCP* 72:125-45.
Loers, V., ed. 1843. *P. Ovidi Nasonis Metamorphoseon Libri XV.* Leipzig.
Luck, G., ed. 1967-77. *P. Ovidius Naso, Tristia.* Wissenschaftliche Kommentare zu griechischen und lateinischen Schriftstellern. Heidelberg.
Ludwig, W. 1965. *Struktur und Einheit der Metamorphosen Ovids.* Berlin.
Lueneburg, A. 1888. *De Ovidio sui imitatore.* Diss., Jena.
Luppe, W. 1984. "Epikureische Mythenkritik bei Philodem-Götterliebschaften in PHerc. 243 II und III." *Cronache Ercolanesi* 14:109-24.
McCarty, W. C. N.d. *Et tu spectabere serpens: Narcissus and his Relations in the Metamorphoses of Ovid.*
McKeown, J.C., ed. 1987-. *Ovid: Amores, Text, Prolegomena and Commentary.* 4 vols. Liverpool and Leeds.
Magnus, H., ed. 1914. *P. Ovidi Nasonis Metamorphoseon Libri XV.* Berlin.
Marouzeau, J. 1958. "Un procédé Ovidien." In *Ovidiana. Recherches sur Ovid, publiées à l'occasion du bimillénaire de la naissance du poète,* edited by N. I. Hersecu. Paris.
Melville, A.D. 1986. *Ovid, Metamorphoses.* Oxford.
Merkelbach, R., and M.L. West, eds. 1970. *Hesiodi, Opera.* Oxford.
Miller, F.J. 1920-21. "Some Features of Ovid's Style." *CJ* 16:464-76.
Mitchell, W.J.T., ed. 1980-81. *On Narrative.* Chicago and London.
Moore-Blunt, J.J. 1977. *A Commentary on Ovid, Metamorphoses II.* Uithoorn.
Murgia, C.E. 1984. "Ovid *Met.* 1.544-547 and the Theory of Double Recension." *Cl. Ant* 3:207-35.
Mynors, R.A.B., ed. 1969. *P. Virgili Maronis, Opera.* Oxford.
Nagle, B.R. 1980. *The Poetics of Exile: Programme and Polemic in the Tristia and Epistulae ex Ponto of Ovid.* Collection Latomus 170. Brussels.
———. 1983. "Byblis and Myrrha: Two Incest Narratives in the *Metamorphoses.*" *CJ* 78:301-15.

———. 1985. "Calliope's 'Rape of Proserpina' as a Miniature *Carmen Perpetuum.*" *American Philological Association Annual Meeting Abstracts.* Decatur, Ga.

———. 1987. Review of *Metaformations: Soundplay and Wordplay in Ovid and Other Classical Poets,* by F. Ahl. *CJ* 82:340–42.

———. 1988a. "A Trio of Love-triangles in Ovid's *Metamorphoses.*" *Arethusa* 21:75–98.

———. 1988b. "Erotic Pursuit and Narrative Seduction in Ovid's *Metamorphoses.*" *Ramus* 17:32–51.

Newlands, C. 1991. "Ovid's Ravenous Raven." *CJ* 86:244–55.

Nisbet, R.G.M., and M. Hubbard. (1970). *A Commentary on Horace, Odes Book I.* Oxford.

———. 1978. *A Commentary on Horace, Odes Book II.* Oxford.

Norden, E., ed. 1957. *P. Virgilius Maro Aeneis Buch VI.* 4th ed. Stuttgart.

O'Hara, J.J. 1986. *Death and the Optimistic Prophecy in the Aeneid.* Ph.D. diss., University of Michigan.

Otis, B. 1970. *Ovid as an Epic Poet.* 2d ed. Cambridge.

Owen, S.G., ed. 1915. *P. Ovidi Nasonis Tristium Libri Quinque, Ibis, Ex Ponto Libri Quattuor, Halieutica, Fragmenta.* Oxford.

Paley, F.A., ed. 1881. *P. Ovidii Nasonis Fastorum Libri Sex.* London.

Palmer, A., ed. 1898. *P. Ovidi Nasonis Heroides.* Oxford.

Papathomopoulos, M., ed. 1968. *Antoninus Liberalis, Les Métamorphoses.* Collection Budé. Paris.

Pfeiffer, R., ed. 1949–53. *Callimachus.* 2 vols. Oxford.

———. 1968. *History of Classical Scholarship.* Oxford.

Plaehn, G. 1882. *De Nicandro aliisque poetis Graecis ab Ovidio in Metamorphosibus conscribendis adhibitis.* Diss., Halle.

Powell, B. 1906. *Erichthonius and the Three Daughters of Cecrops.* Cornell Studies in Classical Philology 17. Ithaca, N.Y.

Prince, G. 1982. *Narratology: The Form and Functioning of Narrative.* Berlin.

Proosdij, B.A. van, ed. 1982. *P. Ovidii Nasonis, Metamorphoseon Libri XV.* Leiden.

Pucci, P. 1987. *Intertextual Readings in the Odyssey and the Iliad.* Cornell.

Reitzenstein, E. 1931. "Zur Stiltheorie des Kallimachos." *Festschrift Richard Reitzenstein.* Leipzig and Berlin.

Ricoeur, P. 1980/1981. "Narrative Time." In *On Narrative,* edited by W.J.T. Mitchell. Chicago.

Robertson, N. 1983. "The Riddle of the Arrhephoria at Athens." *HSCP* 87:241–88.

Ross, D.O. 1975. *Backgrounds to Augustan Poetry: Gallus, Elegy and Rome.* Cambridge.

———. 1987. *Virgil's Elements.* Princeton.

Russell, D.A. 1979. "*De Imitatione.*" In *Creative Imitation and Latin Literature,* edited by D.A. West and A.J. Woodman. Cambridge.

Saylor, C. 1967. "*Querelae:* Propertius' Distinctive, Technical Name for his Elegy." *AGON* 1:142–49.

Segal, C.P. 1968. "Ancient Texts and Modern Literary Criticism." *Arethusa* 1:1-25.

———. 1969. *Landscape in Ovid's Metamorphoses: A Study in the Transformations of a Literary Symbol.* Hermes Einzelschriften 23. Wiesbaden.

———. 1981. "Theocritean Criticism and the Interpretation of the Fourth Idyll." *Poetry and Myth in Ancient Pastoral:* 85-109. Princeton. First published in *Ramus* 1 (1972):1-25.

Shelmerdine, S. 1981. *The 'Homeric Hymn to Hermes': A Commentary (1-114) with Introduction.* Ph.D. diss., University of Michigan.

Simmons, C., ed. 1887. *P. Ovidii Nasonis Metamorphoseon XIII & XIV.* London.

Simon, E. 1983. *Festivals of Attica.* Madison.

Smith, B.H. 1968. *Poetic Closure.* Chicago.

———. 1978. *On the Margins of Discourse: the Relation of Literature to Language.* Chicago.

———. 1980-1981. "Narrative Versions, Narrative Theories." In *On Narrative,* edited by W.J.T. Mitchell. Chicago.

Snyder, J.M. 1980. *Puns and Poetry in Lucretius' De Rerum Natura.* Amsterdam.

Solodow, J.B. 1988. *The World of Ovid's Metamorphoses.* Chapel Hill, N.C.

Stankiewicz, L. 1979. "Imiona Pasterskie w Sielankach Teokryta." *Eos* 67:267-78.

Steiner, G. 1988. "The Good Books." *The New Yorker,* 11 Jan. 1988:94-98.

Steiner, G. 1958. "Ovid's *Carmen Perpetuum.*" *TAPA* 89:218-36.

Stitz, M. 1962. *Ovid und Virgils Aeneis.* Diss., Freiburg.

Syme, R. 1978. *History in Ovid.* Oxford.

Thomas, R.F. 1979. "New Comedy, Callimachus, and Roman Poetry." *HSCP* 83:179-206.

———. 1982. "Catullus and the Polemics of Poetic Reference." *AJP* 103:144-64.

———. 1983. "Callimachus, the *Victoria Berenices,* and Roman Poetry." *CQ* n.s. 33:92-113.

———. 1985. "From *recusatio* to Commitment: the Evolution of the Virgilian Programme." *PLLS* 5:61-73.

———. 1986. "Virgil's Georgics and the Art of Reference." *HSCP* 90:171-98.

———, ed. 1988. *Virgil: Georgics.* 2 vols. Cambridge.

Thompson, D.W. 1936. *A Glossary of Greek Birds,* new ed. Oxford.

Todorov, T. 1971. *La poétique de la prose.* Paris.

Trypanis, C.A. 1958. *Callimachus, Fragments.* The Loeb Classical Library. 2 vols. London and Cambridge, Mass.

von Albrecht, M. 1964. *Die Parenthese in Ovids Metamorphosen und ihre dichterische Funktion.* Spudasmata 7. Hildesheim.

von Albrecht, M., and E. Zinn, ed. 1968. *Ovid.* Wege der Forschung 92. Darmstadt.

Walde, A., and J.B Hofmann. 1938-56. *Lateinisches Etymologisches Wörterbuch.* 3 vols. Heidelberg.

Wallace-Hadrill, A. 1982. "*Civilis Princeps:* Between Citizen and King." *JRS* 72:32-48.

West, M.L., ed. 1966. *Hesiod, Theogony.* Oxford.
Wilkinson, L.P. 1955. *Ovid Recalled.* Cambridge.
———. 1958. "The World of the *Metamorphoses.*" In *Ovidiana. Recherches sur Ovide, publiées à l'occasion du bimillénaire de la naissance du poète,* edited by N.I. Herescu, Paris.
———. 1969. *The Georgics of Virgil. A critical survey.* Cambridge.
———. 1970. "Pindar and the proem to the Third Georgic." *Festschrift K. Büchner.* Wiesbaden: 286-90.
———. 1982. "The *Georgics.*" In *Latin Literature,* edited by E.J. Kenney. The Cambridge History of Classical Literature Volume 2. Cambridge.
Williams, F., ed. 1978. *Callimachus, Hymn to Apollo.* Oxford.
Williams, G. 1978. *Decline and Change.* Berkeley.
———. 1983. "Roman Poets as Literary Historians: Some Aspects of *Imitatio.*" *ICS* 8:211-37.
Wimmel, W. 1960. *Kallimachos in Rom: die Nachfolge seines apologetischen Dichtens in der Augusteerzeit.* Hermes Einzelschriften 16. Wiesbaden.
———. 1962. "Aglauros in Ovids Metamorphosen." *Hermes* 90:326-33.
Winkler, J.J. 1986. *Auctor and Actor: A Narratological Reading of Apuleius' Metamorphoses.* Berkeley.
Wiseman, T.P. 1969. *Catullan Questions.* Leicester.
———. 1979. *Clio's Cosmetics.* Leicester.
———. 1985. *Catullus and His World, A Reappraisal.* Cambridge.
Wormell, D.E.W. 1979. "Ovid and the *Fasti.*" *Hermathena* 127:39-50.
Young, D. 1968. *Three Odes of Pindar.* Leiden.
Zetzel, J.E.G. 1983. "Catullus, Ennius, and the Poetics of Allusion." *ICS* 8:251-66.
———. 1987. Review of *Supplementum Hellenisticum,* by H. Lloyd-Jones and J. Rea. *CP* 82:347-62.

Index

Aesculapius, 54, 63-64, 67-77, 92-93, 103, 135, 149

Aglauros, 6, 13-14, 35, 97, 117-33, 135, 149. *See also* Cecropids

Allusion, as *imitatio* or *aemulatio,* 17-20, 29-31, 36-37, 43-45, 67, 83n.41, 108-11, 113-14, 121, 124, 129, 138-39, 145; as cross-reference, *See* Cross-reference.

Apollonius of Rhodes, 108, 111

Battus, 6, 95-118, 132, 135, 149-50

Bucolic, 112-14

Callimachus: *Hecale,* 6, 9-20, 30n.65, 43-45, 151-52; other works, 20, 30, 124-25, 128, 141

Cecropids, 6, 10, 13-15, 17-18, 21-22, 24, 27-29, 35, 55-56, 66, 97-98, 117-35, 149-50

Cercopes, 147-50

Chiron, 6, 63-64, 76-81, 92-93, 96, 135, 150

Chronology of Ovid's early career, 48n.17

Coroneus, 23-25, 35-36, 66, 150

Coronis, 11-12, 19, 41n.4, 44, 47, 51-60, 63, 66, 96-99, 125, 150

Cross-reference: to *Fasti,* 48-52, 69-71, 75-81; to *Metamorphoses,* 40-43, 68, 71-74, 76, 118-23, 137-46, 147-50

Crow, 6-7, 9-37, 48-50, 52-53, 55-61, 66, 82, 97-99, 101-3, 106, 115, 118-25, 132-33, 135, 149-50

Elegy, 140-45

Etymological wordplay, 6, 32-36, 49n.19, 52-53, 55, 58-59, 64-66, 72-74, 85-92, 103-6, 115, 125-27, 143-45, 149-50

Footnote, Alexandrian, 29-30, 52-53, 106-7

Garrulity, 12, 22, 26, 28-31, 47-50, 52, 54, 61, 92, 99-101, 103-5, 115, 120, 131-33, 149

Herse, 13-14, 35, 97, 118-21, 123-24, 126, 149. *See also* Cecropids

Hesiod, 108, 111-12, 130

Homer, 107-8, 138, 148

Informer. *See* Garrulity

Invidia, 124-31

Loquacity, indiscreet. *See* Garrulity

Narrative, collocative, 28, 95-99, 115-18, 133, 135; embedded, 3-5, 6-7, 9-37, 55-61, 63-82, 102-3, 118-23; first-layer (embedding), 3-5, 39-61, 119-23; motivated by greed, 6, 54n.32, 56-57, 101-4, 110, 126; narratives about, 28-31, 48, 52, 84-92, 104-7; temporal sequentiality in, 26-28, 45-46, 61, 64, 72-74, 96, 118-23, 137-46

Nicander, 35n.79, 108-14

Nyctimene, 25-27, 31-33, 56, 125

Ocyroe, 6, 63-99, 101-3, 115, 133, 135, 147, 149-50

Owl, 16, 19, 22, 32-33, 49-50. *See also* Nyctimene

Pandrosos, 13-14, 35, 97, 118-21, 124, 149. *See also* Cecropids

Peacock, 39-42, 64, 92, 121-22

163

Prophecy, 6, 15, 19-20, 53, 66-84, 99, 147, 149

Raven, 6, 11, 16-20, 39-61, 63-67, 97-99, 101-4, 106, 115, 117, 121-22, 125, 132-33, 135, 149-50

Ring Composition, 55, 93, 133-34, 147-50

Sibyl, 82-84, 147-48

Swans, 11, 42-44, 47, 92, 121-22, 137-46

Theocritus, 95, 112-14

Transitions between episodes, 5, 22-28, 39-47, 63-67, 92-96, 114-23, 133-34

Varro, 32, 65, 85-91, 104-6, 126n.18

Virgil, 29-30, 88-89, 122n.8, 128-29, 144-45